CHOCTAW BY BLOOD

ENROLLMENT CARDS

1898-1914

VOLUME II

TRANSCRIBED BY

JEFF BOWEN

NATIVE STUDY
Gallipolis, Ohio
USA

Originally published:
Baltimore, Maryland
2015

Reprinted by:

Native Study LLC
Gallipolis, OH
www.nativestudy.com

Library of Congress Control Number: 2020911767

ISBN: 978-1-64968-002-0

Made in the United States of America.

**This series is dedicated to
Mike Marchi,
who keeps my spirits up.**

CREEK CENSUS.

SECOND NOTICE.

Members of the Dawes Commission will be present at the following times and places for the purpose of enrolling Creek citizens, as required by Act of Congress of June 10, 1896:

At Muskogee, Nov. 8 to 30, 1897, inclusive.
At Wagoner, Nov. 8 to 13, " inclusive.
At Eufaula, Nov. 8 to 13, " inclusive.
At Sapulpa, Nov. 15 to 20, " inclusive.
At Wetumpka, Nov. 15 to 20, " inclusive.
At Okmulgee, Nov. 22 to 30, " inclusive.

All persons who have not heretofore enrolled before the Dawes Commission should appear and enroll. Parents and guardians can enroll their families and wards.

TAMS BIXBY,
FRANK C. ARMSTRONG,
A. S. McKENNON,
THOS. B. NEEDLES,
Commissioners.

The above illustration is similar in nature to what was found throughout Indian Territory for different tribes as far as postings on bulletin boards, public centers, or wherever they could be read so people would be notified of where and when they needed to be for enrollment with the Dawes Commission.

This is a picture of the Dawes Commission at Camp Jones in Stonewall, Indian Territory on September 8, 1898.

The images below are of two of the original cards given on the microfilm. The cards given in this book have been formatted to fit on one page and still give all the information found on the original cards.

.

Introduction

This series of Choctaw Enrollment Cards for the Five Civilized Tribes 1898-1914 has been transcribed from National Archive Film M-1186 Rolls 39-46.

The series contains more than 6100 Choctaw enrollment cards. All of the cards list age, sex and degree of blood, the parties' Dawes Roll Numbers, and date of enrollment by the Secretary of Interior for each person. The contents also give the enrollee's parents' names as well as miscellaneous notes pertaining to the enrollee's circumstances, when needed. Most entries indicate whether or not a spouse is an Intermarried White, with the initials I.W.

Enrollment wasn't as simple a process as most would think just by going through these pages. The relationships between the Five Tribes and the Dawes Commission were weak at best. There were political battles going on between the tribes and the U.S. Government as it was, but the struggles didn't stop there. Each tribe had its own political factions pulling it from every direction. On top of everything else, people from every corner of the United States were trying to figure how to get in on the spoils (Money and Land Allotment) by means of political favor. Kent Carter, author of *The Dawes Commission*, describes the continuous effort required to enroll the different tribes and the pressure the Commission incurred from people all over the country who tried to insinuate themselves into the equation:

"In May 1896 the Dawes Commission Returned To Indian Territory for its third visit, establishing its headquarters at Vinita in the Cherokee Nation. It now had to process applications for citizenship in addition to negotiating allotment agreements; these circumstances make the narrative of events more confusing because the commission attempted the two tasks concurrently. The commissioners resumed making their usual speeches to tribal officials and public gatherings to promote negotiations, but now they inevitably had to respond to questions about how the application process for citizenship would work. They also began receiving letters from people all over the United States asking how they could 'get on the rolls' so they could 'get Indian land'."[1]

For the actual process of Choctaw enrollment, "A commission was appointed in each county of the Choctaw Nation under an act of September 18 to make separate rolls of citizens by blood, by intermarriage, and freedmen; it was to deliver them to recently elected Chief Green McCurtain by October 20, but he rejected them even before they were completed because of charges that people were being left off for political reasons. On October 30, the National Council authorized establishment of a five-member

---

[1] *The Dawes Commission* by Kent Carter, page 15, para. 1

commission to revise the rolls within ten days and then directed McCurtain to turn them over to the Dawes Commission on November 11, 1896. The Choctaws hired the law firm of Stuart, Gordon, and Hailey, of South McAlester to represent the tribe at all proceedings held by the Dawes Commission,"[2] another indication that throughout the Commission's efforts there was always controversy between the tribes and the negotiators.

When completed, this multi-volume series will contain thousands of names, all of them accounted for in the indexes carefully prepared by the author. Hopefully this work will help many researchers find their ancestors and satisfy the questions that so many have had about their Native American heritage.

Jeff Bowen
Gallipolis, Ohio
NativeStudy.com

---

[2] *The Dawes Commission* by Kent Carter, page 16, para. 5

Choctaw By Blood Enrollment Cards 1898-1914

RESIDENCE: Chickasaw Nation ~~COUNTY.~~ **Choctaw Nation**   Choctaw Roll   CARD NO.
POST OFFICE: Wynnewood, Ind. Ter.   (Not Including Freedmen)   FIELD NO. **301**

Dawes' Roll No.	NAME		Relationship to Person First Named	AGE	SEX	BLOOD	TRIBAL ENROLLMENT		
							Year	County	No.
15374	1 Norman, Ida	27	Named	23	F	1/2			
15375	2 " Alvy	4	son	8wks	M	1/4			
15376	3 " Clayton	2	Son	2mo	M	1/4			
15377	4 " Raymond	1	Son	2wks	M	1/4			
15777	5 " Oren		"	9	"	1/4			
15778	6 " Byron		"	7	"	1/4			
	7								
	8	ENROLLMENT							
	9	OF NOS. 1-2-3-4 HEREON APPROVED BY THE SECRETARY							
	10	OF INTERIOR May 9 1904							
	11	No.1 admitted by Dawes Com. Case No 822; and no appeal taken.							
	12								
	13								
	14	ENROLLMENT							
	15	OF NOS. 5 and 6 HEREON APPROVED BY THE SECRETARY							
	16	OF INTERIOR Mar 15, 1905							
	17								

TRIBAL ENROLLMENT OF PARENTS

	Name of Father	Year	County	Name of Mother	Year	County
1	B.F. Stanley	Dead	Choctaw roll	Sylva Robison ^Stanley		non citizen
2	J.A. Norman		non citizen	No. 1		
3	" " "		" "	No. 1		
4	" " "		" "	No. 1		
5	" " "		" "	No. 1		
6	" " "		" "	No. 1		
7						
8	Oren and Byron Norman children of No. 1 on Choctaw Card #R.216					
9	No.3 Enrolled April 10, 1901 Born Aug 24, 1898					
10	No.4 Born Aug. 31, 1902; enrolled Sept. 11, 1902.					
	~~Correct given name of No.2 is Alvy~~					
11	Nos 5 and 6 originally listed for enrollment on Choctaw Card R.216 and					
12	transferred to this card Jan. 28, 1905. See decision of Jan. 12, 1905.					
13	For child of No.1 see N.B. (Apr 26, 1906) Card No. 197					
	" " " " " " (March 3, 1905) " " 1138					
14						
15						
16	P.O. Woolsey Okla 11/26/06 G F 40675-1911			Date of Application for Enrollment.		Sept. 23/98
17	Sulphur, I.T.					1&2

P.O. Palmer I.T. 4/17/05

1

Choctaw By Blood Enrollment Cards 1898-1914

RESIDENCE: Atoka COUNTY.
POST OFFICE: Atoka, Ind. Ter.

Choctaw Nation

Choctaw Roll (Not Including Freedmen)

CARD No.
FIELD No. 400

Dawes' Roll No.	NAME	Relationship to Person First Named	AGE	SEX	BLOOD	TRIBAL ENROLLMENT		
						Year	County	No.
								CCR #2
767	1 Folsom, Alfred Emerson 58		54	M	3/8		Atoka	189
768	2 " , Ollie 38	wife	24	F	1/16		"	"
769	3 " , Eunis 10	dau	6	"	7/32		"	"
	4							
	5							
	6							
	7							
	8							
	9							
	10							
	11							
	12							
	13							
	14							
	15							
	16							
	17							

ENROLLMENT
OF NOS. 1, 2 and 3 HEREON
APPROVED BY THE SECRETARY
OF INTERIOR Dec 12, 1902

No1 1896 Atoka 4436 as A. E. Folsom
No2 1896 " 4437
No3 1896 " 4440
No 1 is father of children on Chickasaw Card #1255.

TRIBAL ENROLLMENT OF PARENTS

	Name of Father	Year	County	Name of Mother	Year	County
1	Israel Fulsom[sic]	Dead	Choctaw roll	Louvisey Folsom	Dead	Choctaw roll
2	J.L.C. Pate		non citizen	Ella A. Pate	"	Choctaw roll
3	No 1			No 2		
4						
5						
6						
7						
8						
9						
10						
11						
12						
13						
14						
15				Date of Application for Enrollment.		Oct 14/98
16						
17	P.O. Caddo I.T. 4/9/03					

100

Choctaw By Blood Enrollment Cards 1898-1914

RESIDENCE: Tobucksy   COUNTY.
POST OFFICE: Hartshorn, Ind. Ter

Choctaw Nation

Choctaw Roll
(Not Including Freedmen)

CARD NO.
FIELD NO. **302**

Dawes' Roll No.	NAME	Relationship to Person First Named	AGE	SEX	BLOOD	TRIBAL ENROLLMENT		
						Year	County	No.
VOID. 1	Carney, Philip	Named	19	M	1/2			
2								
3								
4								
5								
6	On Chickasaw roll, Page 71, transferred to Choctaw roll by Dawes Com.							
7								
8								
9								
10								
11								
12								
13								
14								
15								
16								
17								

TRIBAL ENROLLMENT OF PARENTS

	Name of Father	Year	County	Name of Mother	Year	County
1	William Carney		Chick. residing in Choctaw N. 1st Dist	Silsey Carney	Dead	Choctaw roll
2						
3						
4						
5						
6						
7						
8						
9						
10						
11						
12						
13						
14						
15			Date of Application for Enrollment.			Sept. 28/98
16						
17						

Transferred to Choctaw Card 1602 Oct. 13, 1902

CANCELLED

Choctaw By Blood Enrollment Cards 1898-1914

RESIDENCE: Chickasaw Nation ~~COUNTY.~~ **Choctaw Nation**   Choctaw Roll   CARD NO.
POST OFFICE: Purcell, Ind. Ter.   *(Not Including Freedmen)*   FIELD NO. 303

Dawes' Roll No.	NAME		Relationship to Person First Named	AGE	SEX	BLOOD	TRIBAL ENROLLMENT		
							Year	County	No.
14528	1 Berry, Dena	23	First Named	19	F	1/16	1896	Choctaw residing in Chickasaw District	1845
14529	2 " Roy	6	Son	2 ½	M	1/32	1896	" "	1846
14530	3 " May	5	Dau	7ᵐᵒ	F	1/32			
14531	4 " Gipson	1	Son	6wks	M	1/32			
IW697	5 " John	32	Husb	32	M	I.W.			
	6								
	7	ENROLLMENT OF NOS. 1,2,3 and 4 HEREON APPROVED BY THE SECRETARY OF INTERIOR May 20, 1903							
	8								
	9								
	10	ENROLLMENT OF NOS. ~ 5 ~ HEREON APPROVED BY THE SECRETARY OF INTERIOR May 7, 1904							
	11								
	12								
	13								
	14								
	15								
	16								
	17								

TRIBAL ENROLLMENT OF PARENTS

Name of Father	Year	County	Name of Mother	Year	County
1 George Johnson	Dead	Chickasaw Roll	Elizabeth Cochran		Choctaw residing in Chickasaw District
2 John Berry		White man	No 1		
3 " "		" "	No 1		
4 " "		" "	No 1		
5 George G. Berry		non-citizen	Lucy A. Berry		non citizen
6					
7		~~No 1 on Choctaw roll as Siney Berry; Wife of John Berry Choctaw Card No D53~~			
8		No3 Born January 28, 1898. See affidavit of Mother dated Sept 26, 1898 on file			
9		with papers in this case.			
10		No4 Enrolled Sept 5, 1901			
11		~~No5 transferred from Choctaw Card #D53. See decision of Feby 27, 1904.~~			
		~~For children of Nos 1&5 see NB (Mar 3'05) #553~~			
12					
13					
14					#1 to 3
15					Date of Application for Enrollment.
16					Sept. 28/98
17 P.O. McGee I.T. 3/28/05					

3

Choctaw By Blood Enrollment Cards 1898-1914

RESIDENCE: Chickasaw Nation ~~COUNTY~~.
POST OFFICE: Waupaunuka[sic], Ind. Ter.

Choctaw Nation

Choctaw Roll
(Not Including Freedmen)

CARD NO.
FIELD NO. 304

Dawes' Roll No.	NAME	Relationship to Person First Named	AGE	SEX	BLOOD	TRIBAL ENROLLMENT		
						Year	County	No.
VOID.	1 ~~Hawkins, Kingsberry~~		~~38~~	~~M~~	~~Full~~			
	2							
	3							
	4							
	5							
	6 Husband of Ledicy Hawkins, Chickasaw roll, Card No. 757							
	7							
	8 On Chickasaw roll, Pontotoc County, Page 51, transferred to Choctaw roll by Dawes Com							
	9							
	10							
	11							
	12							
	13							
	14							
	15							
	16							
	17							

TRIBAL ENROLLMENT OF PARENTS

	Name of Father	Year	County	Name of Mother	Year	County
1	~~Isum Hawkins~~	~~Dead~~	~~Choctaw roll~~	~~E-ma-to-na~~	~~Dead~~	~~Choctaw roll~~
2						
3						
4						
5						
6						
7						
8						
9						
10						
11						
12						
13						
14						
15				Date of Application for Enrollment.	Sept. 29/98	
16						
17	P O Byrne Ind Ter.					

CANCELLED

Transferred to Chickasaw Card [remainder illegible]

4

Choctaw By Blood Enrollment Cards 1898-1914

RESIDENCE: Chickasaw Nation ~~COUNTY.~~ **Choctaw Nation**   Choctaw Roll   CARD NO.
POST OFFICE: Hickory, Ind. Ter. *(Not Including Freedmen)* FIELD NO. **305**

Dawes' Roll No.	NAME	Relationship to Person First Named	AGE	SEX	BLOOD	TRIBAL ENROLLMENT		
						Year	County	No.
VOID.	1 Bradley, Bruce	Named	17	M	1/2			
VOID.	2 DEAD " , Ellen	Dau	2wks	F	1/4			
	3							
	4	On Chickasaw roll, Tishomingo Co., Page 28, transferred to Choctaw roll by						
	5	Dawes Com.						
	6	No.1 is now the husband of Ida Bradley, non citizen. Evidence						
	7	of marriage filed Sept 28, 1901.						
	8	No2 Enrolled Sept 28, 1901						
	9					Proof of death of No2 filed 11/18/02		
	10							
	11							
	12							
	13							
	14							
	15							
	16							
	17							

TRIBAL ENROLLMENT OF PARENTS

	Name of Father	Year	County	Name of Mother	Year	County
1	John Bradley	Dead	non citizen	Juicy Bradley	Dead	Choctaw roll
2	No1			Ida Bradley		non-citizen
3						
4						
5						
6						
7						
8						
9						
10						
11						
12						
13						
14						
15					Date of Application for Enrollment.	Sept. 29/98
16						
17						

5

Choctaw By Blood Enrollment Cards 1898-1914

RESIDENCE: Chickasaw Nation ~~COUNTY.~~   **Choctaw Nation**   Choctaw Roll   CARD NO.
POST OFFICE: Earl, Ind. Ter.   *(Not Including Freedmen)*   FIELD NO. **306**

Dawes' Roll No.	NAME	Relationship to Person First Named	AGE	SEX	BLOOD	TRIBAL ENROLLMENT		
						Year	County	No.
Void	1 Norton, Yancey M.	Named	42	M	I.W.			
Void	2 " , Sealy	wife	45	F	1/2			
Void	3 " , Thomas Owen	son	10	M	1/4			
Void	4 " , Henry Taylor	"	8	"	1/4			
Void	5 " , Lewis Bird	"	6	"	1/4			
Void	6 " , Jesse Melton	"	2	"	1/4			
	7							
	8							
	9	No 1 on Chickasaw roll as Yancey N Norton						
	10	No 2 " " " Sealy Morton						
	11	No 3 " " " Thomas Oin "						
	12	No 4 " " " Henry T "						
	13	No 5 " " " Lewis B "						
	14	No 6 " " " Jessie M "						
	15							
	16							
	17							

TRIBAL ENROLLMENT OF PARENTS

Name of Father	Year	County	Name of Mother	Year	County
1 John F. Norton	Dead	non citizen	Lucy E Norton	Dead	non citizen
2 J.E. Anderson	:	Chickasaw Roll	Jiney Anderson	"	Choctaw roll
3 No 1			No 2		
4 No 1			No 2		
5 No 1			No 2		
6 No 1			No 2		
7					
8					
9	No1 on Chickasaw roll, Tishomingo County, Page 79				
10	All others " " " " " "			33	
11	All transferred to Choctaw roll by Dawes Com.				
12					
13					
14					
15				Date of Application for Enrollment.	Sept. 29/98
16					
17					

CANCELLED

Transferred to Chickasaw #8664 June 30 - 1902

6

RESIDENCE: Chickasaw Nation ~~COUNTY.~~ **Choctaw Nation** Choctaw Roll CARD No.
POST OFFICE: Wiley, Ind. Ter. (Not Including Freedmen) FIELD No. 307

Dawes' Roll No.	NAME	Relationship to Person First	AGE	SEX	BLOOD	TRIBAL ENROLLMENT		
						Year	County	No.
VOID. 1	Smith, Wood	Named	43	M	I.W.			
VOID. 2	", Serena DEAD	wife	38	F	1/4			
VOID. 3	", Frank	Son	19	M	1/8			
VOID. 4	" Mollie	Dau	16	F	1/8			
VOID. 5	" Birdie	"	14	"	1/8			
VOID. 6	" Richard	Son	10	M	1/8			
VOID. 7	" Rector	"	8	"	1/8			
VOID. 8	" Cheadle	"	5	"	1/8			
DEAD 9	" Almirena DEAD	Dau	3	F	1/8			
VOID. 10	" Dewey	"	4mo	"	1/8			
VOID. 11	" Katie	Dau	3mo	F	1/8			
12	Parents of No.11 are Nos. 1 and 2							
13								
14	No 1 on Chickasaw roll, Pontotoc Co, Page 81, transferred to Choctaw roll by Dawes Com.							
15	All others " " " " 49; " " " " " "							
16								
17								

TRIBAL ENROLLMENT OF PARENTS

	Name of Father	Year	County	Name of Mother	Year	County
1	Thomas Smith	Dead	non-citizen	Letitia Smith	Dead	non-citizen
2	Thomas Cheadle	"	Chickasaw roll	Rebecca Cheadle	"	Choctaw roll
3	No 1			No 2		
4	No 1			No 2		
5	No 1			No 2		
6	No 1			No 2		
7	No 1			No 2		
8	No 1			No 2		
9	No 1			No 2		
10	No 1			No 2		
11	No 1			No 2		
12	Certified copy of marriage license and certificate to be supplied.					
13	No.2 died Nov. 1 1901: Evidence of death filed Jany. 20, 1902.					
14	No.11 born Nov. 1st, 1901: Enrolled Jany. 20, 1902.					
15	No. 9 died Oct. 20, 1900: proof of death filed Aug. 2, 1902.					
16				Date of application for enrollment Sept. 29/98		
17				No-10 enrolled Mar 6/99		

CANCELLED

Choctaw By Blood Enrollment Cards 1898-1914

RESIDENCE: Chickasaw Nation ~~COUNTY.~~

POST OFFICE: Tishomingo Ind. Ter.

Choctaw Nation

Choctaw Roll *(Not Including Freedmen)*

CARD NO.

FIELD NO. **308**

Dawes' Roll No.	NAME	Relationship to Person First Named	AGE	SEX	BLOOD	TRIBAL ENROLLMENT		
						Year	County	No.
DEAD	1 ~~Fisher, David Osborne~~		73	M	3/8		Choctaw residing in Chickasaw District	CCR#2 194
IW1081	2 Fisher, Matilda Olive 57	wife	53	F	I.W.		" "	C.I. Roll 33
647	3 Muldrow, Mary Daisy 26	Dau	22	"	3/16		" "	CCR#2 194
VOID	4 ~~Fisher, Agnes John~~	"	19	"	3/16		" "	"
648	5 Fisher, Blanche 17	"	13	"	3/16		" "	"
649	6 Muldrow, Osborn Fisher 3	grandson	4mo	M	3/32		" "	"
IW220	7 " Henry L. Jr.	Husband of No.3	30	M	I.W.			
	8 Aug 14/99 No.3 is now the wife of				No 1	1896	Chickasaw Dist	4560
	9 Henry L Muldrow, Jr. who is on				No 2	1896	" "	14549
	10 Card No. D.316.				No 3	1896	" "	4562
	11 ENROLLMENT OF NOS. 3, 5 and 6 HEREON APPROVED BY THE SECRETARY				No 4	1896	" "	4563
	12 OF INTERIOR Dec 12 1902				No 5	1896	" "	4564
	13 No7 transferred from Choctaw Card D316 August 5, 1903. See Decision of July 20, 1903							
	14 Affidavit of Father Lawrence Smyth, Forth Smith Ark Who Performed the							
	15 Marriage Ceremony to be supplied - Received Oct. 11/98							
	16 No4 taken from this card and transferred							
	17 to Choctaw #3366 with her husband Benjamin H Colbert Nov. 26, 1900							

(left margin: No. 1 hereon dismissed under order of the Commission to the Five Civilized Tribes of March 31, 1905)

TRIBAL ENROLLMENT OF PARENTS

	Name of Father	Year	County	Name of Mother	Year	County
1	~~Joseph Fisher~~	Dead	Non-Citizen	~~Martha Fisher~~	Dead	Choctaw roll
2	Peter McSweeney	"	" "	Joanna McSweeney	"	Non Citizen
3	No.1			No.2		
4	~~No.1~~			~~No.2~~		
5	No.1			No.2		
6	Henry L Muldrow Jr			No.3		
7	Robert Muldrow	Dead	Non-Citizen	Annie Muldrow		Non-Citizen
8	No1 on Choctaw roll as David O. Fisher					
9	No2 " " " " Mattie O. "			ENROLLMENT OF NOS ~~~2~~ HEREON APPROVED BY THE SECRETARY		
10	No3 " " " " Daisy M. "			OF INTERIOR Nov 16 1904		
11	No.1 Died Oct. 24, 1898. Evidence of death					
12	filed Nov. 7, 1901					
13	For child of Nos. 3 and 7 see N.B. (Apr 26,06) Card #7.				Date of Application for Enrollment.	
14	No. 6 Enrolled May 24, 1900.				Sept. 29/98	
15	ENROLLMENT OF NOS. 7 HEREON APPROVED BY THE SECRETARY OF INTERIOR Sep 12 1908					
16						
17						

For child of Nos. 3&7 see N.B. (Mar. 3-05)Card #76

8

Choctaw By Blood Enrollment Cards 1898-1914

RESIDENCE: Chickasaw Nation ~~COUNTY~~. **Choctaw Nation** Choctaw Roll CARD NO.
POST OFFICE: Cumberland, Ind. Ter. *(Not Including Freedmen)* FIELD NO. 309

Dawes' Roll No.	NAME (Ara, I.T.)	Relationship to Person First Named	AGE	SEX	BLOOD	TRIBAL ENROLLMENT Year	TRIBAL ENROLLMENT County	TRIBAL ENROLLMENT No.
650	1 Spain, Granger ²⁷		23	M	1/32		Atoka	CCR#2 431
I.W. 555	2 " , Lula M. ²⁶	Wife	23	F	I.W.			
	3				(No. 1	1896	Atoka	11654)
651	4 Spain, Annie M. ⁷	Dau	3	F	1/64	1896	"	11658
652	5 " , Agnes ²	Dau	1 yr	F	1/64			
	6							
	7	ENROLLMENT			No 5 Enrolled Aug 9, 1901			
	8	OF NOS. 1, 4 and 5 HEREON APPROVED BY THE SECRETARY			No 4 on Choc Roll as Annie Spain			
	9	OF INTERIOR Dec 12, 1902						
	10				No 1 descendant of Mary M. Spain Who was admitted by Act of			
	11				Choctaw Council of Oct. 31, 1877.			
	12				For child of Nos. 1 & 2 see NB (Apr 26-06) Card #444.			
	13							
	14	ENROLLMENT OF NOS. 2 HEREON						
	15	APPROVED BY THE SECRETARY OF INTERIOR Feb. 8, 1904						
	16							
	17							

TRIBAL ENROLLMENT OF PARENTS

Name of Father	Year	County	Name of Mother	Year	County
1 W.H.H. Spain	Dead	Choctaw Roll	Lou Spain		Non Citizen
2 C. Shelton		Non-Cit	Mary Shelton		" "
3 No 1			No 2		
4 No 1			No 2		
5					
6					
7					
8					
9					
10					
11					
12					
13				#1 to 4	
14				Date of Application for Enrollment. Sept. 29/98	
15					
16					
17					

9

Choctaw By Blood Enrollment Cards 1898-1914

RESIDENCE: Chickasaw Nation ~~COUNTY~~. **Choctaw Nation** Choctaw Roll CARD NO.
POST OFFICE: Emmet, Ind. Ter. *(Not Including Freedmen)* FIELD NO. **310**

Dawes' Roll No.	NAME	Relationship to Person First Named	AGE	SEX	BLOOD	TRIBAL ENROLLMENT		
						Year	County	No.
653	1 Taylor, Lousina J. ⁵⁶	First Named	52	F	1/16		Choctaw residing in Chickasaw District	CCR #2 452
654	2 " , Ruel Fenton ¹⁹	Son	15	M	1/32		" "	"
655	3 " , Sallie ¹⁵	Dau	11	F	1/32		" "	"
656	4 " , Lurel E. ¹³	Son	9	M	1/32		" "	"
657	5 " , Carrie D ¹⁰	Dau	6	F	1/32		" "	"
658	6 " , Wayne Oscar ⁸	Son	4	M	1/32		" "	"
I.W. 1082	7 " , Epps ⁴⁷	Husband	47	M	I.W.	1896	Chick Dist	15125
	8 ~~ENROLLMENT~~				No 1	1896	Chickasaw Dist	12559
	9 ~~OF NOS. 1,2,3,4,5 and 6 HEREON~~ ~~APPROVED BY THE SECRETARY~~				No 2	"	" "	12561
	10 ~~OF INTERIOR~~ Dec 12, 1902							
	11 ~~No7 transferred from Choctaw Card #D-56 Oct~~							
	12 ~~31, 1904: See decision of Oct. 15, 1904~~							
	13							
	14 ~~ENROLLMENT~~					No7 also on 1896 Choc census roll as		
	15 ~~OF NOS. 7 HEREON~~ ~~APPROVED BY THE SECRETARY~~					E. Taylor Page 401 #15124 Chick Dist.		
	16 ~~OF INTERIOR~~ Nov. 16, 1904							
	17							

TRIBAL ENROLLMENT OF PARENTS

	Name of Father	Year	County	Name of Mother	Year	County
1	Dave Harkins	Dead	Choctaw Roll	Belle Harkins	Dead	Choctaw Roll
2	Epps Taylor		White Man	No 1		
3	" "		" "	No 1		
4	" "		" "	No 1		
5	" "		" "	No 1		
6	" "		" "	No 1		
7	M.C. Taylor	dead	Non Citizen	Mary Taylor	Dead	Non Citizen
8						
9	No1 on Choctaw Roll as L. J. Taylor					
10	No2 " " " " Reed "					
11	~~No4 " " " " Letha "~~					
12	No5 " " " " Dee "					
13	No6 " " " " I.W. "					
14	No3 1896 Chickasaw Dist 12562 as Silly Taylor					
	~~No4 1896 " " 12563~~					
15	No5 1896 " " 12564				#1 to 6	
	No6 1896 " " 12565				Date of Application for Enrollment.	
16						Sept. 29/98
17	No2 is now husband of Maggie Collins on Chickasaw card #787 Nov. 21, 1902					

No7 P.O. Durant I.T. 11/19/02

Choctaw By Blood Enrollment Cards 1898-1914

RESIDENCE: Chickasaw Nation ~~COUNTY~~. POST OFFICE: Sulphur, Ind. Ter. **Choctaw Nation** — Choctaw Roll *(Not Including Freedmen)* — CARD NO. / FIELD NO. **311**

Dawes' Roll No.	NAME	Relationship to Person First Named	AGE	SEX	BLOOD	TRIBAL ENROLLMENT Year	County	No.
VOID	1 Hilton, Charles N.	Named	31	M	I.W.			
VOID	2 " , Minnie	wife	24	F	1/4			
VOID	3 Flemmings, Joe	Stepson	5	M	1/8			
VOID	4 Hilton, Lonia Ruth	Dau	4mo	F	1/8			
	5							
	6							
	7							
	8	No2 on Chickasaw roll, Tishomingo County, Page 29 as Minnie Flemmings;						
	9	transferred to Choctaw roll by Dawes Com.						
	10	No.3 also on Chickasaw roll, same Page						
	11							
	12							
	13							
	14							
	15							
	16							
	17							

TRIBAL ENROLLMENT OF PARENTS

Name of Father	Year	County	Name of Mother	Year	County
1 Wm D. Hilton		non citizen	Sarah R Hilton	Dead	non citizen
2 Hamp Willis	Dead	Chickasaw roll	Delilah Willis now Davis		Towson County Choctaw roll
3 Will Flemmings	"	non citizen	No 2		
4 No. 1			No. 2		
5					
6					
7					
8					
9					
10					
11					
12					
13					
14					
15				Date of Application for Enrollment.	Sept. 29/98
16			No.4 Enrolled May 24, 1900		
17					

11

Choctaw By Blood Enrollment Cards 1898-1914

RESIDENCE: Chickasaw Nation ~~COUNTY~~.
POST OFFICE: Tishomingo, Ind. Ter.

Choctaw Nation

Choctaw Roll *(Not Including Freedmen)*

CARD NO.
FIELD NO. **312**

Dawes' Roll No.	NAME	Relationship to Person First Named	AGE	SEX	BLOOD	TRIBAL ENROLLMENT		
						Year	County	No.
VOID. 1	Folsome, John		38	M	1/2			
2								
3								
4								
5								
6								
7								
8								
9								
10								
11								
12								
13								
14								
15								
16								
17								

TRIBAL ENROLLMENT OF PARENTS

	Name of Father	Year	County	Name of Mother	Year	County
1	Loom Folsome		Blue	Rhoda Morris		Choctaw residing in Chickasaw Dist
2						
3						
4						
5						
6						
7						
8						
9						
10						
11						
12						
13						
14						
15				Date of Application for Enrollment.	Sept. 29/98	
16						
17						

CANCELLED

Transferred to [remainder illegible]

12

RESIDENCE: Chickasaw Nation ~~COUNTY~~
POST OFFICE: McGee, Ind. Ter.

Choctaw Nation

Choctaw Roll
(Not Including Freedmen)

CARD NO.
FIELD NO. **313**

Dawes' Roll No.	NAME	Relationship to Person First Named	AGE	SEX	BLOOD	TRIBAL ENROLLMENT		
						Year	County	No.
659	₁ Impson, Isaac ³⁶	First Named	32	M	Full		Choctaw residing in Chickasaw District	CCR #2 266
ᴵᵂ1083	₂ " , Mary J. ²⁹	Wife	25	F	I.W.			
	3							
	4							
	5							
	6					No 1	1896	Blue	6311
	7							
	8							
	9							
	10							
	11							
	12							
	13	For child of No 1 see NB (Apr 26-06) Card #756.						
	14	" " " " " " (Mar 3-05) " #1288.						
	15	Nos 1 and 2 have separated. See testimony taken 11/17/02.						
	16							
	17							

ENROLLMENT
OF NOS. 1 HEREON
APPROVED BY THE SECRETARY
OF INTERIOR Dec 12, 1902

ENROLLMENT
OF NOS. 2 HEREON
APPROVED BY THE SECRETARY
OF INTERIOR Nov 16, 1904

TRIBAL ENROLLMENT OF PARENTS

	Name of Father	Year	County	Name of Mother	Year	County
1	Kellop Impson	Dead	Choctaw Roll	Malina Freeney		Blue
2	A. Blackwell		Non-Citizen	Margaret Blackwell		Non-Citizen
3						
4						
5						
6						
7						
8						
9						
10						
11						
12						
13						
14						
15						
16						
17	P.O. Stonewall I.T.					

Date of Application for Enrollment.
Sept. 29/98

13

Choctaw By Blood Enrollment Cards 1898-1914

RESIDENCE: Tobucksy COUNTY. **Choctaw Nation** Choctaw Roll CARD NO.
POST OFFICE: Stewart, Ind. Ter. (Not Including Freedmen) FIELD NO. **314**

Dawes' Roll No.	NAME	Relationship to Person First Named	AGE	SEX	BLOOD	TRIBAL ENROLLMENT Year	County	No.
660	1 Quincy, Melvina 46	First Named	42	F	Full	1896	Tobucksy	10660
661	2 " , Jerome Ervin 25	son	21	M	1/2	1896	"	10667
662	3 " , Magdelene 23	Dau	19	F	1/2	1896	"	10661
663	4 " , Martha 21	"	17	"	1/2	1896	"	10662
664	5 " , Erasmus 15	son	11	M	1/2	1896	"	10663
665	6 " , Vada 12	Dau	8	F	1/2	1896	"	10664
666	7 " , Alice 10	"	6	"	1/2	1896	"	10665
667	8 " , Julia 8	"	4	"	1/2	1896	"	10666
668	9 " , Wm Warren 5	G. Son	9mo	M	3/4			
NB650	10 " Jackson							
	11	ENROLLMENT						
	12	OF NOS. 1,2,3,4,5,6,7,8 and 9 HEREON APPROVED BY THE SECRETARY						
	13	OF INTERIOR Dec 12 1902						
	14							
	15	For child of No.3 see NB (Apr 26-06) card #650						
	16	" " " No.2 " " (Mar 3-05) " #1291						
	17							

TRIBAL ENROLLMENT OF PARENTS

	Name of Father	Year	County	Name of Mother	Year	County
1	Bill Pusley	Dead	Atoka	Julia Pusley	Dead	Tobucksy
2	Herbert M. Quincy	1897	Chick residing in Choctaw N. 1st Dist	No. 1		
3	" " "	1897	" " " "	No. 1		
4	" " "	1897	" " " "	No. 1		
5	" " "	1897	" " " "	No. 1		
6	" " "	1897	" " " "	No. 1		
7	" " "	1897	" " " "	No. 1		
8	" " "	1897	" " " "	No. 1		
9	No. 2			Rebecca Quincy	Dead	Tobucksy
10	Nicholas Woolridge [sic]			No. 3	Born	Aug 23-05
11	No1 on Choctaw roll as Melvina Quincy					
12	No1 wife of Herbert M Quincy, Chickasaw roll Card No. 812					
	No2 on Choctaw roll as Ervin Quincy					
13	No3 " " " " Maggie "					
14	No5 " " " " Arasmus "					
15	No8 " " " " Hortona "					
16	No2 is the husband of Daisy Quincy on Choctaw card #4585					Date of Application for Enrollment.
	P.O. Address, Roff, Ind. Ter. Feby. 7, 1902					
17	Evidence of birth of No. 9 received and filed Feby 14, 1902.					Sept. 29, 1898

Choctaw By Blood Enrollment Cards 1898-1914

RESIDENCE: Tobucksy   COUNTY.   **Choctaw Nation**   **Choctaw Roll**   CARD NO.
POST OFFICE: Stewart, Ind. Ter.   *(Not Including Freedmen)*   FIELD NO. **315**

Dawes' Roll No.	NAME Stuart	Relationship to Person First Named	AGE	SEX	BLOOD	TRIBAL ENROLLMENT		
						Year	County	No.
								CCR #2
669	1 Gates, Gaines 22	First Named	18	M	Full		Tobucksy	200
	2							
	3	ENROLLMENT				1896	Tobucksy	4707
	4	OF NOS. I HEREON APPROVED BY THE SECRETARY						
	5	OF INTERIOR Dec 12, 1902						
	6							
	7							
	8							
	9							
	10							
	11							
	12							
	13							
	14							
	15							
	16							
	17							

TRIBAL ENROLLMENT OF PARENTS

Name of Father	Year	County	Name of Mother	Year	County
1 Sim-Li-e-shubby		Tobucksy		Dead	Choctaw Roll
2					
3					
4					
5					
6					
7					
8					
9					
10					
11					
12					
13				Date of Application for Enrollment.	
14				Sept. 29/98	
15					
16					
17					

Choctaw By Blood Enrollment Cards 1898-1914

RESIDENCE: Atoka COUNTY. **Choctaw Nation**   Choctaw Roll   CARD No.
POST OFFICE: Waupaunuka[sic] Ind. Ter.   (Not Including Freedmen)   FIELD No. 316

Dawes' Roll No.	NAME	Relationship to Person First Named	AGE	SEX	BLOOD	TRIBAL ENROLLMENT		
						Year	County	No.
670	1 Billis, Jackson 49	First Named	45	M	Full		Atoka	CCR #2 74
	2							
	3 ENROLLMENT					1896	Atoka	1819
	4 OF NOS. 1 HEREON APPROVED BY THE SECRETARY							
	5 OF INTERIOR DEC 12 1902							
	6							
	7							
	8							
	9 Husband of Louvina Billis, Chickasaw roll, Card No 819							
	10							
	11							
	12							
	13							
	14							
	15							
	16							
	17							

TRIBAL ENROLLMENT OF PARENTS

	Name of Father	Year	County	Name of Mother	Year	County
1	Billis	Dead	Choctaw roll	Ste-ma-che	Dead	Cedar
2						
3						
4						
5						
6						
7						
8						
9						
10						
11						
12						
13						
14					Date of Application for Enrollment.	Sept. 29/98
15						
16						
17						

16

Choctaw By Blood Enrollment Cards 1898-1914

RESIDENCE: Chickasaw Nation ~~COUNTY~~.   **Choctaw Nation**   Choctaw Roll *(Not Including Freedmen)*   CARD NO.
POST OFFICE: Wiley, Ind Ter.   FIELD NO. 317

Dawes' Roll No.	NAME	Relationship to Person First Named	AGE	SEX	BLOOD	TRIBAL ENROLLMENT		
						Year	County	No.
VOID.	1 Fillmore, Jacob		28	M	1/2			
	2							
	3							
	4							
	5							
	6	Husband of Selan Fillmore, Chickasaw roll, Card No. 832						
	7	On Chickasaw roll, Pontotoc County, Page 59; transferred to Choctaw						
	8	roll by Dawes Com.						
	9							
	10							
	11							
	12							
	13							
	14							
	15							
	16							
	17							

[Illegible]

CANCELLED

TRIBAL ENROLLMENT OF PARENTS

	Name of Father	Year	County	Name of Mother	Year	County
1	Millet Fillmore	Dead	Choctaw roll	Lottie Fillmore	Dead	Choctaw roll
2						
3						
4						
5						
6						
7						
8						
9						
10						
11						
12						
13						
14						
15						
16						
17						

Date of Application for Enrollment. 1898

17

Choctaw By Blood Enrollment Cards 1898-1914

RESIDENCE: Chickasaw Nation ~~COUNTY~~.
POST OFFICE: Wiley, Ind. Ter.

Choctaw Nation

Choctaw Roll
(Not Including Freedmen)

CARD NO.
FIELD NO. 318

Dawes' Roll No.	NAME	Relationship to Person First Named	AGE	SEX	BLOOD	TRIBAL ENROLLMENT		
						Year	County	No.
671	1 Cealey, Susan 27	First Named	23	F	Full		Blue	CCR #2 117
	2							
	3 ENROLLMENT					1896	Blue 2877 as Susan Cealy	
	4 OF NOS. 1 HEREON APPROVED BY THE SECRETARY							
	5 OF INTERIOR DEC 12 1902							
	6							
	7 Wife of Cephus Cealey. Chickasaw roll, Card No 840							
	8							
	9							
	10							
	11							
	12							
	13							
	14							
	15							
	16							
	17							

TRIBAL ENROLLMENT OF PARENTS

	Name of Father	Year	County	Name of Mother	Year	County
1	Simeon Pis-sa-chabby	Dead	Choctaw roll	Sally	Dead	Choctaw roll
2						
3						
4						
5						
6						
7						
8						
9						
10						
11						
12						
13						
14						
15				Date of Application for Enrollment.		Sept. 29/98
16						
17						

Choctaw By Blood Enrollment Cards 1898-1914

RESIDENCE: Atoka   COUNTY.   **Choctaw Nation**   **Choctaw Roll**   CARD NO.
POST OFFICE: Waupaunuka[sic] Ind. Ter.   (Not Including Freedmen)   FIELD NO. **319**

Dawes' Roll No.	NAME	Relationship to Person First Named	AGE	SEX	BLOOD	TRIBAL ENROLLMENT Year	County	No.
672	₁ Thornton, Sylvia ³⁰		26	F	3/4	Blue		CCR #2 383
673	₂ Goforth, Andrew ⁴	son	5mo	M	7/8			
674	₃ Thornton, Luther ²	son	1	M	7/8			
14881	₄ Ridley, William Munroe ¹	son	7mo	M	7/8			
	5				No 1	1896 Blue 9824 as Sopha Nelson		
	6	ENROLLMENT						
	7	OF NOS. 1,2 and 3 HEREON APPROVED BY THE SECRETARY						
	8	OF INTERIOR Dec 12 1902						
	9	ENROLLMENT						
	10	OF NOS. 4 HEREON APPROVED BY THE SECRETARY						
	11	OF INTERIOR May 21 1903						
	12							
	13							
	14							
	15							
	16							
	17							

TRIBAL ENROLLMENT OF PARENTS

	Name of Father	Year	County	Name of Mother	Year	County
₁	Wᵐ Morrison	Dead	Choctaw roll	Becky Morrison	dead	Choctaw roll
₂	Wᵐ Goforth		Blue	No. 1		
₃	Ed A Thornton		intermarried	No. 1		
₄	H. M. Ridley		non-citizen	No. 1		
5						
6	No 1 on Choctaw roll as Sophia Nelson					
7	No1 is now the wife of Edwin A. Thornton on Choctaw card #D.400				Nov. 25, 1901	
8	No. 3 born July 25, 1900. Enrolled Nov. 25, 1901.					
9						
10	No.4 Born Aug. 12, 1902, proof of birth received Oct. 2, 1902 returned for					
11	further information relative to the mother, returned and filed March 14, 1903.					
12						
13						
14						#1&2
15						Date of Application for Enrollment.
16						Sept. 29/98
₁₇	P.O. Tishomingo I.T.					

19

Choctaw By Blood Enrollment Cards 1898-1914

RESIDENCE: Chickasaw Nation ~~COUNTY~~.
POST OFFICE: Tishomingo, Ind Ter.

Choctaw Nation

Choctaw Roll (Not Including Freedmen)

CARD NO.
FIELD NO. 320

Dawes' Roll No.	NAME	Relationship to Person First Named	AGE	SEX	BLOOD	TRIBAL ENROLLMENT		
						Year	County	No.
DEAD. 1	McCurtain, Ada L		3	F	1/4		Sugar Loaf	CCR #2 363
2								
3	CIVILIZED TRIBES OF MARCH 31, 1905.							
4	ORDER OF THE COMMISSION TO THE FIVE HEREON DISMISSED UNDER No. 1							
5								
6	No. 1 HEREON DISMISSED UNDER							
7	ORDER OF THE COMMISSION TO THE FIVE CIVILIZED TRIBES OF MARCH 31, 1905.							
8								
9								
10								
11	Nº 1 Died May 15, 1900, proof of death filed Dec 24, 1902							
12								
13								
14	Joshua McCurtain on card 9-1454 Thos and Willie McCurtain							
15	children of Joshua McCurtain on card 7-2887							
16								
17								

TRIBAL ENROLLMENT OF PARENTS

Name of Father	Year	County	Name of Mother	Year	County
1 Joshua McCurtain		Sugar Loaf	Lottie McCurtain		non-citizen
2					
3					
4					
5					
6					
7					
8					
9					
10					
11					
12					
13					
14					
15			Date of Application for Enrollment.		Sept 30/98
16					
17					

CANCELLED

Dated prior to Sept. 25, 1902

Choctaw By Blood Enrollment Cards 1898-1914

RESIDENCE: Chickasaw Nation ~~COUNTY~~.
POST OFFICE: Waupaunuka[sic], Ind. Ter. **Choctaw Nation** **Choctaw Roll** *(Not Including Freedmen)* CARD NO.
FIELD NO. 321

Dawes' Roll No.	NAME	Relationship to Person First Named	AGE	SEX	BLOOD	TRIBAL ENROLLMENT		
						Year	County	No.
I.W. 198	1 Howell, Sallie 32		28	F	I.W.			
	2							
	3							
	4							
	5	ENROLLMENT OF NOS. ~~1~~ HEREON APPROVED BY THE SECRETARY OF INTERIOR DEC 24 1903						
	6							
	7							
	8	Admitted by Dawes Com Case No. 1348 and no appeal taken.						
	9							
	10	Married to Chas W. Howell, a U.S. citizen in 1893 (before admission by Dawes Com.)						
	11	Choctaw husband Joseph H Riley deceased, father of Joanna Riley						
	12	on Choctaw card #56.						
	13							
	14							
	15							
	16							
	17							

TRIBAL ENROLLMENT OF PARENTS

	Name of Father	Year	County	Name of Mother	Year	County
1	James Moore		non citizen	Elizabeth Moore		non citizen
2						
3						
4						
5						
6						
7						
8						
9						
10						
11						
12						
13						
14						
15						Sept. 30/98
16						
17						

21

Choctaw By Blood Enrollment Cards 1898-1914

RESIDENCE: Chickasaw Nation ~~COUNTY.~~ **Choctaw Nation**   **Choctaw Roll**   CARD No.

POST OFFICE: Emmet, Ind. Ter.   (Not Including Freedmen)   FIELD No.   322

Dawes' Roll No.	NAME	Relationship to Person First Named	AGE	SEX	BLOOD	TRIBAL ENROLLMENT		
						Year	County	No.
1	~~Keel, Easmon~~ Eastman		41	M	Full	1893	Chick Dist	339
2								
3								
4								
5								
6								
7								
8								
9								
10								
11								
12								
13								
14								
15								
16								
17								

TRIBAL ENROLLMENT OF PARENTS

	Name of Father	Year	County	Name of Mother	Year	County
1	Cah-non-tom-by	Dead	Choctaw roll	Sally	Dead	Choctaw roll
2						
3						
4						
5						
6						
7						
8						
9						
10						
11						
12						
13						
14						
15				Date of Application for Enrollment.		Sept. 30/98
16						
17						

CANCELLED

#965 and transferred to Chickasaw Card Aug 10, 1903

Choctaw By Blood Enrollment Cards 1898-1914

RESIDENCE: Chickasaw Nation ~~COUNTY~~. **Choctaw Nation** Choctaw Roll — CARD NO.
POST OFFICE: Waupaunuka[sic], Ind. Ter. (Not Including Freedmen) FIELD NO. 323

Dawes' Roll No.	NAME	Relationship to Person First Named	AGE	SEX	BLOOD	TRIBAL ENROLLMENT		
						Year	County	No.
VOID. 1	~~Fillmore, Silas~~		54	M	3/4		Choctaw residing in Chickasaw District	CCR #2
2							"	C.I. Roll
3								
4								
5								
6								
7	Husband of Mary Ann Fillmore, Chickasaw Roll Card No 888.							
8	On Chickasaw roll, Pontotoc County, Page 58; transferred to Choctaw roll by Dawes Com							
9								
10								
11								
12								
13								
14								
15								
16								
17								

TRIBAL ENROLLMENT OF PARENTS

	Name of Father	Year	County	Name of Mother	Year	County
1	~~Millard Fillmore~~	Dead	~~Choctaw roll~~	~~Lottie Fillmore~~	Dead	Choctaw residing in Chickasaw Dist
2						
3						
4						
5						
6						
7						
8						
9						
10						
11						
12						
13						
14						
15				Date of Application for Enrollment.		Sept. 30/98
16						
17						

CANCELLED

Transferred to. [remainder illegible]

Choctaw By Blood Enrollment Cards 1898-1914

RESIDENCE: Chickasaw Nation ~~COUNTY~~.   **Choctaw Nation**   Choctaw Roll   CARD No.
POST OFFICE: Wiley, Ind. Ter.   (Not Including Freedmen)   FIELD No. 324

Dawes' Roll No.	NAME	Relationship to Person First Named	AGE	SEX	BLOOD	TRIBAL ENROLLMENT		
						Year	County	No.
VOID.	1 Fillmore, Elias		40	M	1/2			
	2							
	3							
	4							
	5							
	6							
	7							
	8	Husband of Epsie Fillmore, Chickasaw Card No 893						
	9							
	10	On Chickasaw roll, Pontotoc County, Page 59; transferred to Choctaw roll by Dawes Com.						
	11							
	12							
	13							
	14							
	15							
	16							
	17							

TRIBAL ENROLLMENT OF PARENTS

Name of Father	Year	County	Name of Mother	Year	County
1 Millard Fillmore	Dead	Chickasaw roll	Maria Fillmore	Dead	Choctaw roll
2					
3					
4					
5					
6					
7					
8					
9					
10					
11					
12					
13					
14					
15				Date of Application for Enrollment.	Sept. 30/98	
16					
17					

CANCELLED

transferred to [remainder illegible]

24

Choctaw By Blood Enrollment Cards 1898-1914

RESIDENCE: Chickasaw Nation ~~COUNTY~~. **Choctaw Nation** Choctaw Roll CARD NO.

POST OFFICE: Spanish Fort, Texas *(Not Including Freedmen)* FIELD NO. 325

Dawes' Roll No.	NAME	Relationship to Person First Named	AGE	SEX	BLOOD	TRIBAL ENROLLMENT Year	County	No.
675	1 Ady, Marie Jane ⁴⁹	First Named	45	F	1/4		Sugar Loaf	CCR #2 168
676	2 Johnson, Maude L ²²	Dau	18	"	1/8		" "	CCR #2 277
677	3 " , Victor M ²⁵	Son	21	M	1/8		" "	CCR #2 434
678	4 " , Jennie ¹	Gran.dau	4mo	F	1/16			
IW 1496	5 " , Dicie E	Wife of No3	19	F	I.W.			
	6							
	7	ENROLLMENT OF NOS. 1 2 3 and 4 HEREON			No 1 on Choctaw roll as Mary Jane Folley			
	8	APPROVED BY THE SECRETARY						
	9	OF INTERIOR DEC 12 1902						
	10	ENROLLMENT						
	11	OF NOS. ~~5~~ HEREON APPROVED BY THE SECRETARY						
	12	OF INTERIOR NOV 27 1905						
	13							
	14							
	15							
	16							
	17							

TRIBAL ENROLLMENT OF PARENTS

	Name of Father	Year	County	Name of Mother	Year	County
1	Geo. Grubbs	Dead	non citizen	Nancy Ann Grubbs	Dead	Blue
2	Stephen H Johnson	"	" "	No 1		
3	" " "	"	" "	No 1		
4	No.3			Dicie Johnson		white woman
5	Joshua W Walker		non citizen	Dicie E Walker		noncitizen
6						
7	No3 is now married to Dicie Johnson, a white woman Dec 3rd, 1900					
8	No1 1896 Sugar Loaf 3973 as Mary J. Folley					
9	No2 1896 " " 6567 " Maud L Johnson					
10	No3 1895 " " 11780 " Victor M. Staytahm[sic].					
11	No.4 Enrolled December 3rd, 1900					
12	No.3 also on 1896 Choctaw roll, Wade County, page 292. #11344 as Richard Stidham.					
13	No 5 placed hereon June 22, 1905 by an order of the Commission of that date holding					
14	that application was made for her enrollment within the time provided by the act of					
15	Congress approved July 1, 1902 (32 Stat 641)					Date of Application for Enrollment.
16	№2 P O Tishomingo I T					
17	P.O. Guertie, I T					Sept. 30/98

Choctaw By Blood Enrollment Cards 1898-1914

RESIDENCE: Chickasaw Natn COUNTY.
POST OFFICE: Regan, I.T.

Choctaw Nation

Choctaw Roll CARD NO.
(Not Including Freedmen) FIELD NO. 326

Dawes' Roll No.	NAME	Relationship to Person First Named	AGE	SEX	BLOOD	TRIBAL ENROLLMENT		
						Year	County	No.
1	Gaddis, Will	Named	28	M	1/2		Choctaw residing in Chickasaw District	CCR #2 216
2								
3								
4								
5	No. 1 also on 1896 Chickasaw roll page 38 as Willie Gaddis							
6								
7								
8	Nº1 is the husband of Sallie McKinney on Chickasaw card #830							
9								
10								
11								
12								
13								
14								
15								
16								
17								

TRIBAL ENROLLMENT OF PARENTS

	Name of Father	Year	County	Name of Mother	Year	County
1	Jack Gaddis	1897	Chu ku [illegible]	Melvina Johnson	1897	Choc. residing in Chickasaw District
2						
3						
4						
5						
6						
7						
8						
9						
10						
11						
12						
13						
14						
15						
16						
17	Alhambra I.T.				Date of Application for Enrollment.	9 - 30 - 98

CANCELLED

No1 transferred to Chickasaw card 830 March 19, 1904

Choctaw By Blood Enrollment Cards 1898-1914

RESIDENCE: Chickasaw Natn ~~COUNTY.~~
POST OFFICE: Tishomingo, I.T.

Choctaw Nation

Choctaw Roll *(Not Including Freedmen)*

CARD NO.
FIELD NO. 327

Dawes' Roll No.	NAME	Relationship to Person First Named	AGE	SEX	BLOOD	TRIBAL ENROLLMENT		
						Year	County	No.
1	Thompson, Jacob Loren	Named	24	M	1/16	1896	Choc. residing in Chickasaw Dist	12560
2								
3								
4								
5	On Chickasaw Roll, Tishomingo County, Page 32. Transferred to Choctaw							
6	Roll by Dawes Commission							
7	On Chickasaw roll Jacob L Thompson							
8	No.1 on 1896 Choctaw census roll, page 328: No. 12560 as L. Thompson							
9	No.1 is now the husband of Mattie Cheadle on							
10	Chickasaw card #910. April 6, 1900							
11								
12								
13								
14								
15								
16								
17								

TRIBAL ENROLLMENT OF PARENTS

	Name of Father	Year	County	Name of Mother	Year	County
1	T. J. Thompson	Dead	Tishomingo	Lou J. Thompson	1897	Choc. residing in Tishomingo
2						
3						
4						
5						
6						
7						
8						
9						
10						
11						
12						
13						
14						
15					Date of Application for Enrollment.	
16						
17					9 - 30 - 98	

CANCELLED

Transferred to Chickasaw Card 1896 February 8

RESIDENCE: Chickasaw Nation ~~COUNTY~~.
POST OFFICE: Palmer, Ind. Ter.

Choctaw Nation

Choctaw Roll
(Not Including Freedmen)

CARD No.
FIELD No. 328

Dawes' Roll No.	NAME		Relationship to Person First Named	AGE	SEX	BLOOD	TRIBAL ENROLLMENT		
							Year	County	No.
679	1 Sheegog, Myrtie	22	First Named	18	F	1/4		Choctaw residing in Chickasaw Dist	CCR #2 375
680	2 " , May Eula	4	Dau	13 days	"	1/8			
681	3 " , James Bland	2	Son	2mo	M	1/8			
682	4 " , Maggie Lillie	1	Dau	1½	F	1/8			
I.W. 174	5 " , Charley		Husband	29	M	I.W.			
	6		ENROLLMENT	No.1 1896 Chickasaw Dist 9501 as Myrtle McClung					
	7		OF NOS. 1 2 3 and 4 HEREON APPROVED BY THE SECRETARY						
	8		OF INTERIOR Dec 12 1902						
	9								
	10		ENROLLMENT						
	11		OF NOS. 5 ~~~~~ HEREON APPROVED BY THE SECRETARY						
	12		OF INTERIOR Jun 13, 1903						
	13		#3 "Died prior to September 25, 1902: not entitled to land or money"						
	14		See Indian office letter May 13, 1910. D.C. #667-1910.						
	15		No1 is the wife of Charley Sheegog on Choctaw card #D58. No2 affidavit of attending physician to be supplied - Received Oct 21/98						
	16		No3 Enrolled Oct. 16th, 1900.						
	17		No4 Born May 15" 1902: Enrolled July 1st 1902.						

TRIBAL ENROLLMENT OF PARENTS

Name of Father	Year	County	Name of Mother	Year	County
1 Lundey McClung		Non Citizen	Emma McClung		Choctaw residing in Chickasaw Dist
2 Charly[sic] Sheegog		White Man	No 1		
3 " " "		Charley"Sheegog on Choctaw card #D58	No 1		
4 " " "			No 1		
5 Jim Sheegog	Dead	non Citizen	Lantha Sheegog		non Citizen
6					
7					
8 No2 Full correct given name is May Eula. See copy of letter from Patchell & Pyeatt filed Aug 13, 1902.					
9 No3 died November 1 1900: Proof of death filed October 25, 1902					
10 No5 transferred from Choctaw card #D58. See decision of May 5, 1903.					
11 For child of Nos 1&5 see NB (Apr 26-06) Card #654.					
12					
13					
14					#1&2
15				Date of Application for Enrollment.	Oct 1/98
16					
17					

RESIDENCE: Chickasaw Nation ~~COUNTY~~.   **Choctaw Nation**   **Choctaw Roll**   CARD NO.
POST OFFICE: Norton, Ind. Ter.   *(Not Including Freedmen)*   FIELD NO. 329

Dawes' Roll No.	NAME	Relationship to Person First Named	AGE	SEX	BLOOD	TRIBAL ENROLLMENT		
						Year	County	No.
VOID. 1	~~Brawdy, Johnson~~		27	M	1/4			
VOID. 2	" , Ada	Wife	18	F	I.W.			
VOID. 3	" Dave	Son	5mo	M	1/8			
4								
5	No 1 on Chickasaw roll as Johnson Broady.							
6	On Chickasaw roll, Tishomingo County, age 33; transferred to Choctaw							
7	roll by Dawes Com							
8	Full name of No2 is Ada Catherine Brawdy. See letter from her filed Oct. 1, 1902.							
9	No. 3 Enrolled Oct 1, 1901.							
10								
11								
12								
13								
14								
15								
16								
17								

TRIBAL ENROLLMENT OF PARENTS

	Name of Father	Year	County	Name of Mother	Year	County
1	John Brawdy	Dead	non citizen	Sealy Brawdy now Norton		Choctaw residing in Chickasaw Dist
2	Frank Caldwell		"	Ada Caldwell	Dead	Non Citz
3	No 1			No 2		
4						
5						
6						
7						
8						
9						
10						
11						
12						
13						
14					Date of Application for Enrollment.	
15					Oct 1/98	
16					No2 enrolled Aug 15/99	
17						

Choctaw By Blood Enrollment Cards 1898-1914

RESIDENCE: Chickasaw Nation <s>COUNTY.</s> **Choctaw Nation** Choctaw Roll CARD No.
POST OFFICE: Oakland, Ind. Ter. (Not Including Freedmen) FIELD No. **330**

Dawes' Roll No.	NAME	Relationship to Person First Named	AGE	SEX	BLOOD	TRIBAL ENROLLMENT		
						Year	County	No.
15209	1 Buckholts, John M ⁴⁸	First Named	44	M	1/16		Choctaw residing in Chickasaw district	CCR #2 80
IW 874	2 " , Frances E. ⁴⁴	wife	40	F	I.W.		" "	C.I. Roll 11
15210	3 " , Everett ²¹	son	17	M	1/32		" "	CCR #2 80
15211	4 " , William Lee ¹¹	"	7	"	1/32		" "	"
15212	5 " , Fannie Olive ⁷	dau	5	F	1/32		" "	"
15213	6 " , John B. Jr. ⁶	son	2	M	1/32		" "	"
	see opinion of Atty Genl of Feb. 10 '04 and letter of Secy of Interior of Feby 24 '04 in case of James M Buckholts et al 7-5738							
	9							
	10 #1 not admitted by							
	11 Supreme Court in Oct 1872 when his							
	12 father William		No1 1896 Chickasaw Dist			1991 as John Buckholtz		
	13 Buckholts, R.T.		No2 1896 "		"	14353 " Francis E. "		
	14 Jonir[sic] & John		No3 1896 "		"	1993 " Everid "		
	Null alone were		No4 1896 "		"	1994 " William "		
	15 admitted		No5 1896 "		"	1995 " Fannie "		
	16		No6 1896 "		"	1996		
	17							

TRIBAL ENROLLMENT OF PARENTS

	Name of Father	Year	County	Name of Mother	Year	County
1	Wᵐ Buckholts		Blue	Matilda Buckholts	dead	non citizen
2	George Price	dead	non citizen	Manerva Price	"	"
3	No 1			No 2		
4	No 1			No 2		
5	No 1			No 2		
6	No 1			No 2		
7						
8	No3 on Choctaw roll as Everd Buckholts					
9	No4 " " " " William "					
	No5 " " " " Fannie "					
10						
11						
12						
13			See affidavit of No2 and that of attending physicians			
14			as to her inability to appear at Tishomingo, before the			
15			Commission in person, filed Nov. 6, 1902			
16						
17	11/6/02 Madill I.T. Evidence of marriage between Nos 1 and 2 filed Nov. 14, 1902					

ENROLLMENT OF NOS. 2 HEREON APPROVED BY THE SECRETARY OF INTERIOR Aug 3 1904

ENROLLMENT OF NOS. 1-3-4-5-6 HEREON APPROVED BY THE SECRETARY OF INTERIOR May 9, 1904

Date of Application for Enrollment.

Oct 1/98

RESIDENCE: Chickasaw Nation ~~COUNTY.~~ **Choctaw Nation** Choctaw Roll CARD No.

POST OFFICE: Chickasha, Ind. Ter. *(Not Including Freedmen)* FIELD NO. 331

Dawes' Roll No.	NAME	Relationship to Person First Named	AGE	SEX	BLOOD	TRIBAL ENROLLMENT		
						Year	County	No.
VOID. 1	~~Perry, Charley~~		23	M	1/2			
2								
3								
4								
5								
6								
7	On Chickasaw roll, Panola County, Page 7; transferred to Choctaw roll by							
8	Dawes Com.							
9								
10								
11								
12								
13								
14								
15								
16								
17								

TRIBAL ENROLLMENT OF PARENTS

	Name of Father	Year	County	Name of Mother	Year	County
1	~~Levi Perry~~	Dead	Choctaw residing in Chickasaw Dist	~~Ellen Willis Perry~~	Dead	Choctaw residing in Chickasaw District
2						
3						
4						
5						
6						
7						
8						
9						
10						
11						
12						
13						
14						
15				Date of Application for Enrollment,		Oct 1/98
16						
17						

Choctaw By Blood Enrollment Cards 1898-1914

RESIDENCE: Chickasaw Natn ~~COUNTY~~. **Choctaw Nation** Choctaw Roll CARD NO.

POST OFFICE: Tishomingo, I.T. *(Not Including Freedmen)* FIELD NO. 332

Dawes' Roll No.	NAME	Relationship to Person First Named	AGE	SEX	BLOOD	TRIBAL ENROLLMENT		
						Year	County	No.
VOID.	1 Chapman, Thos. Jefferson	Named	48	M	I.W.			
VOID.	2 " Susan	Wife	46	F	3/4			
VOID.	3 " Edward	Son	18	M	3/8			
VOID.	4 " Ellen	Dau	15	F	"			
VOID.	5 " James Thomas	Son	12	M	"			
VOID.	6 " John Napoleon	"	9	"	"			
	7							
	8 No1 - Affidavit of Judge Brown as to license to be supplied - Received Oct 21/98							
	9							
	10 No1 on Chickasaw Roll as T.J. Chapman No5 on Chick roll as James Chapman							
	No3 " " " " Edwin Chapman No6 " " " " John Chapman							
	11							
	12							
	13							
	14							
	15							
	16							
	17							

TRIBAL ENROLLMENT OF PARENTS

	Name of Father	Year	County	Name of Mother	Year	County
1	G.W. Chapman	18__	Non-Citz	Liza Chapman	Dead	Non-Citz
2	John E. Anderson	Dead	Tishomingo	Jincy Hayes	"	Tishomingo
3	No 1			No 2		
4	No 1			No 2		
5	No 1			No 2		
6	No 1			No 2		
7						
8						
9						
10						
11	No1 - On Chickasaw roll, Pickens County, Page 79 transferred to Choctaw Roll by Dawes Com					
12	Nos2-3-4 " " " Tishomingo County, Page 35 " " " " " "					
13	Nos 5-6 " " " " " 34 " " " " " "					
14						
15						
16						
17				Date of Application for Enrollment	10 - 1 - 98	

CANCELLED (watermark)

Transferred to [remainder illegible] (watermark)

Choctaw By Blood Enrollment Cards 1898-1914

RESIDENCE: Chickasaw Nation ~~COUNTY.~~   **Choctaw Nation**   Choctaw Roll   CARD NO.
POST OFFICE: Oakland, I.T.   (Not Including Freedmen)   FIELD NO.   333

Dawes' Roll No.	NAME	Relationship to Person First Named	AGE	SEX	BLOOD	TRIBAL ENROLLMENT		
						Year	County	No.
15214	₁ Murphy, Burly Sedelia ²³		19	F	1/32	1897	Choctaw residing in Chickasaw Dist	CCR #2 18
I.W. 875	₂ " James C. ⁴⁰	Hus.	40	M	I.W.	1896	Chick. Dist	14841
						1896	Chickasaw Dist	8899
	☞ ₄ See opinion of Atty Genl of Feb. 18 '04 and letter of Secy of Interior							
	of Feby 24 '04 in case of James M Buckholts et al 7-5738							
	₅							
	₆							
	₇							
	₈							
	₉							
	₁₀							
	₁₁							
	₁₂							
	₁₃							
	₁₄	ENROLLMENT OF NOS. 1 HEREON APPROVED BY THE SECRETARY OF INTERIOR MAY 9 1904	ENROLLMENT OF NOS. ~~2~~ HEREON APPROVED BY THE SECRETARY OF INTERIOR AUG 3 1904					
	₁₅							
	₁₆							
	₁₇							

TRIBAL ENROLLMENT OF PARENTS

Name of Father	Year	County	Name of Mother	Year	County
₁ John M Buckholtz	1897	Pickens	Frances Buckholtz	1897	Pickens
₂ John Murphy	1897	Non Citizen	Elizabeth Murphy	Dead	Non citizen
₃					
₄					
₅					

₆ No1 is the Grand-daughter of Wᵐ Buckholts admitted by Supreme Court Choctaw Nation Oct '72

₇ On roll as Burly Murphy

₈

₉ No.1 is the wife of James C. Murphy on Choctaw card #D.60

₁₀ No.2 transferred from Choctaw card #D-60 July 7, 1904. See decision of June 21, 1904.

₁₁

₁₂

₁₃

₁₄

₁₅

₁₆ No2 P.O. Connerville I.T. 11/20/02

₁₇ P.O [Illegible.] 7/13/0[?]

Date of Application for Enrollment 10 -1 -98

Choctaw By Blood Enrollment Cards 1898-1914

RESIDENCE: Chickasaw Nation ~~COUNTY~~.   **Choctaw Nation**   Choctaw Roll   CARD NO.
POST OFFICE: Buckchitto[sic], I.T.   *(Not Including Freedmen)*   FIELD NO. 334

Dawes' Roll No.	NAME	Relationship to Person First Named	AGE	SEX	BLOOD	TRIBAL ENROLLMENT		
						Year	County	No.
VOID.	1 Thompson, Selena Isabella		8	F	1/2			
	2							
	3							
	4							
	5							
	6	On Chickasaw Roll, Tishomingo County, Page 3___ transferred						
	7	to Choctaw Roll by the Dawes Com.						
	8							
	9	On Chickasaw roll Selena Thompson						
	10	See Choctaw Card #3807.						
	11							
	12							
	13							
	14							
	15							
	16							
	17							

TRIBAL ENROLLMENT OF PARENTS

	Name of Father	Year	County	Name of Mother	Year	County
1	Thos. B. Thompson	189_	Tishomingo Chickasaw roll	Isabella Thompson	1897	Blue
2						
3						
4						
5						
6						
7						
8						
9						
10						
11						
12						
13						
14						
15						
16						
17				Date of Application for Enrollment.		10-1-98

CANCELLED

Transferred to [remainder illegible]

Choctaw By Blood Enrollment Cards 1898-1914

RESIDENCE: Chickasaw Nation ~~COUNTY.~~ **Choctaw Nation** **Choctaw Roll** CARD No.

POST OFFICE: Emet, I.T. *(Not Including Freedmen)* FIELD No. 335

Dawes' Roll No.	NAME	Relationship to Person First Named	AGE	SEX	BLOOD	TRIBAL ENROLLMENT		
						Year	County	No.
1	Walker, Theodore D		27	M	1/4	1896	Atoka	13990
2								
3								
4								
5								
6								
7	On Chickasaw Roll, Pontotoc County, Page 43, transferred							
8	to Choctaw Roll by the Dawes Com.							
9								
10	On 1896 roll, Page 367 as Theodore Walker							
11								
12								
13								
14								
15								
16								
17								

TRIBAL ENROLLMENT OF PARENTS

	Name of Father	Year	County	Name of Mother	Year	County
1	Trudy C Walker	1897	Pontotoc	Adeline Walker	Dead	Pontotoc
2						
3						
4						
5						
6						
7						
8						
9						
10						
11						
12						
13						
14						
15						
16						
17					Date of Application for Enrollment	10-1-98

Choctaw By Blood Enrollment Cards 1898-1914

RESIDENCE: Chickasaw Nation ~~COUNTY.~~ **Choctaw Nation**   **Choctaw Roll**   CARD No.

POST OFFICE: Marietta, Ind. Ter.   *(Not Including Freedmen)*   FIELD No. **336**

Dawes' Roll No.	NAME	Relationship to Person First Named	AGE	SEX	BLOOD	TRIBAL ENROLLMENT		
						Year	County	No.
VOID.	₁ East, Frances		67	F	1/2			
VOID.	₂ Green, Daniel	son	24	M	1/4			
VOID.	₃ Adams, Charles	"	18	"	1/4			
	4							
	5							
	6	No 1 on Chickasaw roll as Francis East.						
	7							
	8	All on Chickasaw roll, Pickens County, Page 26, transferred to Choctaw						
	9	roll by Dawes Com.						
	10							
	11							
	12							
	13							
	14							
	15							
	16							
	17							

TRIBAL ENROLLMENT OF PARENTS

	Name of Father	Year	County	Name of Mother	Year	County
₁	David Colbert	Dead	Chickasaw roll	Mamie Colbert	Dead	Choctaw roll
₂	Daniel Green	"	non citizen	No 1		
₃	Charles Adams	"	" "	No 1		
4						
5						
6						
7						
8						
9						
10						
11						
12						
13						
14						
15						Date of Application for Enrollment. Oct 3/98
16						
17						

Choctaw By Blood Enrollment Cards 1898-1914

RESIDENCE: Chickasaw Nation ~~COUNTY~~.
POST OFFICE: Bob, Ind Ter.

Choctaw Nation

Choctaw Roll *(Not Including Freedmen)*

CARD No.
FIELD No. 337

Dawes' Roll No.	NAME	Relationship to Person First Named	AGE	SEX	BLOOD	TRIBAL ENROLLMENT		
						Year	County	No.
Void	1 Green, Redie Jackson	Named	28	M	1/4			
Void	2 ", William Elvie	son	8	"	1/8			
Void	3 ", Myrtle Emma	Dau	6	F	1/8			
	4							
	5	No1 married under name of Dutch Green.						
	6	No2 on Chickasaw roll as Wm E. Green						
	7	No3 " " " Myrtle E "						
	8	No1 is the husband of Etta Green on Choctaw card #D.61						
	9	No1 Chickasaw Pay Roll No 2, Page 90						
	10	No2 " " " No 2 " 90						
	11	No3 " " " No 2 " 90						
	12							
	13							
	14							
	15							
	16							
	17							

TRIBAL ENROLLMENT OF PARENTS

	Name of Father	Year	County	Name of Mother	Year	County
1	Daniel Green	Dead	non citizen	Frances East		Choctaw residing in Chickasaw Dist
2	No 1			Etta Green		white woman
3	No 1			" "		" "

Date of Application for Enrollment. Oct 3/98

37

Choctaw By Blood Enrollment Cards 1898-1914

RESIDENCE: Chickasaw Nation ~~COUNTY~~.
POST OFFICE: Johnson, Ind. Ter.

Choctaw Nation

Choctaw Roll
(Not Including Freedmen)

CARD NO.

FIELD NO. 338

Dawes' Roll No.	NAME	Relationship to Person First Named	AGE	SEX	BLOOD	TRIBAL ENROLLMENT		
						Year	County	No.
void	1 ~~Thompson, Minnie Lee~~	~~First Named~~	~~24~~	~~F~~	~~1/4~~			
void	2 ~~", Mamie Frances~~	~~dau~~	~~7~~	~~"~~	~~1/8~~			
void	3 ~~", Robert Lee~~	~~son~~	~~5~~	~~M~~	~~1/8~~			
void	4 ~~", Charles William~~	~~"~~	~~3~~	~~"~~	~~1/8~~			
void	5 ~~", Emma Augusta~~	~~dau~~	~~1~~	~~F~~	~~1/8~~			
void	6 ~~", Jessie May~~	~~"~~	~~5mo~~	~~"~~	~~1/8~~			
	7							
	First four on Chickasaw roll, Pontotoc Co, Page 61, transferred to Choctaw roll by Dawes Com.							
	No. 5_9 " " " " " " 86 " " " " " "							
	10 No2 on Chickasaw roll as Francis							
	11 No3 " " " " R. L.							
	12 No4 " " " " C. W.							
	13 No1 was also admitted as a Chickasaw by blood by							
	14 U.S. Court Sou. Dist. Ind. Ter. March 12, 1898, in							
	15 Court case #54							
	16 Aug 13, 1900 Evidence of birth of No.5 received and filed							
	17							

TRIBAL ENROLLMENT OF PARENTS

Name of Father	Year	County	Name of Mother	Year	County
1 ~~Daniel Green~~	~~Dead~~	~~non-citizen,~~	~~Frances East~~		Choctaw residing in Chickasaw Dist
2 ~~J. W. Thompson~~		~~white man~~	~~No 1~~		
3 " "		"	No 1		
4 " "		"	No 1		
5 " "		"	No 1		
6 " "		"	No 1		
7					
8					
9					
10					
11					
12				Date of Application for Enrollment.	
13					
14			On Chickasaw card Sept. 16/98		
15			" Choctaw " Oct. 3/98		
16			No6 enrolled Nov. 1/99		
17 See Chickasaw C #9					

38

RESIDENCE: Chickasaw Nation ~~COUNTY~~.   **Choctaw Nation**   Choctaw Roll   CARD NO.
POST OFFICE: Pickens, Ind Ter   *(Not Including Freedmen)*   FIELD NO. **339**

Dawes' Roll No.	NAME	Relationship to Person First Named	AGE	SEX	BLOOD	TRIBAL ENROLLMENT		
						Year	County	No.
IW 1282	Mayo, James D. ~~42~~ ~~DIED PRIOR TO SEPTEMBER 25, 1902~~	First Named	37	M	I.W.		Choctaw residing in Chickasaw District	
~~683~~	2 " N.J. Wallace ~~40~~	~~wife~~	~~36~~	~~F~~	~~1/4~~	~~1896~~	" "	~~8918~~
684	3 Goldstan, Estella ~~20~~	dau	16	"	1/8	1896	" "	8924
685	4 Scott, Phoebe Ethel ~~18~~	"	14	"	1/8	1896	" "	8925
686	5 Mayo, James L. ~~13~~	son	9	M	1/8	1896	" "	8926
687	6 " , Ida Preston ~~11~~	"	7	"	1/8	1896	" "	8927
688	7 " , John Edward ~~8~~	"	4	"	1/8	1896	" "	8928
689	8 " , William Phillip ~~6~~	"	1	"	1/8	ENROLLMENT OF NOS. 2,3,4,5,6,7,8 and 9 HEREON APPROVED BY THE SECRETARY OF INTERIOR Dec 12, 1902		
690	9 Scott, Lorena ~~1~~	grand dau	1/2	F	1/16			
	10							
	11 No1 marriage license and certificate to be supplied.							
	No4 on Choctaw roll as Theblin Mayo. For child of No4 see N.B. (March 3, 1905) #1161.							
	12 No6 " " " " I. Foster "					ENROLLMENT		
	13 No7 " " " " Jno Edmund "					OF NOS. 1 HEREON APPROVED BY THE SECRETARY		
	No1 " " " " W.G.Walker "					OF INTERIOR Mar 14 1905		
	14 Dec 10/98 Affidavit of R.J. Hogue as to marriage received							
	15 No4 the wife of ~~Chopling Scott on Choctaw D578 7 5797~~							
	16 Marriage license filed this date, June 20, 1900							
	17 No5 on Choctaw roll as Jas. L. Mayo							

TRIBAL ENROLLMENT OF PARENTS

Name of Father	Year	County	Name of Mother	Year	County
1 John A. Mayo	dead	non citizen	Phoebe Mayo		non citizen
2 ~~Ed. Wallace~~	~~dead~~	~~" "~~	~~Martha Ann Wallace~~	~~dead~~	~~Choctaw roll~~
3		No. 1			No. 2
4		No. 1			No. 2
5		No. 1			No. 2
6		No. 1			No. 2
7		No. 1			No. 2
8		No. 1			No. 2
9 Chopley Scott		non citz			No. 4
10 No2 died Jan 1-1902· Enrollment cancelled by Department July 8, 1904					
11 For child of No4 see NB (Apr 26-06) card #700					
12 No3 is now the wife of James W. Goldston on					
13 Choctaw card #D.781, Sept 2, 1902 7-6076.					
No1 admitted by act of general council of					
14 Choctaw Nation, approved Oct. 20, 1883					
15 No.9 born June 21, 1901 and					
Enrolled Dec. 5. 1901				Date of Application for Enrollment.	Oct 3/98
16					
17 P.O. Riley I.T. 11/29/04				→	1 to 8 inc

For child of No.3 see N.B. (Mar 3, 1905) #1307

Choctaw By Blood Enrollment Cards 1898-1914

RESIDENCE: Chickasaw Nation ~~COUNTY.~~
POST OFFICE: Kingston, Ind Ter.

Choctaw Nation

Choctaw Roll
(Not Including Freedmen)

CARD NO.
FIELD NO. **340**

Dawes' Roll No.	NAME	Relationship to Person First Named	AGE	SEX	BLOOD	TRIBAL ENROLLMENT		
						Year	County	No.
691	1 Peter, Stephen ⁴⁹	First Named	45	M	Full		Choctaw residing in Chickasaw Dist	CCR #2 405
	2							
	3					1896	Chickasaw Dist	10625
	4							
	5							
	6							
	7	Husband of Martha Peter, Chickasaw roll, card No. 988						
	8							
	9							
	10							
	11							
	12							
	13							
	14							
	15							
	16							
	17							

ENROLLMENT
OF NOS. 1 HEREON
APPROVED BY THE SECRETARY
OF INTERIOR Dec 12 1902

TRIBAL ENROLLMENT OF PARENTS

	Name of Father	Year	County	Name of Mother	Year	County
1	John Peter	dead	Choctaw roll	Viney Peter	dead	Choctaw roll
2						
3						
4						
5						
6						
7						
8						
9						
10						
11						
12						
13						
14						
15					Date of Application for Enrollment. Oct 3/98	
16						
17						

40

Choctaw By Blood Enrollment Cards 1898-1914

RESIDENCE: Chickasaw Nation ~~COUNTY~~. **Choctaw Nation** Choctaw Roll CARD NO.

POST OFFICE: Marietta, Ind. Ter. *(Not Including Freedmen)* FIELD NO. 341

Dawes' Roll No.	NAME	Relationship to Person First Named	AGE	SEX	BLOOD	TRIBAL ENROLLMENT		
						Year	County	No.
VOID.	1 Cochran, William Hunter	Named	30	M	1/4			
VOID.	2 " , Willie	Dau	3	F	1/8			
VOID.	3 " , Vertis	"	8 mos	"	1/8			
VOID.	4 " , Samuel T.	Son	9mo	M	1/8			
	5							
	6 Nos 1 and 2 on Chickasaw roll, Pickens Co, Page 26; transferred to Choctaw							
	7 roll by Dawes Com.							
	8 No.1 on Chickasaw roll as Hunter Cochran.							
	Evidence of marriage between No.1 and Carrie E Hill, non citizen filed July 2, 1901.							
	9 No4 Enrolled July 2, 1901.							
	10 See letter D.G. Bartlett as to given name of No4. filed this day July 16, 1901.							
	Evidence of birth of No.3 received and filed Feby. 13, 1902.							
	11							
	12							
	13							
	14							
	15							
	16							
	17							

TRIBAL ENROLLMENT OF PARENTS

	Name of Father	Year	County	Name of Mother	Year	County
1	Samuel T. Cochran	Dead	non citizen	Frances East		Choctaw residing in Chickasaw Dist
2	No 1			Carrie Cochran		white woman
3	No 1			" "		" "
4	No 1			" "		" "
5						
6						
7						
8						
9						
10						
11						
12						
13						
14						Date of Application for Enrollment. Oct 3/98
15						
16						
17	No1 husband of Carrie Cochran on Choc Card #D62.					

Choctaw By Blood Enrollment Cards 1898-1914

RESIDENCE: Chickasaw Nation ~~COUNTY~~.
POST OFFICE: Pickens, Ind. Ter.

Choctaw Nation

Choctaw Roll
(Not Including Freedmen)

CARD NO.
FIELD No. **342**

Dawes' Roll No.	NAME		Relationship to Person First Named	AGE	SEX	BLOOD	TRIBAL ENROLLMENT		
							Year	County	No.
15215	1 Buckholts, Eley	24	First Named	20	M	1/32		Choctaw residing in Chickasaw District	CCR #2 80
I.W. 1084	2 " , Fannie	26	Wife	22	F	I.W.		" " "	C.I. Roll
15264	3 " , Edward E.	6	Son	2	M	1/64		" " "	CCR #2 80
	4								
	☞ 5 See opinion of Atty Genl of Feb. 18 '04 and letter of Secy of Interior								
	6 of Feby 24 '04 in case of James M Buckholts et al 7-5738								
	7 #1 Not admitted by					No 1	1896	Chickasaw Dist	1992
	8 Supreme Court in					No2	1896	" "	14358
	9 Oct 1872, when his ~~grand father, Wm~~								
	10 ~~Buckholts, R.T.~~								
	11 Jones & John Null								
	12 alone were admitted ~~Son of John Buckholts~~								
	13								
	14								
	15								
	16								
	17								

ENROLLMENT
OF NOS. 1 - 3 HEREON
APPROVED BY THE SECRETARY
OF INTERIOR May 9, 1904

ENROLLMENT
OF NOS. ~~2~~ HEREON
APPROVED BY THE SECRETARY
OF INTERIOR Nov. 16, 1904

TRIBAL ENROLLMENT OF PARENTS

	Name of Father	Year	County	Name of Mother	Year	County
1	John Buckholts	Dead	Choctaw Roll	Frances Buckholts (IW)		Choctaw residing in Chickasaw Dist
2	Sam Williford		Non Citizen	Katie Williford		Non Citizen
3	No 1			No 2		
4						
5	No1 is grand-daughter[sic] of Wm Buckholts who was admitted by Supreme Court					
6	Choctaw Nation Oct 72.					
7	~~No1 on Choctaw Roll as Eli Buckholts~~ ~~No1 died Oct 10, 1902; Proof of death filed Nov. 6, 1902.~~					
8	Evidence of mariage between Nos 1 and 2 received and filed Nov. 14, 1902.					
9	No3 Born July 7, 1897. Proof of birth filed March 21, 1904.					
10	For child of No2 see NB (Apr 26-06) #1114.					
11						
12						
13						
14					Date of Application for Enrollment.	
15					Oct 4/98	
16						
17	Madill, Ind. Ter.					

RESIDENCE: Chickasaw Nation ~~COUNTY~~.
POST OFFICE: Woodville, Ind Ter.

Choctaw Nation
(Not Including Freedmen)

Choctaw Roll
CARD NO.
FIELD NO. **343**

Dawes' Roll No.	NAME	Relationship to Person First Named	AGE	SEX	BLOOD	TRIBAL ENROLLMENT		
						Year	County	No.
14272	1 Askew, Daniel B. 26	First Named	22	M	1/16		Choctaw residing in Chickasaw District	CCR #2 24
14273	2 " , Bill 24	Bro	20	"	1/16		" "	"
14274	3 " , Oscar 22	"	18	"	1/16		" "	"
14275	4 " , Luther 20	"	16	"	1/16		" "	"
14276	5 Key, Lula 18	Sister	14	F	1/16		" "	"
14277	6 Askew, Cleveland 15	Bro	11	M	1/16		" "	"
14278	7 " , Edward A. 2	Nephew	3wks	M	1/32			
14279	8 Key, Clauda 1	son of No 5	1mo	M	1/32			
	9	ENROLLMENT						
	10	OF NOS. 1,2,3,4,5,6,7,8 HEREON						
	11	APPROVED BY THE SECRETARY OF INTERIOR Apr 11, 1903						
	12 For child of No3 see NB (Apr 26-06) Card #337.							
	13 No5 P.O. Madill I.T. 3/30/05.							
	No3 P.O. Colbert I.T. 6/8/04.							
	14							
	15							
	16							
	17							

TRIBAL ENROLLMENT OF PARENTS

	Name of Father	Year	County	Name of Mother	Year	County
1	Aaron Askew	Dead	1/8 Choctaw Indian	Lucy Askew		Non Citizen
2	" "	"	" "	" "		" "
3	" "	"	" "	" "		" "
4	" "	"	" "	" "		" "
5	" "	"	" "	" "		" "
6	" "	"	" "	" "		" "
7	No 3			Arkansas Askew		Intermarried
8	J.H. Key		Non Citizen	No 5		
9	All admitted by Dawes Com Case No 1130 and No appeal taken.					
10	Wife of No.1 is Maxie Askew on Choctaw Card #5860.					
11	Arkansas Askew wife of No.3 on Choctaw Card D#452:- Transferred to 7-5861 Evidence of marriage filed with Choctaw D.452.					
12	No7 Enrolled Aug 23d 1900.					
13	No5 is now the wife of J.H. Key Non-Citizen; Evidence of marriage filed May 17, 1901.					
14	No.8 Enrolled May 17, 1901					#1to6 inc
15	Nos 6-8 inclusive Children of persons so admitted.				Date of Application for Enrollment.	Oct 4/98
16	For children of No5 see NB (Mar 3 '05) #695					
17	No7 P.O. Hogan I.T.	Nos 1-5 inclusive admitted by U.S.Indian Agent Feb 8, 1895.				

Choctaw By Blood Enrollment Cards 1898-1914

RESIDENCE: Chickasaw Nation ~~COUNTY~~.
POST OFFICE: Lebanon, Ind. Ter.

Choctaw Nation

Choctaw Roll (Not Including Freedmen)

CARD NO.
FIELD NO. **344**

Dawes' Roll No.	NAME		Relationship to Person First Named	AGE	SEX	BLOOD	TRIBAL ENROLLMENT		
							Year	County	No.
14280	1 McKenzie, Dora	35	First Named	31	F	1/8		Choctaw residing in Chickasaw Dist	CCR#2 374
14281	2 " , Claudie	15	Dau	11	"	1/16		"	"
14282	3 " , Leonard	12	Son	8	M	1/16		"	"
14283	4 " , Pearl	8	Dau	4	F	1/16		"	"
14284	5 " , William	6	Son	2	M	1/16		"	"
14285	6 " , Arnold	3	Son	2mo	M	1/16		"	"
I.W. 876	7 " , Sam	㊷	Hus	42	M	I.W.		"	C.I. Roll 78
	8 ~~ENROLLMENT~~ No2 on Choctaw roll as Claud McKenzie.								
	9 OF NOS. 1 2 3 4 5 and 6 HEREON APPROVED BY THE SECRETARY No5 " " " " Willie "								
	10 OF INTERIOR Apr. 11, 1903								
	11 All admitted by Dawes Com, Case No.1130 and no appeal taken.								
	12 No7 transferred from Choctaw Card D-63 June 12-1904. See decision of May 27-1904								
	13								
	14 ~~ENROLLMENT~~ 15 OF NOS. 7 HEREON APPROVED BY THE SECRETARY 16 OF INTERIOR Aug 3, 1904								
	17								

TRIBAL ENROLLMENT OF PARENTS

	Name of Father	Year	County	Name of Mother	Year	County
1	Morrill Askew	Dead	Choctaw roll	Liza Askew (IW)		Choctaw residing in Chickasaw District
2	Sam McKenzie		White Man	No 1		
3	" "		" "	No 1		
4	" "		" "	No 1		
5	" "		" "	No 1		
6	" "		" "	No 1		
7	Elijah "	Dead	Non Citizen	Becky McKenzie	Dead	Non Citizen
8						
9	~~See decision of D.M. Wisdom US Indian Agt. filed with Choctaw #3554, Oct. 21, 1902.~~					
10	No.1 admitted by U.S. Indian Agent Feb. 8, 1895 Nos 2-6 inclusive					
11	Children of Person so admitted.					
12						
13						
14						#1 to 5 inc
15					Date of Application for Enrollment.	Oct 4/98
16				No 6 Enrolled May 24, 1900		
17						

RESIDENCE: Chickasaw Nation ~~COUNTY~~.
POST OFFICE: Courtney, Ind. Ter.

Choctaw Nation

Choctaw Roll *(Not Including Freedmen)*

CARD NO.
FIELD NO. **345**

Dawes' Roll No.	NAME	Relationship to Person First Named	AGE	SEX	BLOOD	TRIBAL ENROLLMENT		
						Year	County	No.
~~dead~~	1 ~~Rubottom~~							
14620	2 Rubottom, Matilda E. [39]	wife	35	F	1/8	1896	Choctaw residing in ~~Chickasaw Dist~~	11021
14621	3 Sorrells, Mary Frances [22]	dau	18	"	1/16	1896	" "	11023
14622	4 Langley, Calcie Lee [20]	"	16	"	1/16	1896	" "	11024
14623	5 Rubottom, Rosabelle [17]	"	13	"	1/16	1896	" "	11025
14624	6 " , Ruthie Ruer [13]	"	9	"	1/16	1896	" "	11026
14625	7 " , Minnie Viola [9]	"	5	"	1/16	1896	" "	11027
14626	8 " , Jesse Andrew [6]	son	2	M	1/16	1896	" "	11028
~~DEAD~~	9 ~~" , Alva Estes~~	"	~~8mo~~	"	~~1/16~~	No9 hereon dismissed under order of the Commission to the Five Civilized Tribes of March 31, 1905.		
14627	10 " , Ella Evelyn [3]	dau	4mo	F	1/16			
14628	11 Sorrells, Ethel Lee [2]	gr. dau	5mo	"	1/32	No9 Affidavit of attending physician to be supplied. Received Nov. 17/98.		
14629	12 Langley, Matilda Sarah [1]	" "	3wks	"	1/32			
14630	13 Rubottom, Matilda P. [1]	dau	1mo	"	1/16			

ENROLLMENT
OF NOS. 2,3,4,5,6,7,8,10,11,12 and 13 HEREON
APPROVED BY THE SECRETARY
OF INTERIOR

William P. Rubottom husband of No2 and father of children on his card on Choctaw Card #D.64 now on 7-5985

No2 on Choctaw roll as Matilda E Reuberton
" 3 " " " " M. E. "
" 4 " " " " Calvin "
" 5 " " " " Rose "
" 6 " " " " Ruthie "
" 7 " " " " Minnie "
" 8 " " " " Jesse "

TRIBAL ENROLLMENT OF PARENTS

	Name of Father	Year	County	Name of Mother	Year	County
1						
2	Henry Sorrels (I.W.)		Choctaw residing in ~~Chickasaw Dist~~	Mary Sorrells	dead	Choctaw roll
3	Wᵐ P. Rubottom		white man	No 2		
4	" " "		" "	No.2		
5	" " "		" "	No.2		
6	" " "		" "	No.2		
7	" " "		" "	No.2		
8	" " "		" "	No.2		
9	" " "		" "	~~No.2~~		
10	" " "		" "	No.2		
11	J.J. Sorrells		non-citizen	No.3		
12	Samuel L. Langley		" "	No.4		
13	William P. Rubottom		" "	No.2		

For children of No. see NB (Mar. 3, 1905) 1448

14 [No3] is now the wife of T.J. Sorrells a noncitizen evidence of marriage filed Feb 5, 1901.
[No4] is the wife of S.L. Langley Feb, 20,1901: On Choctaw card #E717 May 7 1902
15 No9 died Aug 24 1899 Proof of death filed Nov 1, 1902.
16 No10 enrolled June 26"1908   No11 enrolled Feb 5, 1901
No12 born Feb 27, 1902. Enrolled March 10" 1902
17 No13 born March 18, 1902 Enrolled May 3, 1902

P.O. Terral I.T. 3/21/05

Date of Application for Enrollment.
Oct. 4/98

For child of No3 see NB (Apr26-06)Card#655   Nos 1 to 8 inclusive admitted by Dawes Com Case #673 no appeal
" " " " 4 " " (Mar3-05) " #75

Choctaw By Blood Enrollment Cards 1898-1914

RESIDENCE: Atoka COUNTY.
POST OFFICE: Owl, Ind. Ter.

Choctaw Nation
(Not Including Freedmen)

Choctaw Roll

CARD No.
FIELD No. **346**

Dawes' Roll No.	NAME	Relationship to Person First Named	AGE	SEX	BLOOD	TRIBAL ENROLLMENT		
						Year	County	No.
692	1 McDonald, Lucy E. ²⁰	First Named	16	F	1/16		Atoka	CCR #2 356
	2							
	3 ENROLLMENT							
	4 OF NOS. 1 HEREON APPROVED BY THE SECRETARY							
	5 OF INTERIOR Dec 12, 1902							
	6			1896 Atoka 8848 as E. Lowena More				
	7							
	8							
	9			For child of No1 see N.B. (March 3, 1905) #1317				
	10							
	11							
	12							
	13							
	14							
	15							
	16							
	17							

TRIBAL ENROLLMENT OF PARENTS

	Name of Father	Year	County	Name of Mother	Year	County
1	Joe Moore	dead	Choctaw residing in Chickasaw District	Nancy M. Roach		non citizen
2						
3						
4						
5						
6						
7						
8						
9						
10						
11						
12						
13						
14						
15						Date of Application for Enrollment.
16	P.O. Wapanucka[sic] 12/23/02					Oct 5/98
17	P.O. Ada I.T. 4/27/05					

P.O. Celestine I.T. 12/16/06

Choctaw By Blood Enrollment Cards 1898-1914

						TRIBAL ENROLLMENT		

RESIDENCE: Chickasaw Nation ~~COUNTY.~~
POST OFFICE: Linn, Ind. Ter.

Choctaw Nation

Choctaw Roll *(Not Including Freedmen)*

CARD NO.
FIELD NO. **347**

Dawes' Roll No.	NAME	Relationship to Person First Named	AGE	SEX	BLOOD	Year	County	No.
693	1 Moore, Thomas ³⁸	First Named	34	M	1/16		Choctaw residing in Chickasaw District	CCR #2 358
I.W. 1085	2 " , Nancy M. ³⁷	Wife	33	F	I.W.		" "	C.I. Roll 72
DEAD	3 " , Elneta DEAD	Dau	13	"	1/32		" "	CCR #2 358
694	4 " , Mary J. ¹⁵	"	11	"	1/32		" "	"
695	5 " , Elizabeth ¹³	"	9	"	1/32		" "	"
696	6 " , Robert Thomas¹⁰	Son	6	M	1/32		" "	"
697	7 " , Benjamin O. ⁷	"	3	"	1/32		" "	"
698	8 " , Henrietta ³	Dau	4mo	F	1/32			
DEAD	9 Smith, Roze Zella DEAD	G.dau	1w	F	1/64			

10 No3 and 9 hereon dismissed under For child of No4 see NB(Apr 26, 1906) Card No 19
11 order of the Commission to the five No3 on Choctaw roll as Ellen Moore.
   civilized tribes of March 31, 1905. No6 " " " Robert J. "
12
13 No3 died Feby 4th, 1901. No3 died Feby 4, 1901. No9 died Feby 25, 1901. See the
14 No9 died Feby 25ᵗʰ, 1901. sworn statement of Albert Smith of July 25, 1901.
15 ENROLLMENT No3 is now the wife of Albert Smith
16 OF NOS. 1,4,5,6,7 and 8 HEREON No5 on Choc roll as Elizabeth More
   APPROVED BY THE SECRETARY No6 " " " Robt. J. " April 4ᵗʰ, 1900.
17 OF INTERIOR Dec 12, 1902.

TRIBAL ENROLLMENT OF PARENTS

Name of Father	Year	County	Name of Mother	Year	County
1 Joseph Moore	Dead	Choctaw residing in Chickasaw District	Mary Moore	Dead	Non Citizen
2 John Turner	"	Non Citizen	Nancy M. Roark		Non Citizen
3		No 1	No 2		
4		No 1	No 2		
5		No 1	No 2		
6		No 1 ENROLLMENT	No 2		
7		No 1 OF NOS. ~~2~~ HEREON	No 2		
8		No 1 APPROVED BY THE SECRETARY	No 2		
9	Albert Smith	OF INTERIOR Nov. 16, 1904	No 3		

10 No1 1896 Chickasaw Dist 8904 as Thos Moore
11 No2 1896 " " 14845
12 No3 1896 " " 8913
   No4 1896 " " 8914 as Mary J More
13 No5 1896 " " 8915 No8 Enrolled May 24, 1900. #1 to 7 inc
14 No6 1896 " " 8916 No9 Enrolled January 19, 1901. Date of Application for Enrollment.
15 No7 1896 " " 8917 as Ben O. Moore Oct 5/98
16 For child of Nos 1&2 see NB (Mar 3-05) #77
17 P.O. Medill[sic] I.T. " " " No4 " " " " " #523

P.O. Cumberland I.T. 1/5/04

47

Choctaw By Blood Enrollment Cards 1898-1914

RESIDENCE: Chickasaw Nation ~~COUNTY~~. **Choctaw Nation** **Choctaw Roll** CARD NO.
POST OFFICE: Lebanon, Ind. Ter. (Orphan Home) *(Not Including Freedmen)* FIELD NO. 348

Dawes' Roll No.	NAME	Relationship to Person First Named	AGE	SEX	BLOOD	TRIBAL ENROLLMENT		
						Year	County	No.
VOID.	1 ~~Kay, Minnie~~		12	F	1/2			
	2							
	3							
	4							
	5							
	6							
	7							
	8							
	9	On Chickasaw roll Tishomingo Co, Page 30, as Minnie Key; transferred to Choctaw						
	10	roll by Dawes Com.						
	11							
	12							
	13							
	14							
	15							
	16							
	17							

TRIBAL ENROLLMENT OF PARENTS

	Name of Father	Year	County		Name of Mother	Year	County
1	~~Charley Kay~~	Dead	non-citizen		~~Minnie Kay~~	Dead	Choctaw roll
2							
3							
4							
5							
6							
7							
8							
9							
10							
11							
12							
13							
14						Date of Application for Enrollment.	
15						Oct 5/98	
16							
17							

CANCELLED

Transferred to Chickasaw Card #4618

Choctaw By Blood Enrollment Cards 1898-1914

RESIDENCE: Chickasaw Nation ~~COUNTY.~~
POST OFFICE: Buckhorn, Ind. Ter.

Choctaw Nation

Choctaw Roll
(Not Including Freedmen)

CARD NO.
FIELD NO. 349

Dawes' Roll No.	NAME	Relationship to Person First Named	AGE	SEX	BLOOD	TRIBAL ENROLLMENT		
						Year	County	No.
VOID. 1	~~Kay, Charley~~		6	M	1/2			
2								
3								
4								
5								
6								
7	On Chickasaw roll as Charley Key, Tishomingo County, Page 27; transferred							
8	to Choctaw roll by Dawes Com.							
9								
10	Lives with W. C. Garrett, U.S. citi...							
11								
12								
13								
14								
15								
16								
17								

TRIBAL ENROLLMENT OF PARENTS

	Name of Father	Year	County	Name of Mother	Year	County
1	~~Charley Kay~~	~~Dead~~	~~non citizen~~	~~Minnie Kay~~	~~Dead~~	~~Choctaw roll~~
2						
3						
4						
5						
6						
7						
8						
9						
10						
11						
12						
13						
14						
15						
16				Date of Application for Enrollment.	Oct	
17						

CANCELLED

Transferred to Chickasaw Card No. 1649   Oct. 14th 1902

Choctaw By Blood Enrollment Cards 1898-1914

RESIDENCE: Chickasaw Nation ~~COUNTY.~~   **Choctaw Nation**   Choctaw Roll   CARD NO.
POST OFFICE: Wynnewood, Ind. Ter.   *(Not Including Freedmen)*   FIELD NO. **350**

Dawes' Roll No.	NAME	Relationship to Person First Named	AGE	SEX	BLOOD	TRIBAL ENROLLMENT		
						Year	County	No.
699	₁ Mouser, Robert B. ²⁴	First Named	20	M	1/4		Choctaw residing in Chickasaw District	CCR #2 259
I.W. 808	₂ " , Lizzie ㉓	Wife	23	F	I.W.			
	3	ENROLLMENT						
	4	OF NOS. 1 HEREON APPROVED BY THE SECRETARY						
	5	OF INTERIOR DEC 12 1902						
	6				1896	Chickasaw Dist 8944 as B. Robert Mouser		
	7							
	8	ENROLLMENT						
	9	OF NOS. 2 HEREON APPROVED BY THE SECRETARY						
	10	OF INTERIOR MAY 21 1904						
	11	No2 transferred from Choctaw card D962 April 16, 1904.						
	12	See decision of March 15, 1904						
	13							
	14	For child of Nos 1&2 see N B (Apr 26-06) Card #936						
	15	" " " " " " (Mar 3-05) " #83						
	16							
	17							

TRIBAL ENROLLMENT OF PARENTS

	Name of Father	Year	County	Name of Mother	Year	County
1	John Mouser		non citizen	Sibbie Holloway	Dead	Tobucksy
2	Warren Pitts		" "			noncitizen
3						
4						
5						
6						
7						
8						
9						
10						
11						
12						
13						
14						
15				Date of Application for Enrollment.		Oct 5/98
16						
17						

Choctaw By Blood Enrollment Cards 1898-1914

RESIDENCE: Chickasaw Nation ~~COUNTY~~. **Choctaw Nation** Choctaw Roll   CARD NO.
POST OFFICE: ~~Cate,~~ Sterrett, Ind. Ter.   *(Not Including Freedmen)* FIELD NO. **351**

Dawes' Roll No.	NAME	Relationship to Person First Named	AGE	SEX	BLOOD	TRIBAL ENROLLMENT		
						Year	County	No.
DEAD	1 ~~Finch, William E.~~		28	M	1/4		Choctaw residing in Chickasaw District	CCR #2 194
700	2 " , Zola ¹¹	dau	7	F	1/8		" "	"
701	3 " , Burton ⁹	son	5	M	1/8		" "	"
DEAD	4 ~~" , Elli~~ ¹	"	9mos	"	1/8		" "	"
	5					No1 and 4 hereon dismissed under		
	6					order of the Commission to the Five		
	7					Civilized Tribes of March 31, 1905.		
	8							
	9					No2 on Choctaw roll as Cely Finch		
	10					No4 - affidavit of attending physician to be supplied. Affidavit of child's grandmother substituted and filed Oct 10/98		
	11							
	12					No1 died Oct. 8, 1898 No4 died July 16, 1899		
	13					Proof of death of Nos. 1 and 4 filed Oct. 8, 1904.		
	14							
	15							
	16							
	17							

ENROLLMENT
OF NOS. 2 and 3 HEREON
APPROVED BY THE SECRETARY
OF INTERIOR Dec 12 1902

TRIBAL ENROLLMENT OF PARENTS

	Name of Father	Year	County	Name of Mother	Year	County
1	~~Major Finch~~	dead	~~non citizen~~	~~Cahchela Finch~~		~~Sugar Loaf~~
2	No 1			Noble M. Finch		non citizen
3	No 1			" " "		" "
4	~~No 1~~			" " "		" "
5						
6			Evidence of death of No1 and 4 requested 8/11/04.			
7			No1 1896 Chickasaw Dist 4565 as W.E. Finch			
8			No2 1896 " " 4566 " Cely "			
9			No3 1896 " " 4567 " Burden "			
10			Nos 2&3 living with S.C. Carshall 7-2401; guardianship papers			
11			to be filed 12/23/02.			
12						
13						Date of Application for Enrollment. Oct 10/98
14						
15						
16						
17						

Choctaw By Blood Enrollment Cards 1898-1914

RESIDENCE: Chickasaw Nation ~~COUNTY.~~
POST OFFICE: Yarnaby, Ind. Ter.

Choctaw Nation

Choctaw Roll *(Not Including Freedmen)*

CARD NO.
FIELD NO. 352

Dawes' Roll No.	NAME	Relationship to Person First Named	AGE	SEX	BLOOD	TRIBAL ENROLLMENT		
						Year	County	No.
VOID.	1 ~~Perry, Eli~~	~~Named~~	~~41~~	~~M~~	~~1/2~~			
VOID.	2 " ~~Lillie Marie~~	~~Dau~~	~~3½ mo~~	~~F~~	~~1/4~~			
VOID.	3 " ~~Hattie Lee~~	~~Dau~~	~~2 mo~~	~~F~~	~~1/4~~			
	4							
	5							
	6							
	7 On Chickasaw roll, Panola County, Page 3; transferred to Choctaw							
	8 roll by Dawes Com							
	9 No2 Enrolled January 2 1901							
	Evidence of marriage of parents of No2 filed Jany 2 1901.							
	10 No3 Born March 13 1902; enrolled May 1, 1902							
	11							
	12							
	13							
	14							
	15							
	16							
	17							

TRIBAL ENROLLMENT OF PARENTS

	Name of Father	Year	County	Name of Mother	Year	County
1	~~Morgan Perry~~	~~Dead~~	Panola County Chickasaw roll	~~Elizabeth Perry~~	~~Dead~~	Choctaw residing in Chickasaw Dist
2	No 1			~~Emma Perry~~		~~white woman~~
3	No 1			" "		" "
4						
5						
6						
7						
8						
9						
10						
11						
12						
13						
14						
15				Date of Application for Enrollment.		Oct 10/98
16	Yuba seems to be P.O. 5/1/02					
17						

52

Choctaw By Blood Enrollment Cards 1898-1914

RESIDENCE:	Blue	COUNTY.	**Choctaw Nation**	**Choctaw Roll**	CARD NO.	
POST OFFICE:	Caddo, Ind. Ter.			*(Not Including Freedmen)*	FIELD NO.	353

Dawes' Roll No.		NAME		Relationship to Person First Named	AGE	SEX	BLOOD	TRIBAL ENROLLMENT		
								Year	County	No.
702	1	Turnbull, Emma	18	First Named	14	F	¾		Blue	CCR #2 449
	2									
	3	ENROLLMENT						1896	Blue	12419
	4	OF NOS. 1 HEREON APPROVED BY THE SECRETARY								
	5	OF INTERIOR DEC 12 1902								
	6									
	7									
	8	Father, Geo. W. Turnbull, on Chickasaw roll, Card No. 1072								
	9									
	10	Also on 1896 roll, Page 323, No. 12407								
	11									
	12									
	13									
	14									
	15									
	16									
	17									

TRIBAL ENROLLMENT OF PARENTS

	Name of Father	Year	County	Name of Mother	Year	County
1	Geo. W. Turnbull	1897	Chick residing in Choctaw N. 3rd Dist	Mary Turnbull		Blue
2						
3						
4						
5						
6						
7						
8						
9						
10						
11						
12						
13						
14						
15				Date of Application for Enrollment.		Oct 10/98
16						
17						

Choctaw By Blood Enrollment Cards 1898-1914

RESIDENCE: Chickasaw Nation ~~COUNTY~~.
POST OFFICE: Silo, Ind. Ter.

Choctaw Nation

Choctaw Roll
(Not Including Freedmen)

CARD NO.
FIELD NO. 354

Dawes' Roll No.	NAME	Relationship to Person First Named	AGE	SEX	BLOOD	TRIBAL ENROLLMENT		
						Year	nty	No.
VOID.	1 Kemp, Roberson		59	M	Full			
	2							
	3							
	4							
	5	On Chickasaw roll, Tishomingo County, Page 31; transferred to Choctaw						
	6	roll by Dawes Com.						
	7	Husband of Julia Kemp, Chickasaw roll Card No. 1073						
	8							
	9							
	10							
	11							
	12							
	13							
	14							
	15							
	16							
	17							

TRIBAL ENROLLMENT OF PARENTS

	Name of Father	Year	County	Name of Mother	Year	County
1	Reuben Kemp	Dead	Chickasaw roll	Becky Turnbull Kemp	Dead	Choctaw roll
2						
3						
4						
5						
6						
7						
8						
9						
10						
11						
12						
13						
14						
15						
16						
17						

CANCELLED

Transferred to Chickasaw Card #1921 Oct. 14, 1902

RESIDENCE: Blue COUNTY.
POST OFFICE: Caddo, Ind. Ter.

Choctaw Nation

Choctaw Roll
(Not Including Freedmen)

CARD NO.
FIELD NO. 355

Dawes' Roll No.	NAME	Relationship to Person First	AGE	SEX	BLOOD	TRIBAL ENROLLMENT Year	County	No.
void.	1 Maytubby, Samuel W.	Named	36	M	1/4			
void.	2 ", Lulu	Wife	33	F	I.W.			
void.	3 ", Samuel W.	Son	6	M	1/8			
void.	4 ", Floyd E.	"	4	"	1/8			
void.	5 ", Dudley	"	2	"	1/8			
DEAD	6 ", Inez Mabel	Dau	7 mos	F	1/8			
void.	7 ", Kalites	Dau	3wk	F	1/8			

No 1 on Chickasaw roll Page 74 as S.W. Maytubby; transferred to
to Choctaw roll by Dawes Com.
Nos. 3,4 and 5 on Chickasaw roll same page.

TRIBAL ENROLLMENT OF PARENTS

Name of Father	Year	County	Name of Mother	Year	County
1 Peter Maytubby		Chick residing in Blue County	Melvina Maytubby	Dead	Blue
2 Jim Mebane	Dead	non citizen	Susan Mebane		non citizen
3	No 1		No 2		
4	No 1		No 2		
5	No 1		No 2		
6	No 1		No 2		
7	No 1		No 2		

Kaliteo Maytubby born Dec 30/99 on
Card No. D4567.
For information as to death of No.6 see letter of S.W. Maytubby dated June 7, 1900.
No7 born December 30, 1899; transferred to this card May 24, 1902

Date of Application for Enrollment. Oct 10/98

55

RESIDENCE: **Blue** COUNTY.
POST OFFICE: **Caddo, Ind. Ter.**

Choctaw Nation

Choctaw Roll
(Not Including Freedmen)

CARD NO.
FIELD NO. **356**

Dawes' Roll No.	NAME	Relationship to Person First Named	AGE	SEX	BLOOD	TRIBAL ENROLLMENT		
						Year	County	No.
VOID. 1	Goforth, William H.		37	M	1/2			
VOID. 2	" , Mary	Dau	16	F	3/4			
VOID. 3	" , Alba	Wife	21	"	I.W.			
VOID. 4	DEAD " , Ora Emily	Dau	4mo	"	1/4			
VOID. 5	" , Lena May	Dau	5mo	F	1/4			
6								
7								
8	Nos 1 and 2 on Chickasaw roll, Page 72, transferred to Choctaw roll by							
9	Dawes Com.							
10	No 1 on Chickasaw roll as W. A. Goforth.							
11								
12								
13								
14								
15								
16								
17								

TRIBAL ENROLLMENT OF PARENTS

	Name of Father	Year	County	Name of Mother	Year	County
1	Solomon Goforth	1897	Chick residing in Choctaw N. 3rd Dist	Caroline Goforth	Dead	Blue
2	No 1			Susie Goforth	"	"
3	Tom Wilfong		Non Citz	Mary Wilfong		Non Citz
4	No 1			No 3		
5	No 1			No 3		
6						
7						
8	No4 Enrolled June 7, 1900					
9	No1 is father of children on Chickasaw card #1098					
10	No5 Born Nov. 22, 1901: enrolled April 22, 1902.					
11						
12						
13						
14					#1 & 2	
15				Date of Application for Enrollment.	Oct 10/98	
16				No3 enrolled Aug 31/99		
17						

Choctaw By Blood Enrollment Cards 1898-1914

RESIDENCE: Jack Fork COUNTY.
POST OFFICE: Antlers, Ind. Ter.

Choctaw Nation

Choctaw Roll CARD NO.
(Not Including Freedmen) FIELD NO. **357**

Dawes' Roll No.	NAME	Relationship to Person First Named	AGE	SEX	BLOOD	TRIBAL ENROLLMENT		
						Year	County	No.
703	1 Anderson, Amanda ²⁹		25	F	Full		Jack Fork	CCR #2 19
704	2 " , Luella ¹³	Dau	9	"	3/4		" "	"
705	3 " , Wilson ¹¹	Son	7	M	3/4		" "	"
706	4 " , Minnie ⁹	Dau	5	F	3/4		" "	"
707	5 " , Ainie ⁶	"	2	"	3/4			
708	6 ~~DIED PRIOR TO SEPTEMBER 25, 1902~~ ~~, Sophy~~	"	~~4mo~~	"	~~3/4~~			
	7							
	8	ENROLLMENT						
	9	OF NOS. 1,2,3,4,5 and 6 HEREON APPROVED BY THE SECRETARY						
	10	OF INTERIOR Dec 12, 1902						
	11						~~Nicholas Anderson~~	
	12	No1 wife of Nicholas Anderson, Chickasaw roll, Card No. 1083 dead						
	13	No1 now the wife of No1 on 7-1529						
	14	No2 on Choctaw roll as Julia Anderson						
		No3 " " " " Willie "						
	15	~~No.6 died Oct - 1899: Enrollment cancelled by Department, July 8-1904~~						
	16							
	17							

TRIBAL ENROLLMENT OF PARENTS

	Name of Father	Year	County	Name of Mother	Year	County
1	Billy Fletcher		Jack Fork	Eliza Fletcher		Jack Fork
2	Nicholas Anderson		Chick residing in Choctaw N. 3rd Dist	No 1		
3	" "		" " "	No 1		
4	" "		" " "	No 1		
5	" "		" " "	No 1		
6	" "		" " "	~~No 1~~		
7						
8			No1 1896 Jacks Fork 464			
9			No2 1896 " 465			
10			No3 1896 " 467			
11			~~No4 1896 " 466~~			
12			No 6 died Oct. 1899: proof of death filed Dec. 5, 1902			
13						
14						
15						Date of Application for Enrollment.
16				No6 enrolled Oct. 6/99		
17						

Choctaw By Blood Enrollment Cards 1898-1914

RESIDENCE: Chickasaw Nation ~~COUNTY.~~ **Choctaw Nation**　　Choctaw Roll　CARD NO.
POST OFFICE:　Kemp, Ind. Ter.　　　　　　　　*(Not Including Freedmen)*　FIELD NO. 358

Dawes' Roll No.	NAME	Relationship to Person First Named	AGE	SEX	BLOOD	ENROLLMENT Year	County	No.
VOID. 1	~~Rains, Catherine~~	~~Named~~	~~50~~	~~F~~	~~1/4~~			
VOID. 2	~~" , Bessie~~	~~Dau~~	~~9~~	~~"~~	~~1/8~~			
3								
4								
5								
6								
7	No1 on Chickasaw roll Page 6; transferred to Choctaw roll by Dawes Com.							
8	No2 "　　　"　　　"　　" 7;	"	"	"	"	"	"	"
9								
10								
11								
12								
13								
14								
15								
16								
17								

TRIBAL ENROLLMENT OF PARENTS

	Name of Father	Year	County	Name of Mother	Year	County
1	~~Morgan Perry~~	~~Dead~~	~~Choctaw roll~~	~~Isabella Perry~~	~~Dead~~	~~Choctaw roll~~
2	~~William Rains~~		~~non citizen~~	~~No 1~~		
3						
4						
5						
6						
7						
8						
9						
10						
11						
12						
13						
14						
15				Date of Application for Enrollment.		Oct 10/98
16						
17	P O Sterrett I.T.					

CANCELLED

Transferred to Chickasaw Card #1624
Oct. 14, 1902

58

Choctaw By Blood Enrollment Cards 1898-1914

RESIDENCE: Chickasaw Nation COUNTY. **Choctaw Nation** Choctaw Roll CARD NO.
POST OFFICE: Lynn, Ind. Ter. (Not Including Freedmen) FIELD NO. **359**

Dawes' Roll No.	NAME	Relationship to Person	AGE	SEX	BLOOD	TRIBAL ENROLLMENT		
						Year	County	No.
I.W. 1086	1 Taylor, Robert H. 51	First Named	47	M	I.W.		Choctaw residing in Chickasaw Dist	C I Roll 107
15378	2 " , Patsey 44	wife	40	F	full		Choctaw residing in Chickasaw District	CCR #2 452
	3							
	4							
	5							
	6	No2 on 1896 Choctaw Census Roll, Kiamitia County as Patsey Thomas No. 12,343						
	7							
	8							
	9							
	10							
	11							
	12							
	13							
	14							
	15							
	16							
	17							

ENROLLMENT OF NOS. 2 ~ HEREON APPROVED BY THE SECRETARY OF INTERIOR May 9-1904

ENROLLMENT OF NOS. 1 HEREON APPROVED BY THE SECRETARY OF INTERIOR Nov 16, 1904

TRIBAL ENROLLMENT OF PARENTS

Name of Father	Year	County	Name of Mother	Year	County
1 Joseph Taylor		non citizen	Martha E. Taylor	Dead	non citizen
2 Lemon Hart		Kiamitia	Mary Hart	Dead	Kiamitia
3					
4					
5					
6					
7					
8					
9					
10					
11					
12					
13					
14					
15					
16			Date of Application for Enrollment.		Oct 11/98
17 P.O. Hart I.T.			No1 enrolled Nov. 24/98		

2-25-02

Choctaw By Blood Enrollment Cards 1898-1914

RESIDENCE: Chickasaw Nation ~~COUNTY~~.
POST OFFICE: Yarnaby, Ind. Ter.

Choctaw Nation

Choctaw Roll
(Not Including Freedmen)

CARD NO.
FIELD NO. 360

Dawes' Roll No.	NAME	Relationship to Person First Named	AGE	SEX	BLOOD	TRIBAL ENROLLMENT		
						Year	County	No.
VOID. Dead	1, Perry, Henry Clay DEAD.	First Named	35	M	1/2			
VOID.	2 ", Emma Frank	Wife	34	F	I.W.			
VOID.	3 ", Willie Clay	Son	12	M	1/4			
VOID.	4 ", Minnie May	Dau	8	F	1/4			
VOID.	5 ", Frank Calvin	Son	3	M	1/4			
VOID. DEAD	6 ", Ray Morgan	"	16 mos	"	1/4			
VOID.	7 ", John Henry	"	6mo	"	1/4			
	8							
	9 No1 on Chickasaw roll, Panola Co, Page 1							
	10 No2 " " Intermarried roll, " 76 transferred to Choctaw roll by Dawes Com							
	11 Nos3,4&5 on " roll Panola Co, " 1							
	12 No6 " " " " " "							
	No 1 Died March 19, 1899: proof of death file Aug. 29, 1902.							
	13							
	14							
	15							
	16							
	17							

TRIBAL ENROLLMENT OF PARENTS

Name of Father	Year	County	Name of Mother	Year	County
1 Morgan Perry	Dead	Panola County Chickasaw Roll	Elizabeth Perry	Dead	Choctaw residing in Chickasaw Dist
2 Frank Webb	"	non-citizen	Polly Webb		non-citizen
3 No 1			No 2		
4 No 1			No 2		
5 No 1			No 2		
6 No 1			No 2		
7 No 1			No 2		
8					
9 No 1 on Chickasaw roll as H. C. Perry					
10 No 2 " " " " E. F. "					
11 No 3 " " " " W. C. "					
No 4 " " " " Minnie "					
12 No 5 " " " " Frank "					
13					
14					Date of Application for Enrollment. Oct 11/98
15					
16					No7 enrolled Nov. 1/99
17 P.O. Sterrell[sic] I.T.					

RESIDENCE: Chickasaw Nation ~~COUNTY.~~ **Choctaw Nation**   **Choctaw Roll**   CARD NO.

POST OFFICE: Emet, Ind. Ter.   (Not Including Freedmen)   FIELD NO. 361

Dawes' Roll No.	NAME	Relationship to Person First Named	AGE	SEX	BLOOD	TRIBAL ENROLLMENT		
						Year	County	No.
VOID. 1	McKinney, Ben F.	Named	31	M	I.W.	1896	Chick Dist.	14889
VOID. 2	", Clara Louisa	Dau	11	F	1/4		Choctaw residing in Chickasaw District	CCR #2 375
VOID. 3	", Ben A	Son	9	M	1/4		" "	"
VOID. 4	", Mattie	Dau	7	F	1/4		" "	"
5	Dec 7/99. The above parents							
6	are to be placed upon Chickasaw							
7	Card							
8	Maggie McKinney having this							
9	day been declared to be a							
10	Chickasaw.							
11	All records hereto attached have been filed with Chickasaw Card							
12	1104.							
13	No1 on Chickasaw Intermarried roll, Pickens Co, Page 79; transferred to Choctaw roll by Dawes Com. Husband of Laura McKinney, Chickasaw Card No 1104							
14								
15								
16								
17								

TRIBAL ENROLLMENT OF PARENTS

	Name of Father	Year	County	Name of Mother	Year	County
1	Alex McKinney	Dead	non citizen	Mattie McKinney		non citizen
2	No 1			Maggie McKinney	Dead	Atoka
3	No 1			" "	" "	
4	No 1			" "	" "	
5						
6						
7				No 2 on Choctaw roll as C. Louisa McKinney		
8				No 1 " Chickasaw " " B. F. McKinney		
9						
10						
11	No2 1896 Chickasaw Dist 9528 as Louisa McKinney					
12	No3 1896 " " 9529					
13	No4 1896 " " 9530					
14	No1 1896 " " 14889 as B.F. McKinney					
15				Date of Application for Enrollment.	Oct 11/98	
16						
17						

CANCELLED

Choctaw By Blood Enrollment Cards 1898-1914

RESIDENCE: Chickasaw Nation ~~COUNTY.~~   **Choctaw Nation**   Choctaw Roll   CARD NO.
POST OFFICE: Silo, Ind. Ter.   (Not Including Freedmen)   FIELD NO.   362

Dawes' Roll No.	NAME	Relationship to Person First Named	AGE	SEX	BLOOD	TRIBAL ENROLLMENT Year	County	No.
I.W. 877	1 Thomas, Andrew Jackson 30		26	M	I.W.		Kiamitia	C.I. Roll 106
709	2 " , Della 24	Wife	20	F	1/4		"	CCR #2 448
710	3 " , Annie Jeanette 5	Dau	10mos	"	1/8			
711	4 " , James M. 2	Son	3wks	M	1/8			
	5							
	6							
	7							
	8							
	9							
	10							
	11							
	12							
	13							
	14							
	15							
	16							
	17							

ENROLLMENT
OF NOS. 2,3 and 4 HEREON
APPROVED BY THE SECRETARY
OF INTERIOR DEC 12 1902

ENROLLMENT
OF NOS 1 HEREON
APPROVED BY THE SECRETARY
OF INTERIOR AUG 3 1904

TRIBAL ENROLLMENT OF PARENTS

	Name of Father	Year	County	Name of Mother	Year	County
1	Jesse Thomas	Dead	non citizen	Elizabeth J Thomas	Dead	non citizen
2	Burrell McIntyre	"	" "	Lucretia McIntyre	"	Kiamitia
3	No 1			No 2		
4	No 1			No 2		
5						
6	No1 1896 Kiamitia 15105 as Andrew J Thomas					
7	No2 1896 " 12344					
8	No.4 Enrolled Sept. 26th, 1900.					
9	For child of Nos 1&2 see NB (Apr 26-06) Card #858					
	" " " " " " " (Mar 3-05) " #1011					
10						
11						
12						
13						
14						
15				Date of Application for Enrollment		Oct 11/98
16						
17						

Choctaw By Blood Enrollment Cards 1898-1914

RESIDENCE: Chickasaw Nation ~~COUNTY~~.
POST OFFICE: Colbert, Ind. Ter.

Choctaw Nation

Choctaw Roll *(Not Including Freedmen)*

CARD NO.
FIELD NO. 363

Dawes' Roll No.	NAME	Relationship to Person First Named	AGE	SEX	BLOOD	TRIBAL ENROLLMENT Year	TRIBAL ENROLLMENT County	TRIBAL ENROLLMENT No.
712	1 Ramseyer, Edward 22	First Named	18	M	1/8		Choctaw residing in Chickasaw Dist	CCR #2 416
	2							
	3					1896	Chickasaw Dist	11022
	4							
	5							
	6							
	7							
	8							
	9							
	10							
	11							
	12							
	13							
	14							
	15							
	16							
	17							

ENROLLMENT OF NOS. 1 HEREON APPROVED BY THE SECRETARY OF INTERIOR DEC 12 1902

TRIBAL ENROLLMENT OF PARENTS

Name of Father	Year	County	Name of Mother	Year	County
1 Gotleit Ramseyer		white man	Martha Ramseyer	Dead	Choctaw residing in Chickasaw District
2					
3					
4					
5					
6					
7					
8					
9					
10					
11					
12					
13					
14					
15			Date of Application for Enrollment.		Oct 11/98
16					
17					

RESIDENCE: Chickasaw Nation ~~COUNTY.~~   **Choctaw Nation**   Choctaw Roll   CARD No.
POST OFFICE: Yarnaby, Ind. Ter.   *(Not Including Freedmen)*   FIELD No.   364

Dawes' Roll No.	NAME	Relationship to Person First Named	AGE	SEX	BLOOD	TRIBAL ENROLLMENT Year	County	No.
VOID. 1	~~Connelly, John William~~	~~Named~~	~~37~~	~~M~~	~~1/2~~			
VOID. 2	" , ~~Hannah~~	~~wife~~	~~36~~	~~F~~	~~I.W.~~			
VOID. 3	" , ~~Elizabeth~~	~~Dau~~	~~14~~	"	~~1/4~~			
VOID. 4	" , ~~Alfred~~	~~Son~~	~~12~~	~~M~~	~~1/4~~			
VOID. 5	" , ~~William~~	"	~~11~~	"	~~1/4~~			
VOID. 6	" , ~~Henry N~~	"	~~9~~	"	~~1/4~~			
VOID. 7	" , ~~Jennie~~	~~Dau~~	~~6~~	~~F~~	~~1/4~~			
VOID. 8	" , ~~Emma May~~	"	~~5~~	"	~~1/4~~			
VOID. 9	" , ~~John W~~	~~Son~~	~~3~~	~~M~~	~~1/4~~			
VOID. 10	" , ~~Irene~~	~~Dau~~	~~10mo~~	~~F~~	~~1/4~~			
VOID. 11	**DEAD** " , ~~James B.~~	~~Son~~	~~1mo~~	~~M~~	~~1/4~~			
VOID. 12	**DEAD** " , ~~Douglas H.~~	~~son~~	~~2mo~~		~~1/4~~			
13	All except No2 on Chickasaw roll. Panola Co Page 3; transferred by Dawes Com.							
14	No2 " " " " " " 76; " " " "							
15								
16	No.12 born Nov. 30, 1901: Enrolled 2?, 1902							
17	Nos.1 and 2 are the parents of No. 12.							

TRIBAL ENROLLMENT OF PARENTS

	Name of Father	Year	County	Name of Mother	Year	County
1	~~Ish-kah-nah~~	~~Dead~~	~~Chickasaw roll~~	~~Elizabeth Hunter~~	~~Dead~~	~~Blue~~
2	~~Ambrose Powell~~		~~non-citizen~~	~~Margaret Powell~~		~~non-citizen~~
3	~~No 1~~			~~No 2~~		
4	~~No 1~~			~~No 2~~		
5	~~No 1~~			~~No 2~~		
6	~~No 1~~			~~No 2~~		
7	~~No 1~~			~~No 2~~		
8	~~No 1~~			~~No 2~~		
9	~~No 1~~			~~No 2~~		
10	~~No 1~~			~~No 2~~		
11	~~No 1~~			~~No 2~~		
12	~~No 1~~			~~No 2~~		
13	No1 on Chickasaw roll as I W. Connelly					
14	No3 " " " " Lizzie "					
15	No5 " " " " Billie "					Date of Application for Enrollment. Oct 11/98
16	~~No8 " " " " Ema "~~			No11 enrolled Nov. 1/99		
17	Evidence of birth of No9 received and filed Feby. 21, 1902.					

Choctaw By Blood Enrollment Cards 1898-1914

RESIDENCE: San[sic] Bois COUNTY. **Choctaw Nation** Choctaw Roll CARD NO.
POST OFFICE: Featherston, Ind. Ter. *(Not Including Freedmen)* FIELD NO. 365

Dawes' Roll No.	NAME	Relationship to Person	AGE	SEX	BLOOD	TRIBAL ENROLLMENT		
						Year	County	No.
								CCR #2
713	1 Carney, Susan 27	First Named	23	F	Full		San Bois	85
714	2 " , Caroline 6	Dau	2	"	3/4		" "	"
	3							
	4	ENROLLMENT						
	5	OF NOS. 1 and 2 HEREON APPROVED BY THE SECRETARY						
	6	OF INTERIOR DEC 12 1902						
	7		No1 1896 Sans Bois 2102 as Susie Carney					
	8		No2 1896 " " 2103 " Adaline "					
	9							
	10							
	11		No1 - wife of Allen Carney, Chickasaw roll, Card No. 1142					
	12		No1 and Allen Carney are separated					
	13							
	14							
	15							
	16							
	17							

TRIBAL ENROLLMENT OF PARENTS

	Name of Father	Year	County	Name of Mother	Year	County
1	Mose Woolidge	Dead	San Bois	Lizzie Carney	Dead	San Bois
2	Allen Carney		Chick residing in Choctaw N. 1st Dist	No 1		
3						
4						
5						
6						
7						
8						
9						
10						
11						
12						
13						
14						
15				Date of Application for Enrollment. Oct 11/98		
16						
17						

Choctaw By Blood Enrollment Cards 1898-1914

RESIDENCE: Chickasaw Nation ~~COUNTY~~.
POST OFFICE: Silo, Ind. Ter.

Choctaw Nation

Choctaw Roll *(Not Including Freedmen)*

CARD NO.

FIELD NO. 366

Dawes' Roll No.	NAME	Relationship to Person First Named	AGE	SEX	BLOOD	TRIBAL ENROLLMENT		
						Year	County	No.
715	1 Gardner, Robert 25		21	M	1/4		Blue	CCR #2 210
716	2 " , William Dempsey 20	Bro	16	"	1/4		"	"
	3							
	4	ENROLLMENT						
	5	OF NOS. 1 and 2 HEREON APPROVED BY THE SECRETARY	No1 1896 Blue 4900 as Robt Gardner					
	6	OF INTERIOR DEC 12 1902	No2 1896 " 4901 " Wᵐ D. "					
	7							
	8	No1, husband of Susie Gardner, Chickasaw roll, Card No. 1143						
	9							
	10	No2 on Choctaw roll as William D. Gardner						
	11	No2 was married to Linnie Barton May 3, 1903						
	12	For child of No1 see Chickasaw NB (March 3, 1905) #183						
	13							
	14							
	15							
	16							
	17							

TRIBAL ENROLLMENT OF PARENTS

	Name of Father	Year	County	Name of Mother	Year	County
1	G. G. Gardner		non citizen	Frances Gardner	Dead	Choctaw roll
2	" " "		" "	" "	"	" " "
3						
4						
5						
6						
7						
8						
9						
10						
11						
12						
13						
14						
15				Date of Application for Enrollment.		Oct 11/98
16						
17						

Choctaw By Blood Enrollment Cards 1898-1914

RESIDENCE: Son[sic] Bois COUNTY.
POST OFFICE: Featherston, Ind. Ter.

Choctaw Nation

Choctaw Roll
(Not Including Freedmen)

CARD NO.
FIELD NO. **367**

Dawes' Roll No.	NAME	Relationship to Person First Named	AGE	SEX	BLOOD	TRIBAL ENROLLMENT Year	TRIBAL ENROLLMENT County	TRIBAL ENROLLMENT No.
717	1 Moore, Lily ³⁰		26	F	Full		San[sic] Bois	CCR #2 345
DEAD	2 " , Jackson DEAD	son	6	M	1/2		" "	"
	3							
	4	ENROLLMENT OF NOS. 1 HEREON						
	5	APPROVED BY THE SECRETARY				No1 1896	Sans Bois	8422
	6	OF INTERIOR Dec. 12, 1902				No2 1896	" "	8423
	7							
	8	No 2 Hereon dismissed under						
	9	order of the Commission to the Five						
	10	Civilized Tribes of March 31, 1905						
	11							
	12							
	13							
	14							
	15							
	16							
	17							

TRIBAL ENROLLMENT OF PARENTS

	Name of Father	Year	County	Name of Mother	Year	County
1	Eastman Charles	Dead	Choctaw roll		Dead	Choctaw roll
2	Austin Moore		Chick residing in Choctaw N. 1ˢᵗ Dist	No 1		
3						
4						
5	No1 - wife of Austin Moore on Chickasaw roll, Card No 1145					
6	No2 - died in August 1899, Proof of death filed Aug. 12 [or 10], 1901					
7	For child of No1 see N.B. (March 3, 1905) #1324					
8						
9						
10						
11						
12						
13						
14						
15					Date of Application for Enrollment.	
16						
17					Oct 11/98	

67

Choctaw By Blood Enrollment Cards 1898-1914

RESIDENCE: Jack Fork   COUNTY.
POST OFFICE: Stringtown, Ind. Ter.   **Choctaw Nation**   Choctaw Roll *(Not Including Freedmen)*   CARD No.   FIELD No. **368**

Dawes' Roll No.	NAME	Relationship to Person First Named	AGE	SEX	BLOOD	TRIBAL ENROLLMENT Year	County	No.
	DIED PRIOR TO SEPTEMBER 25, 1902							CCR #2
~~718~~	₁ Carnes, Ellis Harris ⁴⁶	First Named	42	M	Full		Jack Fork	122
719	₂ " , Julius V ²⁰	Son	16	"	"	" "		"
720	₃ " , Molsie ¹⁵	Dau	11	F	"	" "		"
721	₄ " , Evangeline ⁹	"	5	"	"	" "		"
722	₅ " , Elsie ¹⁸	Niece	14	"	"	" "		"
14532	₆ " , Cillin Bertha Bell¹	Gr Dau	5mo	F	"			
14533	₇ Miller, Stephen ¹	Gr Son	10mo	M	Full			
	₈							
	₉ ENROLLMENT OF NOS. 1,2,3,4 and 5 HEREON					No 1	1896	Jack Fork	2973
	₁₀ APPROVED BY THE SECRETARY					No 2	1896	" "	2975
	₁₁ OF INTERIOR Dec 12 1902					No 3	1896	" "	2976
	₁₂ ENROLLMENT					No 4	1896	" "	2977
	₁₃ OF NOS. 6 and 7 HEREON APPROVED BY THE SECRETARY					No 5	1896	" "	2978
	₁₄ OF INTERIOR May 20 1903							
	₁₅							
	₁₆ For child of No5 see NB (Apr 26-06) Card #644							
	₁₇ " " " No3 " (Mar 3-05) " #831							

TRIBAL ENROLLMENT OF PARENTS

Name of Father	Year	County	Name of Mother	Year	County
₁ Harris Carnes	Dead	Choctaw Roll	Momer Carnes	Dead	Jack Fork
₂ No 1			Lizzie Carnes		" "
₃ No 1			" "		" "
₄ No 1			" "		" "
₅ Lewis Carnes	Dead	Jack Fork	Louvina Carnes	Dead	" "
₆ Alfred Noaby	1896	" "	Nº 3		
₇ Davis Miller	1896	" "	No 5		
₈	No1 husband of Dora Carnes, Chickasaw roll, Card No. 1147				
₉	No1 on Choctaw roll as E. H. Carnes				
₁₀	No3 " " " " Mulsey "				
₁₁	No1 died Oct. 16-1899: Enrollment cancelled by Department July 8-1904				
₁₂					
₁₃	Nº6 Born April 10, 1902: enrolled Sept. 10, 1902. Nº6 is illegitimate				Date of Application for Enrollment.
₁₄	No7 Born Feb. 13, 1902: enrolled Dec. 19, 1902				
₁₅	No5 is now wife of Davis Miller Choc #1749				Oct 11/98
₁₆	Mother of No 2,3 and 4 is Lizzie Choc card #1905 Dec 8/02				
₁₇	Nº1 Died about Oct. 15 1899. Proof of death filed Nov. 4, 1902.				

68

RESIDENCE: Gaines   COUNTY.
POST OFFICE: Hartshorn[sic], Ind. Ter.   **Choctaw Nation** *(Not Including Freedmen)*   **Choctaw Roll**   CARD NO.
FIELD NO. **369**

Dawes' Roll No.	NAME	Relationship to Person First Named	AGE	SEX	BLOOD	TRIBAL ENROLLMENT Year	County	No.
723	1 Thompson, Lucy	First Named	19	F	Full		Gaines	CCR #2 438
~~724~~	DIED PRIOR TO SEPTEMBER 25, 1902 2 ~~, Grant~~	son	~~7mos~~	~~M~~	~~1/2~~			
15749	3 Thompson, Cornelius	son	1	M	Full			
	4							
	5 ENROLLMENT				No 1	1896	Gaines	11989
	6 OF NOS. 1 and 2 HEREON APPROVED BY THE SECRETARY							
	7 OF INTERIOR Dec 12 1902							
	8 ENROLLMENT							
	9 OF NOS. ~~ 3 ~~ HEREON APPROVED BY THE SECRETARY							
	10 OF INTERIOR Dec 15 1904							
	11							
	12 No1. wife of Culberson Thompson Chickasaw roll Card No. 1152							
	13 No.2 died February 23, 1902: Proof of death filed Dec. 23, 1902							
	14 No2 died Feb 23-1902: Enrollment cancelled by Department July 8, 1904							
	15 No3 born March 31, 1901: application for his enrollment was made by father.							
	16							
	17							

TRIBAL ENROLLMENT OF PARENTS

Name of Father	Year	County	Name of Mother	Year	County
1 Charley York		Gaines		Dead	Choctaw roll
~~2 Culberson Thompson~~		Chick residing in Choctaw N. 1st Dist	~~No 1~~		
3 Culberson Thompson		Chick residing in Choctaw N. 1st Dist	No 1		
4					
5					
6 Culberson Thompson at So. McAlester, I.T. Dec. 22d, 1902.					
7 Affidavits as to birth of No3 executed at Hartshorne, I.T. Dec. 24, 1902					
8 and received at office of Commission at Muskogee I.T. Dec. 26, 1902.					
9 No.3 enrolled, Aug. 26, 1904					
10 For child of No.1 see Chickasaw NB (Mar 3, 05) #546					
11					
12					
13				#1&2 Date of Application for Enrollment.	
14					
15				Oct 11/98	
16					
17 Gowen 7/-26-05					

Choctaw By Blood Enrollment Cards 1898-1914

RESIDENCE: Tobucksy COUNTY.							
POST OFFICE: Scipio, Ind. Ter.	**Choctaw Nation**			Choctaw Roll *(Not Including Freedmen)*	CARD No. FIELD No.		**370**

Dawes' Roll No.	NAME	Relationship to Person First Named	AGE	SEX	BLOOD	TRIBAL ENROLLMENT		
						Year	County	No.
725	1 Anderson, Andel 49	First Named	45	M	Full		Tobucksy	CCR #2 5
~~726~~	DIED PRIOR TO SEPTEMBER 25, 1902 2 , Rosa 14	Dau	~~10~~	F	"		"	"
727	3 " , Laura 12	"	8	"	"		"	"
728	4 " , Minnie 18	"	14	"	"		"	"
	5							
	6 ENROLLMENT							
	7 OF NOS. 1,2,3 and 4 HEREON APPROVED BY THE SECRETARY							
	8 OF INTERIOR Dec 12 1902							
	9 No.2 died Oct. 27-1899: Enrollment cancelled by Department July 8 1904							
	10 No 1 Husband of Rhoda Anderson, Chickasaw roll Card No. 1156							
	11 No4 on Choctaw roll as Mamie Anderson							
	~~No2 Died Oct. 27, 1899. Proof of death received and filed Dec 30, 1902.~~							
	12							
	13							
	14				No 1	1896	Tobucksy	128
	15				No 2	1896	"	111
	16				No 3	1896	"	112
	17				No 4	1896	"	113

TRIBAL ENROLLMENT OF PARENTS

Name of Father	Year	County	Name of Mother	Year	County
1 Dan¹ Anderson	Dead	Gained	Liza Anderson	Dead	Tobucksy
2 ~~No 1~~			~~Annie Anderson~~	"	"
3 No 1			" "	"	"
4 No 1			Liza Ann "	"	Gaines
5					
6					
7					
8					
9					
10					
11					
12					
13					Date of Application for Enrollment.
14					
15					Oct 12/98
16					
17					

Choctaw By Blood Enrollment Cards 1898-1914

RESIDENCE: Tobucksy ~~COUNTY.~~ **Choctaw Nation** **Choctaw Roll** CARD NO.

POST OFFICE: McAlester, Ind. Ter. *(Not Including Freedmen)* FIELD NO. **371**

Dawes' Roll No.	NAME	Relationship to Person First Named	AGE	SEX	BLOOD	TRIBAL ENROLLMENT		
						Year	County	No.
~~729~~	DIED PRIOR TO SEPTEMBER 25, 1902 1 Ott, Willie		~~39~~	~~M~~	~~Full~~		~~Tobucksy~~	CCR #2 ~~386~~
	2							
	3 ENROLLMENT					1896	Tobucksy	9921
	4 OF NOS. 1 HEREON APPROVED BY THE SECRETARY							
	5 OF INTERIOR Dec 12 1902							
	6							
	7 Husband of Kitsie Ott Chickasaw roll, Card No. 1157							
	8							
	9 No 1 Died before Sept. 25, 1902, Enrollment cancelled by Department May 2 1906.							
	10							
	11							
	12							
	13							
	14							
	15							
	16							
	17							

TRIBAL ENROLLMENT OF PARENTS

Name of Father	Year	County	Name of Mother	Year	County
1 ~~Sam Ott~~	~~Dead~~	~~Gaines~~	~~Liza Ott~~	~~Dead~~	~~Tobucksy~~
2					
3					
4					
5					
6					
7					
8					
9					
10					
11					
12					
13					
14					
15			Date of Application for Enrollment.	Oct 12/98	
16					
17					

Choctaw By Blood Enrollment Cards 1898-1914

RESIDENCE: Blue   COUNTY.   **Choctaw Nation**   Choctaw Roll   CARD NO.

POST OFFICE: Cale, Ind. Ter.   *(Not Including Freedmen)*   FIELD NO. **372**

Dawes' Roll No.	NAME	Relationship to Person First Named	AGE	SEX	BLOOD	TRIBAL ENROLLMENT Year	County	No.
void	1 Moore, Mary Ellen	Named	25	F	1/2			
void	2 ", Harold	son	11mo	M	1/4			
void	3 ", Claude M	"	1mo	"	1/4			
void	4 ", Floy	Dau	1mo	F	1/4			
	5							
	6							
	7							
	8							
	9	No1 on Chickasaw roll Page 75, as Mary Moore transferred to						
	10	Choctaw roll by Daws[sic] Com						
	11	No1 is the wife of John C Moore on Chickasaw card #1511						
	12	No4 born Dec 13, 1901; Enrolled July. 17. 1902						
	13							
	14							
	15							
	16							
	17							

TRIBAL ENROLLMENT OF PARENTS

	Name of Father	Year	County	Name of Mother	Year	County
1	Peter Maytubby	1897	Chick residing in Choctaw N. 3rd Dist	Refina Maytubby	Dead	Blue
2	John C. Moore		on citizen	No 1		
3	" " "		" "	No 1		
4	" " "		" "	No 1		
5						
6						
7						
8						
9						
10						
11						
12						
13						
14					Date of Application for Enrollment.	
15					Oct 12/98	
16					No3 enrolled Oct. 12/99	
17						

Transferred to Chickasaw Card No 1627 Oct. 14 1902

CANCELLED

72

Choctaw By Blood Enrollment Cards 1898-1914

RESIDENCE: Chickasaw Nation ~~COUNTY.~~ **Choctaw Nation**   **Choctaw Roll**   CARD NO.
POST OFFICE: Lynn, Ind. Ter.   *(Not Including Freedmen)*   FIELD NO. 373

Dawes' Roll No.	NAME	Relationship to Person First Named	AGE	SEX	BLOOD	TRIBAL ENROLLMENT Year	TRIBAL ENROLLMENT County	TRIBAL ENROLLMENT No.
I.W. 1201	1 Whiteside, Levicia	First Named	18	F	I.W.			
14534	2 Moore, Frank	son	2	M	1/32			
	3							
	4	ENROLLMENT						
	5	OF NOS. 2 HEREON APPROVED BY THE SECRETARY						
	6	OF INTERIOR May 20 1903						
	7							
	8	ENROLLMENT						
	9	OF NOS. ~1~ HEREON APPROVED BY THE SECRETARY						
	10	OF INTERIOR Dec 13 1904						
	11	No1 divorced wife of Joseph R. Moore Choctaw #4289 (12002)						
	12	No2 son " " " " " # "						
	13	No1 is now wife of P.L. Whiteside a non citizen 11/19/02						
	14	~~No.1 originally listed on this card as Levicia Moore~~						
	15							
	16							
	17	B/A for #2 in file						

TRIBAL ENROLLMENT OF PARENTS

	Name of Father	Year	County	Name of Mother	Year	County
1	Saml Bumgardner		non citizen	Mary Bumgardner		non citizen
2	J.R. Moore		Choctaw residing in ~~Chickasaw Dist~~	No 1		
3						
4						
5						
6						
7						
8						
9						
10						
11						
12						
13					Date of Application for Enrollment.	
14						
15					Oct 12/98	
16						
17	P.O. Alderson I.T.					

Choctaw By Blood Enrollment Cards 1898-1914

RESIDENCE: Blue   COUNTY.   **Choctaw Nation**   **Choctaw Roll**   CARD NO.
POST OFFICE: Bennington, Ind. Ter.   *(Not Including Freedmen)*   FIELD NO.   374

Dawes' Roll No.	NAME	Relationship to Person First Named	AGE	SEX	BLOOD	TRIBAL ENROLLMENT		
						Year	County	No.
730	1 Folsom, Alfred Wright [62]		58	M	Full		Blue	CCR #2 186
	2							
	3	ENROLLMENT				1896	Blue	4356
	4	OF NOS. 1 HEREON APPROVED BY THE SECRETARY						
	5	OF INTERIOR DEC 12 1902						
	6							
	7							
	8	Husband of Levina C. Folsom, Chickasaw roll, Card No. 1163						
	9							
	10	On Choctaw roll as A. W. Folsom						
	11							
	12							
	13							
	14							
	15							
	16							
	17							

TRIBAL ENROLLMENT OF PARENTS

	Name of Father	Year	County	Name of Mother	Year	County
1	Sam Folsom	Dead	Choctaw roll	Annie Folsom	Dead	Choctaw roll
2						
3						
4						
5						
6						
7						
8						
9						
10						
11						
12						
13						
14				Date of Application for Enrollment		Oct 12/98
15						
16						
17						

74

Choctaw By Blood Enrollment Cards 1898-1914

RESIDENCE: Atoka COUNTY.
POST OFFICE: Caney, Ind. Ter.

Choctaw Nation

Choctaw Roll
(Not Including Freedmen)

CARD NO.
FIELD NO. **375**

Dawes' Roll No.	NAME	Relationship to Person First Named	AGE	SEX	BLOOD	TRIBAL ENROLLMENT		
						Year	County	No.
731	1 Summer, Amanda L.M 24	First Named	20	F	1/32		Choctaw residing in Chickasaw Dist	CCR #2 433
732	2 " , Minnie 7	Dau	3	"	1/64		" "	"
15822	3 " , Mirtle May	"	2	"	1/64			
	4							
	5							
	6	ENROLLMENT OF NOS. 1 and 2 HEREON APPROVED BY THE SECRETARY OF INTERIOR Dec. 12, 1902						
	7							
	8							
	9							
	10							
	11							
	12							
	13							
	14	ENROLLMENT OF NOS. 3 HEREON APPROVED BY THE SECRETARY OF INTERIOR Jun 12, 1905						
	15							
	16							
	17							

TRIBAL ENROLLMENT OF PARENTS

	Name of Father	Year	County	Name of Mother	Year	County
1	John Moore	Dead	Choctaw roll	Mary Jane Thompson		white woman
2	Jim Summer		non citizen	No 1		
3	James Summers		" "	No 1		
4						
5			No 1 1896 Chickasaw Dist 11729 as Amand L. M. Summer			
6			No 2 1896 " " 11730			
7			No 3 born Oct. 11, 1900, application made May 2, 1905 under Act of Congress approved March 3, 1905			
8			For child of No. 1 see N.B. (Apr 26, 1906) Card No. 29			
9			" " " " " " (March 3 1905) " " 1406			
10						
11						
12						
13						
14						
15				Date of Application for Enrollment.	For Nos 1 and 2	
16					Oct 12/98	
17	P.O. Linn, I.T.					

Choctaw By Blood Enrollment Cards 1898-1914

RESIDENCE: Chickasaw Nation ~~COUNTY.~~

POST OFFICE: Yarnaby, Ind. Ter.

Choctaw Nation

Choctaw Roll
(Not Including Freedmen)

CARD NO.

FIELD NO. 376

Dawes' Roll No.	NAME	Relationship to Person First Named	AGE	SEX	BLOOD	TRIBAL ENROLLMENT		
						Year	County	No.
VOID.	1 ~~Hamblin, Albert H.~~		21	M	1/4			
	2							
	3							
	4							
	5							
	6							
	7 On Chickasaw roll, Panola County, Page 5; transferred to Choctaw roll by							
	8 Dawes Com.							
	9							
	10							
	11							
	12							
	13							
	14							
	15							
	16							
	17							

TRIBAL ENROLMENT OF PARENTS

	Name of Father	Year	County	Name of Mother	Year	County
1	~~Henry Hamblin~~ (I.W.)		~~Blue~~	~~Mollie Hamblin~~	~~Dead~~	Choctaw residing in Chickasaw District
2						
3						
4						
5						
6						
7						
8						
9						
10						
11						
12						
13						
14						
15				Date of Application for Enrollment		Oct 12/98
16						
17						

CANCELLED

Transferred to Chickasaw card No. 1628 Oct 14, 1902

76

Choctaw By Blood Enrollment Cards 1898-1914

RESIDENCE: Tobucksy COUNTY.
POST OFFICE: Stewart, Ind. Ter.

Choctaw Nation

Choctaw Roll (Not Including Freedmen)

CARD NO.
FIELD NO. **377**

Dawes' Roll No.	NAME	Relationship to Person First Named	AGE	SEX	BLOOD	TRIBAL ENROLLMENT		
						Year	County	No.
14535	1 Wesley, Siley	First Named	33	F	Full	1896	Tobucksy	CCR #2 443
14536	2 " , Selin	Dau	2	"	3/4	1896	"	10231
14537	3 Primer, Moses	Son	6	M	Full	1896	Tobucksy	CCR #2 395
15565	4 Watson, Wilburn	"	3	"	"			
14538	5 Wesley, Stephen	"	3mo	"	1/2			
14539	6 " , Silas	Son	4m	"	1/2			
	7							
	8					No 1	1896	Tobucksy	13001
	9 ENROLLMENT OF NOS. 1,2,3,5 and 6 HEREON APPROVED BY THE SECRETARY					No 3	1896	"	10230
	10 OF INTERIOR May 20 1903							
	11	No1 wife of Elias Wesley Chickasaw roll Card No. 1169						
	12							
	13	No1 on Choctaw roll as Sallie Wesley.						
	14 ENROLLMENT OF NOS. 4 ~ HEREON APPROVED BY THE SECRETARY							
	15 OF INTERIOR Sep 22 1904							
	16							
	17	No 4 Born Mch 15 1894 proof of birth filed May 4, 1904						

TRIBAL ENROLLMENT OF PARENTS

	Name of Father	Year	County	Name of Mother	Year	County
1	Tecumseh Leader	Dead	Atoka	Salina Leader	Dead	Atoka
2	Elias Wesley		Chick residing in Choctaw N. 1st Dist	No 1		
3	Calson Primer	Dead	Atoka	No 1		
4	Elliot Watson	"	"	No 1		
5	Elias Wesley		Chickasaw	No 1		
6	" "		Card 1169	No 1		
7						
8	No2 on 1896 Choctaw Census roll, page 260; No 10231 as Sallie Primer					
9	No4 is a duplicate of No1 on Choctaw Card #D.69					
10	No 6 Born March 3rd 1902: Enrolled July 17th 1902					
11	For child of No.1 see NB (March 3, 1905) #1387					
12						
13						#1to3 Date of Application for Enrollment.
14						
15						Oct 12/98
16						Nos 4-5 enrolled Aug 8/99
17						

Choctaw By Blood Enrollment Cards 1898-1914

RESIDENCE: Chickasaw Nation ~~COUNTY~~.
POST OFFICE: Kemp, Ind. Ter.

Choctaw Nation

Choctaw Roll
(Not Including Freedmen)

CARD NO.
FIELD NO. 378

Dawes' Roll No.	NAME	Relationship to Person First Named	AGE	SEX	BLOOD	TRIBAL ENROLLMENT		
						Year	County	No.
733	1 Turnbull, Sam 15	First Named	11	M	1/4		Blue	CCR #2 450
	2							
	3 ENROLLMENT							
	4 OF NOS. 1 HEREON APPROVED BY THE SECRETARY							
	5 OF INTERIOR Dec 12 1902							
	6				1896	Blue	2427 as Samuel Turnbull	
	7							
	8							
	9							
	10							
	11							
	12 Mother, Mary Ellis, on Choctaw Card No. D70, see evidence							
	13 thereto attached.							
	14 For child of No1 see N.B. (Apr 26-06) Card #781							
	15							
	16							
	17							

TRIBAL ENROLLMENT OF PARENTS

	Name of Father	Year	County	Name of Mother	Year	County
1	Sam Turnbull	Dead	Choctaw residing in Chickasaw District	Mary Ellis		white woman
2						
3						
4						
5						
6						
7						
8						
9						
10						
11						
12						
13					Date of Application for Enrollment.	
14						
15					Oct 12/98	
16						
17						

RESIDENCE: Blue   COUNTY.   **Choctaw Nation**   **Choctaw Roll** *(Not Including Freedmen)*   CARD NO.
POST OFFICE: Durant, Ind. Ter.   FIELD NO. 379

Dawes' Roll No.	NAME	Relationship to Person First Named	AGE	SEX	BLOOD	TRIBAL ENROLLMENT Year	County	No.
VOID. 1	Marshall, J. Horace	Named	23	M	I.W.			
VOID. 2	", Lillie	wife	20	F	1/8			
VOID. 3	", Hazel	Dau	1	"	1/16			
VOID. 4	", Colbert	Son	4mo	M	1/16			

No2 on Chickasaw roll, Panola Co. Page 4 as Lillie Colbert; transferred to Choctaw roll by Dawes Com
No.4 Enrolled April 20, 1901.
Correct way of spelling given name of No2 is "Lyllie" See letter of No1 filed this day May 7, 1901.

TRIBAL ENROLLMENT OF PARENTS

	Name of Father	Year	County	Name of Mother	Year	County
1	Wm H Marshall		non citizen	Martha Marshall		non citizen
2	Dave Colbert	Dead	Choctaw residing in Chickasaw Dist	Rebecca Colbert (I.W.)		Choctaw residing in Chickasaw Dist
3	No 1			No 2		
4	No 1			No 2		

Date of Application for Enrollment.
Oct 12/98
No3 enrolled Oct 6/99
PO Colbert I.T.

79

Choctaw By Blood Enrollment Cards 1898-1914

RESIDENCE: San[sic] Bois COUNTY.
POST OFFICE: Featherston, Ind. Ter.

Choctaw Nation

Choctaw Roll
(Not Including Freedmen)

CARD NO.
FIELD NO. 380

Dawes' Roll No.	NAME		Relationship to Person First Named	AGE	SEX	BLOOD	TRIBAL ENROLLMENT		
							Year	County	No.
734	1 Moore, Mary	26	First Named	22	F	Full		San[sic] Bois	CCR #2 345
735	2 " , Dora	8	Dau	4	"	1/2		" "	"
736	3 Carney, Malinda	11	"	7	"	1/2		" "	"
737	4 Moore, Sampson	5	Son	8mos	M	1/2			
	5								
	6 ENROLLMENT OF NOS. 1,2,3 and 4 HEREON								
	7 APPROVED BY THE SECRETARY OF INTERIOR DEC 12 1902								
	8								
	9								
	10								
	11						No 1	1896	Sans Bois	8418
	12						No 2	1896	" "	8420
	13						No 3	1896	" "	8419
	14								
	15								
	16								
	17								

TRIBAL ENROLLMENT OF PARENTS

	Name of Father	Year	County	Name of Mother	Year	County
1	Charley Caney		Atoka		Dead	Choctaw roll
2	Joseph Moore		Chick residing in Choctaw N. 1st Dist	No 1		
3	Allen Carney		" " " "	No 1		
4	Joseph Moore		" " " "	No 1		
5						
6	No1 wife of Joseph Moore, Chickasaw roll, Card No. 1191					
7						
8	No3 on Choctaw roll as Malinda Moore					
9						
10						
11						
12						
13					Date of Application for Enrollment	
14						
15					Oct 12/98	
16	For child of No1 see NB (Mar 3-05) Card #84					
17	P.O. Quinton, I.T. 11/16/07					

RESIDENCE: Atoka COUNTY.
POST OFFICE: Boggy Depot, Ind. Ter.

Choctaw Nation

Choctaw Roll
(Not Including Freedmen)

CARD NO.
FIELD NO. 381

Dawes' Roll No.	NAME	Relationship to Person First Named	AGE	SEX	BLOOD	TRIBAL ENROLLMENT Year	County	No.
738	1 Culberson, Eliza 21		17	F	Full		Atoka	CCR #2 253
15379	2 " Josiah 4	son	1	M	1/2			
	3				No 1/2	1896	Atoka	5973
~~739~~	4 ~~Culberson, Willis~~ DIED PRIOR TO SEPTEMBER 25, 1902	~~son~~	~~3mo~~	~~M~~				
	5							
	6	ENROLLMENT OF NOS. 1 and 4 HEREON APPROVED BY THE SECRETARY OF INTERIOR Dec 12 1902						
	7							
	8							
	9	wife of James Culberson, Chickasaw roll, Card No.1194						
	10							
	11	On Choctaw roll as Eliza Hoyubbie						
	12							
	13							
	14	ENROLLMENT OF NOS. 2 HEREON APPROVED BY THE SECRETARY OF INTERIOR May 9 1904						
	15							
	16							
	17							

TRIBAL ENROLLMENT OF PARENTS

	Name of Father	Year	County	Name of Mother	Year	County
1	Willis Hoyubbi	Dead	Atoka	Georgeanna Hoyubbi		Atoka
2	James Culberson		Chick Roll	No. 1		
3						
4	~~James Culberson~~		~~Chick roll~~	~~No. 1~~		
5						
6						
7						
8						
9						
10	No2 enrolled Dec 19/99. Affidavit irregular					
11	and returned for correction.					
12	No2 born Dec. 7, 1898, proof of birth filed Feby 24, 1904.					
13	~~No1 has taken her allotment in Chick Nation. She filed proof of death of No4 at that time~~ Is not No2 dead?				Date of Application for Enrollment.	
14	No4 Enrolled July 7th, 1900.					
15	No4 died Nov. 13-1900. Enrollment cancelled by Department July 8-1904.			Oct 12/98		
16						
17						

Choctaw By Blood Enrollment Cards 1898-1914

RESIDENCE: Tobucksy COUNTY. **Choctaw Nation** Choctaw Roll CARD NO.
POST OFFICE: Krebs, Ind. Ter. *(Not Including Freedmen)* FIELD NO. 382

Dawes' Roll No.	NAME	Relationship to Person First Named	AGE	SEX	BLOOD	TRIBAL ENROLLMENT		
						Year	County	No.
740	DIED PRIOR TO SEPTEMBER 25, 1902 1 Pope, Nancy	First Named	25	F	Full		Tobucksy	CCR #2 395
741	DIED PRIOR TO SEPTEMBER 25, 1902 2 , Rusley	Son	4 mos	M	3/4			
	3							
	4 ENROLLMENT							
	5 OF NOS. 1 and 2 HEREON APPROVED BY THE SECRETARY					No 1	1896 Tobucksy	10238
	6 OF INTERIOR DEC 12 1902							
	7							
	8							
	9							
	10 No1 wife of Frank Pope, Chickasaw roll, Card No 1199							
	11							
	12 No.2 Died May 7, 1900. Proof of death filed Dec. 30, 1902							
	13 No.1 Died Dec 17, 1900. Proof of death filed Dec. 30, 1902.							
	14							
	15							
	16							
	17							

TRIBAL ENROLLMENT OF PARENTS

	Name of Father	Year	County	Name of Mother	Year	County
1		Dead	Choctaw roll	Siley Barkus		Tobucksy
2	Frank Pope		Chick residing in Choctaw N. 1st Dist	No 1		
3						
4						
5						
6						
7						
8						
9						
10						
11	No2 died May 7-1900: No1 died Dec. 17-1900: Enrollment cancelled					
12						
13						
14					Date of Application for Enrollment.	
15						
16					Oct 12, 1898	
17						

Choctaw By Blood Enrollment Cards 1898-1914

RESIDENCE: Chickasaw Nation ~~COUNTY~~. **Choctaw Nation** POST OFFICE: Kemp, Ind. Ter.

Choctaw Roll CARD NO.
(Not Including Freedmen) FIELD NO. 383

Dawes' Roll No.	NAME	Relationship to Person First Named	AGE	SEX	BLOOD	TRIBAL ENROLLMENT		
						Year	County	No.
Void	1 ~~Shico, Martin~~	~~Named~~	~~27~~	~~M~~	~~1/4~~			
	2							
	3							
	4							
	5	On Chickasaw roll, Panola Co, Page 7, as Bud Shico, transferred to						
	6	Choctaw roll by Dawes Com						
	7							
	8							
	9							
	10							
	11							
	12							
	13							
	14							
	15							
	16							
	17							

TRIBAL ENROLLMENT OF PARENTS

Name of Father	Year	County	Name of Mother	Year	County
1 ~~Charles Shico~~	~~Dead~~	~~Chickasaw roll~~	~~Catherine Raines~~		~~Choctaw residing in Chickasaw Dist~~
2					
3					
4					
5					
6					
7					
8					
9					
10					
11					
12					
13					
14					
15					
16			Date of Application for Enrollment.	Oct 13/98	
17 P.O. Durant I.T.					

CANCELLED

Transferred to Chickasaw Card #630 Oct. 14, 1903

83

Choctaw By Blood Enrollment Cards 1898-1914

RESIDENCE: Gaines COUNTY.	**Choctaw Nation**	**Choctaw Roll** *(Not Including Freedmen)*	CARD No. FIELD NO. 384
POST OFFICE: Hartshorne, Ind. Ter.			

Dawes' Roll No.	NAME	Relationship to Person	AGE	SEX	BLOOD	TRIBAL ENROLLMENT		
						Year	County	No.
742	1 Pickens, Isom 27	First Named	25	M	Full		Gaines	CCR #2 393
	2							
	3	ENROLLMENT				1896	Gaines	10165
	4	OF NOS. 1 HEREON APPROVED BY THE SECRETARY						
	5	OF INTERIOR DEC 12 1902						
	6							
	7							
	8	Husband of Guicy Pickens, Chickasaw roll, Card No 1207						
	9							
	10	On Choctaw roll as Isham Pickens						
	11	For child of No1 see NB (March 3, 1905) #474						
	12							
	13							
	14							
	15							
	16							
	17							

TRIBAL ENROLLMENT OF PARENTS

	Name of Father	Year	County	Name of Mother	Year	County
1	Pis-sok-no-ubby	Dead	Choctaw roll	Oklatona Pissoknoubby	Dead	Gaines
2						
3						
4						
5						
6						
7						
8						
9						
10						
11						
12						
13						
14						
15					Date of Application for Enrollment.	Oct 13/98
16						
17	3/7/08 P.O. Blanco.					

Choctaw By Blood Enrollment Cards 1898-1914

RESIDENCE:	Blue	COUNTY.	**Choctaw Nation**	**Choctaw Roll**	CARD No.	
POST OFFICE:	Durant, Ind. Ter.			(Not Including Freedmen)	FIELD NO.	385

Dawes' Roll No.	NAME	Relationship to Person First Named	AGE	SEX	BLOOD	TRIBAL ENROLLMENT		
						Year	County	No.
743	1 Robinson, Emeline E [64]		58	F	1/2		Blue	CCR #2 414
	2							
	3	ENROLLMENT				1896	Blue	10943
	4	OF NOS. 1 HEREON APPROVED BY THE SECRETARY						
	5	OF INTERIOR Dec 12, 1902						
	6							
	7							
	8							
	9	On Choctaw roll as Emeline Robinson						
	10							
	11							
	12							
	13							
	14							
	15							
	16							
	17							

TRIBAL ENROLLMENT OF PARENTS

	Name of Father	Year	County	Name of Mother	Year	County
1	Jeremiah Folsom	Dead	Choctaw roll	Mary Ann Folsom	Dead	Choctaw roll
2						
3						
4						
5						
6						
7						
8						
9						
10						
11						
12						
13						
14						
15				Date of Application for Enrollment.		Oct 13/98
16						
17	P.O. Doyle I.T.					

85

Choctaw By Blood Enrollment Cards 1898-1914

RESIDENCE: **Blue** COUNTY. **Choctaw Nation** Choctaw Roll *(Not Including Freedmen)* CARD NO. FIELD NO. **386**
POST OFFICE: **Durant, Ind. Ter.**

Dawes' Roll No.	NAME		Relationship to Person First Named	AGE	SEX	BLOOD	TRIBAL ENROLLMENT		
							Year	County	No.
15041	₁ Roberts, Emely F.	39	First Named	35	F	3/8	1896	Blue	10944
744	₂ " , Myrtle	11	dau	7	"	3/16	1896	"	10945
745	₃ " , Maud	9	"	5	"	3/16	1896	"	10946
746	₄ " , Minnie	7	"	3	"	3/16	1896	"	10947
747	₅ " , Mamie	5	"	8mos	"	3/16			
748	₆ White, Eddie	17	son	13	M	3/16	1896	Blue	13906
749	₇ " , Willie	15	"	11	"	3/16	1896	"	13907
750	₈ Roberts, Ethel	2	dau	1mo	F	3/16			
751	₉ " , Mildred	1	dau	1mo	F	3/16			
	10								
	11	ENROLLMENT OF NOS. 2,3,4,5,6,7,8 and 9 HEREON APPROVED BY THE SECRETARY OF INTERIOR Dec 12, 1902							
	12								
	13								
	14								
	15	ENROLLMENT OF NOS. ____ HEREON APPROVED BY THE SECRETARY OF INTERIOR Feb. 16, 1904							
	16								
	17								

TRIBAL ENROLLMENT OF PARENTS

	Name of Father	Year	County	Name of Mother	Year	County
₁	James Robinson	Dead	Blue	Emeline E Robinson		Blue
₂	Rufus Roberts		non citizen	No. 1		
₃	" "		" "	No. 1		
₄	" "		" "	No. 1		
₅	" "		" "	No. 1		
₆	Ed White	Dead	" "	No. 1		
₇	" "		"	" "	No. 1		
₈	Rufus Roberts		" "	No. 1		
₉	" "		" "	No. 1		

10   No1 also on Choctaw Pay Roll, No4 Page 79 No. 642 as Emely F Robets[sic]
11   No2 "   "   "   "   "   No4   "   79 "   645
12   No5 affidavit of attending physician to be supplied - Received Oct. 17/98
13   No1 on 1896 Choctaw Roll as Emily F. Roberts
14   No2 " 1896   "   "   " Myrtle F   "
       Date of Application for Enrollment.
15   No6 " 1896   "   "   " Eddy White
      No7 " 1896   "   "   " Wibley   "
       Oct 13/98
16   No8 Enrolled June 11ᵗʰ 1900
17   No9 Born June 19, 1902; enrolled July 25, 1902.   For child of No1 see N.B.(Mar 3-05) card #85

RESIDENCE: Chickasaw Nation ~~COUNTY~~.
POST OFFICE: Silo, Ind. Ter.

Choctaw Nation

Choctaw Roll
(Not Including Freedmen)

CARD NO.
FIELD NO. **387**

Dawes' Roll No.	NAME	Relationship to Person First Named	AGE	SEX	BLOOD	TRIBAL ENROLLMENT		
						Year	County	No.
I.W. 1087	1 Gardner, Minnie 25		21	F	I.W.		Blue	C.I. Roll 38
752	2 " , Mary 10	Dau	6	"	1/8		"	CCR #2 210
753	3 " Margaret Frances 8	"	4	"	1/8		"	"
754	4 " , Roy 6	Son	2	M	1/8		"	"
	5 William A							
	6							
	7	ENROLLMENT				No3 on Choctaw roll as Margarette		
	8	OF NOS. 2, 3, and 4 HEREON APPROVED BY THE SECRETARY						
	9	OF INTERIOR Dec. 12, 1902						
	10					No1	1896	Blue	14580
	11	ENROLLMENT OF NOS. ~1~ HEREON				No2	1896	"	4898
	12	APPROVED BY THE SECRETARY OF INTERIOR Nov. 16, 1904				No3	1896	"	4899
	13							
	14							
	15							
	16							
	17							

TRIBAL ENROLLMENT OF PARENTS

	Name of Father	Year	County	Name of Mother	Year	County
1	Bill Scroggins		non citizen	Margaret Scroggins	Dead	non citizen
2	Jesse D. Gardner	Dead	Blue	No 1		
3	" " "	"	"	No 1		
4	" " "	"	"	No 1		
5						
6						
7						
8						
9						
10						
11						
12						
13	No1 admitted as an intermarried citizen and No3 as a					Date of Application for Enrollment.
14	citizen by blood by Dawes Commission in 1896: Choctaw					
15	Case #272. no appeal. Evidence of birth of No 4 received and filed Feby. 7 1902					Oct 13/98
16						
17						

For child of No1 see N.B. (Apr. 26-06) #1108

RESIDENCE: Chickasaw Nation ~~COUNTY.~~
POST OFFICE: Yarnaby, Ind. Ter.

Choctaw Nation

Choctaw Roll
(Not Including Freedmen)

CARD No.
FIELD No. 388

Dawes' Roll No.	NAME	Relationship to Person First Named	AGE	SEX	BLOOD	TRIBAL ENROLLMENT		
						Year	County	No.
1	~~Potts, Fannie~~	~~Named~~	23	F	1/8			
2	~~" , Nina June~~	~~Dau~~	3	"	1/16			
3	~~" , Maude~~	"	9mo	"	1/16			
4	~~" , Lela~~	"	7mo	"	1/16			
5	~~" , Joel Cecil~~	~~Son~~	2wks	M	1/16			
6								
7						No 11		
8	Nos 1 and 2 on Page 11 Original roll of Panola County Chickasaw Nation, Sept 22/96							
9	No2 on Chickasaw roll as Tennie Potts							
10								
11								
12								
13								
14								
15								
16								
17								

TRIBAL ENROLLMENT OF PARENTS

	Name of Father	Year	County	Name of Mother	Year	County
1	~~Charley Shico~~	Dead	Chickasaw roll	Catherine Raines	1896 Panola Page 43	Panola County Chickasaw Roll
2	~~Edward Forest Potts~~		White man	No 1		
3	" " "		" "	No 1		
4	" " "		" "	No 1		
5	" " "		" "	No 1		
6						
7						
8						
9						
10						
11						
12						
13						
14		No.4 Enrolled May 24, 1900				
15		No 5 Born Jul 19, 1902: Enrolled July 31, 1902				
16	transfer to Chick				Date of Application for Enrollment	Oct 13/98
17						

CANCELLED Nov 20 1903 to Chickasaw card #1694 and Nos 1 top 5 inclusive transferred

88

Choctaw By Blood Enrollment Cards 1898-1914

RESIDENCE: Chickasaw Nation COUNTY.
POST OFFICE: Yarnaby, Ind. Ter.
Choctaw Nation
Choctaw Roll *(Not Including Freedmen)*
CARD NO.
FIELD NO. **389**

Dawes' Roll No.	NAME	Relationship to Person First Named	AGE	SEX	BLOOD	TRIBAL ENROLLMENT		
						Year	County	No.
void	1 Powell, Thomas Porter	Named	37	M	I.W.			
void	2 " , Ellen Jane	wife	30	F	1/4			
void	3 " , Annie Viola	dau	13	"	1/8			
void	4 " , Charles Ambrose	son	11	M	1/8			
void	5 " , Roy	"	9	"	1/8			
void	6 " , Rutha	dau	5	F	1/8			
void	7 " , Preston	son	3	M	1/8			
void	8 " , Mary	dau	3mos	F	1/8			
void	9 " , Thomas Clifford	son	6mo	M	1/8			
	10							
	11							
	12							
	13							
	14							
	15							
	16							
	17							

TRIBAL ENROLLMENT OF PARENTS

	Name of Father	Year	County	Name of Mother	Year	County
1	Ambrose Powell	Dead	non citizen	Easter Powell	dead	non citizen
2	Charley Shico		Chickasaw roll	Catherine Raines		Choctaw residing in Chickasaw Dist
3	No 1			No 2		
4	No 1			No 2		
5	No 1			No 2		
6	No 1			No 2		
7	No 1			No 2		
8	No 1			No 2		
9	No 1			No 2		
10						
11						
12	All except Nos 1 and 8 on Chickasaw roll, Panola Co, Page 1; transferred to					
13	Choctaw roll by Dawes Com.					
14	No 1 on Chickasaw Doubtful List, Panola Co, Page 83 as T.B. Powell					
15	No 2 " Chickasaw roll as E.J. Powell					
16	No 3 " " " " Ola "					
17	No 4 " " " " Charles "					
	No 9 enrolled July 8, 1901.					

Date of Application for Enrollment Oct 13/98

89

Choctaw By Blood Enrollment Cards 1898-1914

RESIDENCE: Jack Fork   COUNTY. **Choctaw Nation**   **Choctaw Roll**   CARD NO.
POST OFFICE: Hartshorne, Ind. Ter.   *(Not Including Freedmen)*   FIELD NO. **390**

Dawes' Roll No.	NAME	Relationship to Person First Named	AGE	SEX	BLOOD	TRIBAL ENROLLMENT		
						Year	County	No.
15380	1 James, Ellen 34	First Named	30	F	Full		Jack Fork	CCR #2 307
755	2 " , Walton 17	Son	13	M	1/2		" "	CCR #2 76
756	3 DIED PRIOR TO SEPTEMBER 25, 1902 , Cohen	Step Son	18	"	1/2		" "	CCR #2 307
	4							
	5 ENROLLMENT OF NOS. 2 and 3 HEREON							
	6 APPROVED BY THE SECRETARY OF INTERIOR DEC 12 1902							
	7							
	8 ENROLLMENT							
	9 OF NOS. ~~~1~~~ HEREON APPROVED BY THE SECRETARY							
	10 OF INTERIOR MAY 9 1904							
	11							
	12							
	13							
	14							
	15					No1	1896	Jacks Fork	7346
	16					No2	1896	" "	1891
	17 No					No3	1896	" "	7347

TRIBAL ENROLLMENT OF PARENTS

	Name of Father	Year	County	Name of Mother	Year	County
1	Captain Pis-stam-by	Dead	Choctaw roll	Hun-ma-ta-ho-ke	Dead	Jack Fork
2	Wesley James	1897	Chickasaw residing in Choctaw Nation	No 1		
3	" "	1897	" "	Phoebe James	Dead	Jack Fork
4						
5						
6	No1 - wife of Wesley James, Chickasaw roll, Card No. 1220					
7	No.3 died April 8-1902. Enrollment cancelled by Department [remainder illegible]					
8	No1 on Choctaw roll as Allen James					
9	No2 " " " " Walton Burris, (Raised by his aunt Eliza Burris)					
	No1 not dead.. Appeared and gave Testimony at Atoka Jan 15 '04					
10						
11						
12						
13						
14						
15				Date of Application for Enrollment. Oct 13/98		
16						
17						

P.O. Calvin, I.T.

Choctaw By Blood Enrollment Cards 1898-1914

RESIDENCE: Atoka COUNTY. **Choctaw Nation** Choctaw Roll CARD No.
POST OFFICE: Atoka, Ind. Ter. *(Not Including Freedmen)* FIELD No. 391

Dawes' Roll No.	NAME	Relationship to Person First Named	AGE	SEX	BLOOD	TRIBAL ENROLLMENT Year	County	No.
757	1 Sexton, Emmerson 34	First Named	30	M	Full		Atoka	CCR #2 431
	2							
	3				1896 Atoka 11644 as Emerson Sexton			
	4	ENROLLMENT OF NOS. 1 HEREON APPROVED BY THE SECRETARY OF INTERIOR Dec 12 1902						
	5							
	6							
	7							
	8	Husband of Annie Sexton, Chickasaw roll, Card No 1225.						
	9							
	10							
	11							
	12							
	13							
	14							
	15							
	16							
	17							

TRIBAL ENROLLMENT OF PARENTS

	Name of Father	Year	County	Name of Mother	Year	County
1	Holly Sexton	Dead	Choctaw roll	Selis Sexton	Dead	Choctaw roll
2						
3						
4						
5						
6						
7						
8						
9						
10						
11						
12						
13						
14						
15					Date of Application for Enrollment.	
16					Oct 13/98	
17						

Choctaw By Blood Enrollment Cards 1898-1914

RESIDENCE:	Jack Fork	COUNTY.	Choctaw Nation			Choctaw Roll	CARD NO.	
POST OFFICE:	Tuskahoma, Ind. Ter.					(Not Including Freedmen)	FIELD NO.	392

Dawes' Roll No.	NAME		Relationship to Person First Named	AGE	SEX	BLOOD	TRIBAL ENROLLMENT		
							Year	County	No.
758	1 Colbert, Martha	65	First Named	61	F	Full		Jack Fork	CCR #2 124
759	2 " , John	14	son	10	M	1/2		" "	"
	3								
	4 ~~ENROLLMENT~~					No1	1896	Jacks Fork	3036
	5 ~~OF NOS. 1 and 2 HEREON APPROVED BY THE SECRETARY~~					No2	1896	" "	3037
	6 ~~OF INTERIOR Dec. 12 1902~~								
	7								
	8								
	9 Wife of Billie Colbert, Chickasaw roll, Card No. 1227								
	10								
	11								
	12								
	13								
	14								
	15								
	16								
	17								

TRIBAL ENROLLMENT OF PARENTS

	Name of Father	Year	County	Name of Mother	Year	County
1	Joseph Anderson	dead	Choctaw roll	Julia Anderson		Jack Fork
2	Billie Colbert		Chick residing in Choctaw N. 3rd Dist	No. 1		
3						
4						
5						
6						
7						
8						
9						
10						
11						
12						
13						Date of Application for Enrollment
14						Oct 13/98
15						
16						
17						

Choctaw By Blood Enrollment Cards 1898-1914

RESIDENCE: Jack Fork COUNTY. **Choctaw Nation** Choctaw Roll CARD NO.
POST OFFICE: Tuskahoma, Ind. Ter. *(Not Including Freedmen)* FIELD NO. 393

Dawes' Roll No.	NAME	Relationship to Person First Named	AGE	SEX	BLOOD	TRIBAL ENROLLMENT		
						Year	County	No.
760	1 Bohanon, Robert ³²		28	M	1/2		Jack Fork	CCR #2 79
	2							
	3	ENROLLMENT						
	4	OF NOS. 1 HEREON APPROVED BY THE SECRETARY		1896 Jacks Fork 1968 as Robert Bohanan				
	5	OF INTERIOR DEC 12 1902						
	6							
	7	Husband of Liney Bohanon, Chickasaw roll, Card No 1228						
	8	For child of No. 1 see NB (March 3, 1905) #827						
	9							
	10							
	11							
	12							
	13							
	14							
	15							
	16							
	17							

TRIBAL ENROLLMENT OF PARENTS

	Name of Father	Year	County	Name of Mother	Year	County
1	Ellis Bohanon		Jack Fork	Patsey Bohanon	Dead	Wade
2						
3						
4						
5						
6						
7						
8						
9						
10						
11						
12						
13					Date of Application for Enrollment.	
14						
15					Oct 13/98	
16						
17						

93

Choctaw By Blood Enrollment Cards 1898-1914

RESIDENCE: Blue COUNTY. **Choctaw Nation** **Choctaw Roll** CARD No.
POST OFFICE: Durant, Ind. Ter. *(Not Including Freedmen)* FIELD No. 394

Dawes' Roll No.	NAME	Relationship to Person First Named	AGE	SEX	BLOOD	TRIBAL ENROLLMENT		
						Year	County	No.
VOID.	1 Colbert, Charley		35	M	1/4			
	2							
	3							
	4							
	5							
	6	On Chickasaw roll, Panola Co., Page 5; transferred to Choctaw roll by Dawes Com						
	7	No 1 is now the husband of Abbie Colbert on Choctaw Card #D 762; July 22d, 1902						
	8							
	9							
	10							
	11							
	12							
	13							
	14							
	15							
	16							
	17							

TRIBAL ENROLLMENT OF PARENTS

	Name of Father	Year	County	Name of Mother	Year	County
1	Jim Colbert	dead	Chickasaw roll	Athenius Colbert		Choctaw residing in Chickasaw Dist
2						
3						
4						
5						
6						
7						
8						
9						
10						
11						
12						
13						
14				Date of Application for Enrollment.		
15						Oct 13/98
16						
17						

CANCELLED

Transferred to Chickasaw Card No 1632 Oct 14, 1902

94

Choctaw By Blood Enrollment Cards 1898-1914

RESIDENCE:	Jack Fork	COUNTY.					Choctaw Roll		CARD NO.
POST OFFICE:	Tuskahoma, Ind. Ter.	**Choctaw Nation**					*(Not Including Freedmen)*		FIELD NO. 395

Dawes' Roll No.	NAME	Relationship to Person First Named	AGE	SEX	BLOOD	TRIBAL ENROLLMENT		
						Year	County	No.
781	1 Colbert, Alexander 27		23	M	1/2		Jack Fork	CCR #2 124
	2							
	3	ENROLLMENT OF NOS. 1 HEREON				1896	Jacks Fork	3046
	4	APPROVED BY THE SECRETARY						
	5	OF INTERIOR DEC 12 1902						
	6							
	7	Husband of Martha Colbert, Chickasaw roll, Card No. 1235						
	8	N°1 also the father of children on Chickasaw card #1235.						
	9	For children of No.1 see NB (March 3 1905) #1122						
	10							
	11							
	12							
	13							
	14							
	15							
	16							
	17							

TRIBAL ENROLLMENT OF PARENTS

Name of Father	Year	County	Name of Mother	Year	County
1 Billie Colbert		Chick residing in Choctaw N. 3rd Dist	Martha Colbert		Jack Fork
2					
3					
4					
5					
6					
7					
8					
9					
10					
11					
12					
13				Date of Application for Enrollment		
14						
15						Oct 13/98
16						
17						

Choctaw By Blood Enrollment Cards 1898-1914

RESIDENCE: Wade COUNTY. POST OFFICE: Tuskahoma, Ind. Ter. **Choctaw Nation** Choctaw Roll *(Not Including Freedmen)* CARD NO. FIELD NO. **396**

Dawes' Roll No.	NAME	Relationship to Person	AGE	SEX	BLOOD	TRIBAL ENROLLMENT		
						Year	County	No.
	DIED PRIOR TO SEPTEMBER 25, 1902 First							CCR #2
1	Potts, Horace	Named	40	M	Full		Wade	397
2								
3	ENROLLMENT					1896	Wade	10311
4	OF NOS. 1 HEREON APPROVED BY THE SECRETARY							
5	OF INTERIOR DEC 12 1902							
6								
7	Husband of Judy Potts, Chickasaw roll; Card No. 1240							
8	No 1 died Dec 11, 1901; proof of death filed Dec 15, 1902.							
9								
10								
11								
12								
13								
14								
15								
16								
17								

TRIBAL ENROLLMENT OF PARENTS

	Name of Father	Year	County	Name of Mother	Year	County
1	William Potts	Dead	Choctaw roll	Sarah Potts		Wade
2						
3						
4						
5						
6						
7						
8						
9						
10						
11						
12						
13						
14						
15						
16						
17						

Choctaw By Blood Enrollment Cards 1898-1914

RESIDENCE: Chickasaw Nation ~~COUNTY~~.
POST OFFICE: Kemp, Ind. Ter.

Choctaw Nation

Choctaw Roll
(Not Including Freedmen)

CARD NO.
FIELD NO. 397

Dawes' Roll No.	NAME	Relationship to Person First Named	AGE	SEX	BLOOD	TRIBAL ENROLLMENT		
						Year	County	No.
VOID. 1	~~Shico, Robert~~ DEAD		25	M	1/4			
2								
3								
4								
5	On Chickasaw roll, Panola Co., Page 7 as Rob Shico; transferred to Choctaw							
6	roll by Dawes Com.							
7								
8								
9								
10								
11								
12								
13								
14								
15								
16								
17								

TRIBAL ENROLLMENT OF PARENTS

	Name of Father	Year	County		Name of Mother	Year	County
1	Charley Shico	Dead	Chickasaw roll		Catherine Raines		Choctaw residing in Chickasaw Dist
2							
3							
4							
5							
6							
7							
8							
9							
10							
11							
12							
13							
14							
15				Date of Application for Enrollment.			Oct 13/98
16							
17							

97

Choctaw By Blood Enrollment Cards 1898-1914

						TRIBAL ENROLLMENT		
RESIDENCE: Blue COUNTY.								

RESIDENCE: **Blue** COUNTY. **Choctaw Nation**   **Choctaw Roll** CARD NO.
POST OFFICE: **Caddo, Ind. Ter.** *(Not Including Freedmen)* FIELD NO. **398**

Dawes' Roll No.	NAME	Relationship to Person First Named	AGE	SEX	BLOOD	TRIBAL ENROLLMENT		
						Year	County	No.
VOID. 1	Maytubby, Peter, Jr.		25	M	1/4			
2								
3								
4								
5	On Chickasaw roll, Pontotoc County, Page 57, transferred to Choctaw roll by							
6	Dawes Com.							
7								
8								
9								
10								
11								
12								
13								
14								
15								
16								
17								

TRIBAL ENROLLMENT OF PARENTS

	Name of Father	Year	County	Name of Mother	Year	County
1	Peter Maytubby	1897	Chickasaw residing in Choctaw N. 3rd Dist	Rafina Maytubby	Dead	Blue
2						
3						
4						
5						
6						
7						
8						
9						
10						
11						
12						
13						
14						
15				Date of Application for Enrollment.		Oct 14/98
16						
17						

CANCELLED

Transferred to Chickasaw Card No. 1634 Apr. 14, 1902

Choctaw By Blood Enrollment Cards 1898-1914

RESIDENCE: Jack Fork COUNTY.
POST OFFICE: Tuskahoma, Ind. Ter.
Choctaw Nation
Choctaw Roll *(Not Including Freedmen)*
CARD NO.
FIELD NO. **399**

Dawes' Roll No.	NAME	Relationship to Person First Named	AGE	SEX	BLOOD	TRIBAL ENROLLMENT		
						Year	County	No.
763	DIED PRIOR TO SEPTEMBER 25, 1902							CCR #2
~~763~~	₁ ~~McGee, Mollie~~ ⁴¹	~~First Named~~	~~37~~	~~F~~	~~Full~~		~~Jack Fork~~	~~374~~
764	₂ " , David ¹⁶	step son	12	M	1/2		" "	"
765	₃ Anderson, Buster ¹¹	son	7	"	1/2		" "	CCR #2 22
766	₄ McGee, Sophia ⁴	Dau	4mos	F	1/2			
	₅							
	₆ ENROLLMENT					No 1	1896	Jacks Fork	9475
	₇ OF NOS. 1,2,3, and 4 HEREON APPROVED BY THE SECRETARY					No2	1896	" "	9476
	₈ OF INTERIOR Dec 12, 1902					No3	1896	" "	535
	₉							
	₁₀ No1 wife of Fulsome McGee, Chickasaw roll, Card No. 1245.							
	₁₁							
	₁₂							
	₁₃							
	₁₄							
	₁₅							
	₁₆							
	₁₇							

TRIBAL ENROLLMENT OF PARENTS

Name of Father	Year	County	Name of Mother	Year	County
₁ ~~Jos Nuckenatiah~~	~~Dead~~	~~Choctaw Roll~~		~~Dead~~	~~Choctaw roll~~
₂ Fulsome McGee	1897	Chick residing in Choctaw N. 3rd Dist	Susan McGee	"	Jack Fork
₃ Tom Anderson		Chick residing in Choctaw N. 3rd Dist	No 1		
₄ Fulsome McGee	1897	" " " "	No 1		
₅					
₆					
₇ No1 died July 1899; proof of death filed Dec 13, 1902.					
₈ No 1 died July - , 1899; Enrollment cancelled by Department, July 8 - 1904					
₉					
₁₀					
₁₁					
₁₂					
₁₃					
₁₄					
₁₅				Date of Application for Enrollment.	
₁₆				Oct 14/98	
₁₇					

Choctaw By Blood Enrollment Cards 1898-1914

RESIDENCE: Chickasaw Nation ~~COUNTY.~~
POST OFFICE: Colbert, Ind. Ter.

Choctaw Nation

Choctaw Roll
(Not Including Freedmen)

CARD NO.
FIELD NO. **401**

Dawes' Roll No.	NAME	Relationship to Person First Named	AGE	SEX	BLOOD	TRIBAL ENROLLMENT		
						Year	County	No.
void	~~Colbert, Cornie~~	~~Named~~	~~18~~	~~M~~	~~1/4~~			
void	~~2 ", Lela~~	~~sister~~	~~16~~	~~F~~	~~1/4~~			
void	~~3 ", Nancy~~	~~"~~	~~14~~	~~"~~	~~1/4~~			
	4							
	5							
	6							
	7							
	8 All on Chickasaw roll Panola Co. Page 4, transferred to Choctaw roll by Dawes Com.							
	9 No1 " " " " " " 4 as Connie Colbert							
	10 No3 wife of Dan Collins on 9-1122. Evidence of marriage filed Dec 24, 1902							
	11							
	12							
	13							
	14							
	15							
	16							
	17							

TRIBAL ENROLLMENT OF PARENTS

	Name of Father	Year	County		Name of Mother	Year	County	
1	~~David Colbert~~	~~dead~~	~~Choctaw residing in Chickasaw Dist.~~		~~Rebecca Colbert~~		~~white woman~~	
2	" "	"	" " "		" "		" "	
3	" "	"	"		" "		" "	
4								
5								
6								
7								
8								
9								
10								
11								
12								
13								
14								
15				Date of Application for Enrollment.			Oct 14/98	
16								
17								

CANCELLED
Transferred to Chick Card #16 Oct 14, 1902

Choctaw By Blood Enrollment Cards 1898-1914

RESIDENCE: Jack Fork   COUNTY.   **Choctaw Nation**   **Choctaw Roll**   CARD NO.
POST OFFICE: Tuskahoma, Ind. Ter.   *(Not Including Freedmen)*   FIELD NO. **402**

Dawes' Roll No.	NAME	Relationship to Person First Named	AGE	SEX	BLOOD	TRIBAL ENROLLMENT		
						Year	County	No.
770	1 Morris, Joel ⁴¹	First Named	37	M	Full		Jack Fork	CCR #2 357
	2							
	3	ENROLLMENT				1896	Jacks Fork	8885
	4	OF NOS. 1 HEREON APPROVED BY THE SECRETARY						
	5	OF INTERIOR DEC 12 1902						
	6							
	7							
	8							
	9							
	10	Husband of Nehota Morris, Chickasaw roll, Card No. 1266						
	11	Now husband of No 1 Chickasaw card #854						
	12							
	13							
	14							
	15							
	16							
	17							

TRIBAL ENROLLMENT OF PARENTS

Name of Father	Year	County	Name of Mother	Year	County
1 Lem Morris	Dead	Choctaw roll	Becky Morris	Dead	Choctaw roll
2					
3					
4					
5					
6					
7					
8					
9					
10					
11					
12					
13					
14					
15			Date of Application for Enrollment.	Oct 14/98	
16					
17					

102

Choctaw By Blood Enrollment Cards 1898-1914

RESIDENCE: Blue COUNTY.
POST OFFICE: Boggy Depot, Ind. Ter.

Choctaw Nation

Choctaw Roll *(Not Including Freedmen)*

CARD NO.
FIELD NO. **403**

Dawes' Roll No.	NAME	Relationship to Person First Named	AGE	SEX	BLOOD	TRIBAL ENROLLMENT Year	County	No.
771	1 Byington, Emma 26	First Named	22	F	Full		Blue	CCR #2 66
772	2 " , Emmerson 16	Step Son	12	M	1/2	"		"
773	3 " , Malissa 13	" dau	9	F	1/2	"		"
774	4 " , Winnie 8	dau	4	"	1/2	"		"
775	5 " , Lutie 5	"	1	"	1/2			
14540	6 " , Maxwell 1	son	1½yrs	M	1/2			
	7							
	8	ENROLLMENT OF NOS. 1,2,3,4 and 5 HEREON APPROVED BY THE SECRETARY OF INTERIOR Dec. 12, 1902						
	9							
	10	ENROLLMENT OF NOS. 6 HEREON APPROVED BY THE SECRETARY OF INTERIOR May 20 1903						
	11							
	12							
	13							
	14	No1 - wife of Joel Byington Chickasaw roll, Card No. 1270						
	15	" " " " Choctaw card No. 5535						
	16							
	17							

TRIBAL ENROLLMENT OF PARENTS

	Name of Father	Year	County	Name of Mother	Year	County
1	James Pul-hi-ya	Dead	Blue	Susan Lewis		Blue
2	Joel Byington		Chick residing in Choctaw N. 3rd Dist	Sillen Byington	Dead	"
3	" "		" " " "	" "	"	"
4	" "		" " " "	No 1		
5	" "		" " " "	No 1		
6	" "		" " " "	No 1		
7						
8	No1 1896 Blue 1592					
9	No2 1896 " 1593 as Emerson Byington					
10	No3 1896 " 1594 " Melissa "					
11	No4 1896 " 1595					
12	No6 Born June 25, 1901 Proof of birth received and filed Dec 24, 1902					
13	For child of No.1 see N.B. (Apr 26-06) card #669					
14	" " " " " (Mar 3-05) " #471				#1 to 5 inc	
						Date of Application for Enrollment.
15						Oct 14/98
16	P.O. Caddo I.T 10/14/03					
17	P.O. Caney I.T. 2/27/02					

Choctaw By Blood Enrollment Cards 1898-1914

RESIDENCE: Chickasaw Nation ~~COUNTY~~. **Choctaw Nation** Choctaw Roll   CARD NO.
POST OFFICE: Foster, Ind. Ter. *(Not Including Freedmen)* FIELD NO. 404

Dawes' Roll No.	NAME	Relationship to Person First Named	AGE	SEX	BLOOD	TRIBAL ENROLLMENT		
						Year	County	No.
776	1 Wyatt, Ed J. 40	First Named	36	M	1/4		Choctaw residing in Chickasaw District	CCR #2 489
I.W. 1202	2 " , Vancie 31	wife	27	F	I.W.			
777	3 " , Roxsie 10	dau	6	F	1/8		Choctaw residing in Chickasaw District	CCR #2 489
778	4 " , Ed. J, Jr. 8	son	4	M	1/8		" "	"
779	5 " , Mary 4	dau	3mo	F	1/8			
780	6 " , Ernest Montgomery	son	1mo	M	1/8			
	7							
	8		No4 on Choctaw roll as Ed Wyatt, Jr.					
	9	ENROLLMENT OF NOS. 1,3,4,5 and 6 HEREON APPROVED BY THE SECRETARY OF INTERIOR Dec. 12 1902						
	10							
	11	ENROLLMENT OF NOS. ~~2~~ HEREON APPROVED BY THE SECRETARY OF INTERIOR Dec. 13, 1904						
	12							
	13							
	14							
	15							
	16							
	17							

TRIBAL ENROLLMENT OF PARENTS

	Name of Father	Year	County	Name of Mother	Year	County
1	Montgomery Wyatt	Dead	non citizen	Minerva Wyatt	Dead	Red River
2	Joe Allen	" "		Emalisa Allen		noncitizen
3	No.1			Vancie Wyatt (IW)		Choctaw residing in Chickasaw dist.
4	No.1			" "		" " "
5	No.1			" "		" " "
6	No.1			" "		" " "
7						
8	No1 1896 Chickasaw Dist 14153 as Edd Wyatt					
9	No3 1896 " " 14155 " Roxie "					
10	No4 1896 " " 14154 " Edd " Jr.					
	No6 Born March 21, 1902, enrolled April 23, 1902 (Earnest Montgomery)					
11						
12						
13						
14					Date of Application for Enrollment.	#1 3&4
15						Oct 17/98
16					No2 enrolled Oct 19/98	
17	Doyle I.T.				No5 " Oct 13/99	

P.O. Marlow I.T.

Choctaw By Blood Enrollment Cards 1898-1914

RESIDENCE: Chickasaw Nation ~~COUNTY~~.
POST OFFICE: Sulphur ~~Springs~~, Ind. Ter.

Choctaw Nation

Choctaw Roll
(Not Including Freedmen)

CARD NO.
FIELD NO. **405**

Dawes' Roll No.		NAME		Relationship to Person	AGE	SEX	BLOOD	TRIBAL ENROLLMENT		
								Year	County	No.
781	1	Moss, Lurinda	25	First Named	21	F	1/2		Choctaw residing in Chickasaw Dist	CCR #2 360
14541	2	" Lue Willie	5	Dau	2	"	1/4		" "	"
782	3	" Dora May	4	"	1	"	1/4			
IW 1398	4	" Homer		Husband	31	M	IW			
	5									
	6	ENROLLMENT								
	7	OF NOS. 1 and 3 HEREON APPROVED BY THE SECRETARY								
	8	OF INTERIOR Dec. 12, 1902								
	9									
	10	ENROLLMENT ~~OF NOS. 2 HEREON~~								
	11	APPROVED BY THE SECRETARY								
	12	OF INTERIOR May 20 1903								
	13									
	14	ENROLLMENT ~~OF NOS. 4 HEREON~~								
	15	APPROVED BY THE SECRETARY								
	16	OF INTERIOR Jun 12, 1905								
	17									

TRIBAL ENROLLMENT OF PARENTS

	Name of Father	Year	County	Name of Mother	Year	County
1	A. E. Plato (IW)		Choctaw residing in Chickasaw Dist	Louvinia Plato	Dead	Blue
2	Homer Moss		white man	No 1		
3	" "		" "	No 1		
4	J. L. Moss		non citizen	Rose Moss	Dead	non citizen
5						
6						
7						
8	No1 1896 Chickasaw Dist 8970 as Lorinda Moss					
9	Husband of No1 is father of children on this card is					
10	Homer Moss on Choctaw card #D78. ~~No2 proof of birth received and filed Sept 26, 1902~~					
11	No4 originally listed for enrollment on Choctaw card #D-78 Oct. 17/98; transferred					
12	to this card May 15, 1905; see decision of March 27-1905.					
13						
14					Date of Application for Enrollment.	
15					Oct 17/98	
16				No3 enrolled Nov. 1/99		
17						

Choctaw By Blood Enrollment Cards 1898-1914

RESIDENCE: Chickasaw Nation ~~COUNTY.~~ **Choctaw Nation** Choctaw Roll CARD No.
POST OFFICE: Purdy, Ind. Ter. (Not Including Freedmen) FIELD No. **406**

Dawes' Roll No.	NAME	Relationship to Person First Named	AGE	SEX	BLOOD	TRIBAL ENROLLMENT		
						Year	County	No.
14542	1 Blundell, Patsey ²⁸		24	F	1/16		Choctaw residing in Chickasaw District	CCR #2 82
14543	2 " , Earl ⁵	son	2	M	1/32		" "	"
14544	3 Estes, Perry ¹⁰	"	6	"	1/32		" "	CCR #2 162
14545	4 Blundell, Thomas Clyde ²	"	2mo	M	1/32			
I.W. 1283	5 " James H ²⁵	husband	25	M	I.W.		Choctaw residing in Chickasaw District	
	6							
	7	ENROLLMENT OF NOS. 1,2,3 and 4 HEREON APPROVED BY THE SECRETARY OF INTERIOR May 20 1903						
	8							
	9							
	10							
	11	ENROLLMENT OF NOS. 5 HEREON APPROVED BY THE SECRETARY OF INTERIOR Mar 14 1905						
	12							
	13							
	14	No1 on Choctaw roll as Patsey Blundly						
	15	No2 " " " " Earl "						
	16							
	17							

TRIBAL ENROLLMENT OF PARENTS

Name of Father	Year	County	Name of Mother	Year	County
1 Joe Mann	dead	non citizen	Martha Mann	Dead	Choctaw residing in Chickasaw dist
2 James H Blundell		white man	No 1		
3 Joe Estes		non citizen	No 1		
4 James H. Blundell		" "	No.1		
5 Miles Blundell		non citizen	Vetura Blundell		non citizen
6					
7	No1 on 1893 Chick Dist No. 252 as Patsy Mann				
8	Nos 1 and 5 were first married in December 1895, under U.S. law.				
9	" 1 " 5 " remarried Sept 12, 1898, under Chick. law				
10	No3 1896 Chickasaw Dist - 3821 as Perry Esters.				
11	For child of Nos 1&5 see N.B. (Apr. 26-06) card #516				
12	No.4 Enrolled June 23d, 1900				
13					1 to 3 inc
14					Date of Application for Enrollment.
15	Evidence of birth of No.2 received and filed Feby 7ᵗʰ 1902				Oct 17/98
16	No5 originally listed for enrollment on Choctaw card D-79, Oct 17/98				
17 Foster I.T.	transferred to this card Feb 1, 1905; See decision of Jan. 16, 1905.				

For child of Nos 1&5 see N.B. (Mar 3ʳᵈ 1905) card #86.

106

Choctaw By Blood Enrollment Cards 1898-1914

RESIDENCE: **Wade** COUNTY.
POST OFFICE: **Tuskahoma, Ind. Ter**

Choctaw Nation

Choctaw Roll (Not Including Freedmen)

CARD No.
FIELD No. **407**

Dawes' Roll No.	NAME	Relationship to Person First Named	AGE	SEX	BLOOD	TRIBAL ENROLLMENT		
						Year	County	No.
783	1 McCurtain, Allen C. 29		25	M	Full	1896	Wade	CCR #2 367
784	2 " Rebecca 33	Wife	29	F	"	1893	"	#135
	3				No 1	1896	Wade	9233
	4	ENROLLMENT OF NOS. 1 and 2 HEREON						
	5	APPROVED BY THE SECRETARY						
	6	OF INTERIOR DEC 12 1902						
	7							
	8							
	9							
	10							
	11							
	12							
	13	No2 on p. 13 - #135 - 93 - P R Wade Co. as Rebecca Ben.						
	14	Also on 1896 roll Page A7 No 1954 as Bessie						
	15	Ben Jacks Fork Co.						
	16							
	17							

TRIBAL ENROLLMENT OF PARENTS

	Name of Father	Year	County	Name of Mother	Year	County
1	Jackson F. McCurtain	Dead	Wade	Jane McCurtain		Gaines
2	F. Anderson	"	"	T. Anderson	Dd.	Wade
3						
4						
5						
6						
7						
8						
9						
10						
11						
12						
13						
14					Date of Application for Enrollment. 9/6/97	
15					No 1 Oct 17/98	
16					" 2 Sept 5, 1899	
17						

RESIDENCE: Chickasaw Nation ~~COUNTY~~.		Choctaw Nation			Choctaw Roll		CARD No.	
POST OFFICE: Duncan, Ind. Ter					(Not Including Freedmen)		FIELD No. 408	

Dawes' Roll No.	NAME	Relationship to Person	AGE	SEX	BLOOD	TRIBAL ENROLLMENT		
						Year	County	No.
15381	1 Dibrell, James	22 First Named	18	M	1/16		Choctaw residing in Chickasaw District	CCR #2 15
15382	2 Taliaferro, Nora	20 Sister	16	F	1/16		" "	"
15383	3 Taliaferro, Eliza	1 Dau of No2	4das	F	1/32			
I.W. 1203	4 Dibrell, Maude	15 Wife	15	F	I.W.			
	5							
	6 ENROLLMENT							
	7 OF NOS. 1 ~ 2 ~ 3 ~ HEREON APPROVED BY THE SECRETARY							
	8 OF INTERIOR MAY 9 1904							
	9 ENROLLMENT							
	10 OF NOS. ~ 4 ~ HEREON APPROVED BY THE SECRETARY							
	11 OF INTERIOR DEC 13 1904							
	12 No1 1896 Chickasaw Dist 3675 as James Diberal							
	13 No2 1896 " " 3676 " Nora "							
	14 Nos 1&2 Admitted by Dawes Com. Case No. 298, and no appeal taken as to this applicant							
	15 Husband of No2 John D Taliaferro on Choctaw Card ~~No D-48~~ May 9 1901 - 7-5863							
	16 N°3 Born April 22, 1902: enrolled April 26, 1902							
	17 No.1 is now the husband of Maude Dibrell on Choctaw card ⁴D.772; Aug 14, 1902							

TRIBAL ENROLLMENT OF PARENTS

Name of Father	Year	County	Name of Mother	Year	County
1 Joe Dibrell	Dead	Choctaw residing in Chickasaw District	Nancy Dibrell		non citizen
2 " "	"	" " "	" "	" "	" "
3 J.D. Taliaferro		white man	N°2		
4 Ed Kilgore	dead	non-citizen	Kate Tucker		non citizen
5					
6 Mother of N°1 is Nancy Tucker on Choctaw card #5273					
7 Nos 1 and 4 were married April 13, 1902 under a United States license.					
8 No.4 originally listed for enrollment on Choctaw card #D-772 Aug 14, 1902; transferred to this card Nov. 26, 1904. See decision of Nov. 9, 1904.					
9					
10					
11					
12 For child of Nos 1&4 see N B. (Mar 3-05) Card #87					
13 For child of No.2 see NB (March 3, 1905) card #684					
14 " " " " " (April 26 1906) " #137			Date of Application for Enrollment.		
15			Oct 17/98		
16					
17					

Choctaw By Blood Enrollment Cards 1898-1914

RESIDENCE: Chickasaw Nation COUNTY.
POST OFFICE: Arthur, Ind. Ter.

Choctaw Nation

Choctaw Roll (*Not Including Freedmen*)

CARD NO.
FIELD NO. **409**

Dawes' Roll No.	NAME	Relationship to Person	AGE	SEX	BLOOD	TRIBAL ENROLLMENT		
						Year	County	No.
I.W.556	₁ Richerson, John S. ⁵³	First Named	49	M	IW			
14286	₂ " Maggie F ⁴³	Wife	39	F	1/4			
14287	₃ " Bertha Etta ⁵	Dau	7mo	"	1/8	ENROLLMENT OF NOS ~~ 1 ~~ HEREON APPROVED BY THE SECRETARY OF INTERIOR FEB -8 1904		
14288	₄ Sanner, Willie ²⁴	Step Son	20	M	1/8			
14289	₅ " Louie ²²	"	18	"	1/8			
14290	₆ " Jesse ¹⁹	"	15	"	1/8			
14291	₇ " Arie L ¹⁶	Step Dau	12	F	1/8	ENROLLMENT OF NOS. 2,3,4,5,6,7,8,9,10,11 HEREON APPROVED BY THE SECRETARY OF INTERIOR APR 11 1903		
14292	₈ " George ¹³	"	9	"	1/8			
14293	₉ Richerson, John L ²	Son	5mo	M	1/8			
14294	₁₀ Sanner, Lenna Etta ¹	Step Grand Dau	4mo	F	1/16			
14295	₁₁ " Walter ⁹	Son of №2	9	M	1/8			
	₁₂	For child of Nos 1&2 see NB (Mar 3-1905) #26						
	₁₃	№4 is now husband of Lou Sanner, a non-citizen; evidence of marriage filed June 7 1902						
	₁₄	№10 Born Jany 23 1902; enrolled June 7, 1902 — Now on Card #5991						
	₁₅	№11 enrolled Oct. 31, 1902						
	₁₆	№11: This child was included in original application and was admitted by the Commission in 1896 citizenship case #687; See case as written in new docket.						
	₁₇	Age of №11 is as of this date, Oct 31, 1902						

TRIBAL ENROLLMENT OF PARENTS

	Name of Father	Year	County	Name of Mother	Year	County
₁	Wᵐ Richerson	Dead	Non Citizen	Nancy Richerson	Dead	Non Citizen
₂	Carroll Tucker	"	" "	Jane Tucker	"	Choctaw Indian
₃	№1			№2		
₄	Will Sanner	Dead	Non Citizen	№2		
₅	" "	"	" " "	№2		
₆	" "	"	" " "	№2	For children of No4 (Mar 3-05) card #88 see NB	
₇	" "	"	" " "	№2		
₈	" "	"	" " "	№2		
₉	№1			№2		
₁₀	№4			Lou Sanner		Non Citizen
₁₁	Will Sanner	Dead	Non Citizen	№1		

₁₂	Nos1&2 admitted by Dawes Com Case №687 and no appeal taken
₁₃	Marriage license and certificate on file in office of Dawes Com Muskogee Ind Ter. Nos 4,5,6,7 and 8 admitted by Dawes Com Case №687 under name of Sauner and no appeal taken
₁₄	(Daniel Walter Sanner, age 6, omitted from application to Dawes Com) This notation is an error. The
₁₅	name of Walter Sauner is in the original application, but it does not appear on docket in the Case №9 enrolled June 25. 1900
₁₆	1 to 8 May 6 1901
₁₇	Date of Application for Enrollment Oct 17/98

109

Choctaw By Blood Enrollment Cards 1898-1914

RESIDENCE: Chickasaw Nation ~~COUNTY.~~
POST OFFICE: Duncan, Ind Ter.

Choctaw Nation
(Not Including Freedmen)

Choctaw Roll

CARD NO.
FIELD NO. **410**

Dawes' Roll No.	NAME	Relationship to Person	AGE	SEX	BLOOD	TRIBAL ENROLLMENT		
						Year	County	No.
15216	1 Buckholts, William L 55	First Named	51	M	1/16		Choctaw residing in Chickasaw District	CCR #2 82
IW878	2 " Annie J 50	wife	46	F	I.W.		" "	C.I. Roll 11
15217	3 " William E. 30	son	26	M	1/32		" "	CCR #2 82
15218	4 " Albert Lorenzo 27	"	23	"	1/32		" "	
15219	5 Cooksey, William Earnest 11	g.son	7	"	1/64		" "	CCR #2 126
IW1284	6 Buckholts, Carrie L 18	wife of No.4	18	F	I.W.			

See opinion of Atty Genl of Feb. 18, 04 and letter of Secy of Interior of Feby 24'04 in case
of James M Buckholts et al 7-5738   Nos4 and 6 were married Aug 25, 1902
#1-not admitted by Supreme Court in Oct, 1872, when his father, William Buckholts, R. T. Jones & John Null above were admitted.
All admitted by Dawes Com Case No900 and no appeal taken
Nos4and 6 were married Aug 25, 1902
No3 on Choctaw roll as W.E. Buckholts
No4 "   "   "   " Albert L "
No6 originally listed for enrollment on Choc Card D-809 Sept 25 1902 transferred to this card Feb 1, 1905 See decision of Jan 16, 1905.
For child of Nos4&6 see N.B. (Mar 3,05) #969

ENROLLMENT
OF NOS. 1-3-4-5 HEREON
APPROVED BY THE SECRETARY
OF INTERIOR May 9 1904

ENROLLMENT
OF NOS. 6 HEREON
APPROVED BY THE SECRETARY
OF INTERIOR Mar 14 1905

TRIBAL ENROLLMENT OF PARENTS

	Name of Father	Year	County	Name of Mother	Year	County
1	Wm Buckholts		Blue	Matilda Buckholts	dead	Blue
2	J.R. Watkins	dead	no citizen	Mary J Watkins		non citizen
3	No1			No2		
4	No1			No2		
5	John Cooksey	dead	non citizen	Lena Cooksey	dead	Choctaw residing in Chickasaw Dist
6	J.M. Park		non citizen	M.J. Park		non citizen
7	For child of Nos4&6 see N.B. (Apr 26'06) card #445 No4 is the husband of Carrie L Buckholts on Choctaw card #D809 Sept 25, 1902.					
8	No1 1896 Chickasaw Dist 2049 as Wm L. Buckholtz					
9	No2 1896 " " 14357 " Annie J Buckholt					
10	No3 1896 " " 2050 " W.E. Buckholtz					
	No4 1896 " " 2051 " Adelbert "					
11	No5 1896 " " 3148 " William Cookey					

ENROLLMENT
OF NOS 2 HEREON
APPROVED BY THE SECRETARY
OF INTERIOR Aug 3, 1904

Date of Application for Enrollment.

Oct 17/98

[On back of card] Record returned. See opinion of Assistant Attorney General of March 15, 1906 in case of Omer R. Nicholson

Elmore I.T.

10/28/02 Record as to enrollment of No6 forwarded Department, Mar 14,1906 (over)

110

Choctaw By Blood Enrollment Cards 1898-1914

RESIDENCE: Chickasaw Nation ~~COUNTY~~.

POST OFFICE: Duncan, Ind. Ter.

Choctaw Nation

Choctaw Roll *(Not Including Freedmen)*

CARD NO.

FIELD NO. 411

Dawes' Roll No.	NAME	Relationship to Person First Named	AGE	SEX	BLOOD	TRIBAL ENROLLMENT		
						Year	County	No.
785	1 Harrison, Lewis H. ³⁶	First Named	32	M	3/4		Choctaw residing in Chickasaw District	CCR #2 259
I.W. 557	2 " , Edga Lee ³⁰	Wife	26	F	I.W.		" "	C.I. Roll 47
786	3 " , Emmet E. ¹⁰	Son	6	M	3/8		" "	CCR #2 259
787	4 " , Cassie M. ⁸	Dau	4	F	3/8		" "	"
788	5 " , William Doyle ⁶	Son	2	M	3/8		" "	"
789	6 " , Cevera L. ¹½	"	5mo	"	3/8			
	7							
	8	ENROLLMENT						
	9	OF NOS. 1,3,4,5 and 6 HEREON APPROVED BY THE SECRETARY						
	10	OF INTERIOR DEC 12 1902				No 2 on Choctaw roll as Edgar L. Harrison		
	11	ENROLLMENT				No 3 " " " " Emmett "		
	12	OF NOS. ~~2~~ HEREON APPROVED BY THE SECRETARY				No 4 " " " " Kizzie E "		
	13	OF INTERIOR FEB -8 1904				No 5 " " " " William D. "		
	14							
	15							
	16							
	17							

TRIBAL ENROLLMENT OF PARENTS

	Name of Father	Year	County	Name of Mother	Year	County
1	Daniel Harrison	Dead	Choctaw residing in Chickasaw District	Heo-ye-yo-ke	Dead	Kiamitia
2	John Brazill	"	non citizen	Malinda Brazill	"	non citizen
3	No 1			No 2		
4	No 1			No 2		
5	No 1			No 2		
6	No 1			No 2		
7						
8						
9				.		
10						
11				For child of Nos 1&2 see NB (Mar 3-05)		
12	No 1 1896 Chickasaw Dist 6235 as Louis H Harrison					#696
13	No 2 1896 " " 4672					
14	No 3 1896 " " 6236 " Emmett "					
15	No 4 1896 " " 6237 Kizzie E "				Date of Application for Enrollment.	Oct 17/98
16	No 5 1896 " " 6238 Wᵐ D "					
17	Bailey I.T.					

111

Choctaw By Blood Enrollment Cards 1898-1914

RESIDENCE: Chickasaw Nation ~~COUNTY.~~
POST OFFICE: Duncan I.T.

Choctaw Nation

Choctaw Roll
(Not Including Freedmen)

CARD NO.

FIELD NO. 412

Dawes' Roll No.	NAME	Relationship to Person First Named	AGE	SEX	BLOOD	TRIBAL ENROLLMENT		
						Year	County	No.
790	1 Oliver, Ella 26		22	F	1/4		Tobucksy	CCR #2 422
I.W. 698	2 " James R. 25	Husb	25	M	I.W.			
	3					No 1	1896 Tobucksy	11295
	4	ENROLLMENT OF NOS. 1 HEREON APPROVED BY THE SECRETARY OF INTERIOR DEC 12 1902						
	5							
	6	ENROLLMENT OF NOS. 2 HEREON APPROVED BY THE SECRETARY OF INTERIOR MAY -7 1904						
	7							
	8							
	9							
	10	On Choctaw roll as Ella Shelby						
	11	No2 transferred from Choctaw card #D301. See decision of Feby 27, 1904.						
	12							
	13							
	14							
	15							
	16							
	17							

TRIBAL ENROLLMENT OF PARENTS

Name of Father	Year	County	Name of Mother	Year	County
1 Sam Shelby		non Citz.	Rebecca Shelby		Choctaw residing in Chickasaw Nat
2 L.C. Oliver		" "	Phoebe Oliver		non-citz.
3					
4					
5					
6					
7					
8					
9					
10					
11					
12					
13					
14				Date of Application for Enrollment.	August 7-99
15					
16					
17				August 7, 1899	

112

Choctaw By Blood Enrollment Cards 1898-1914

RESIDENCE: Chickasaw Nation ~~COUNTY~~.
POST OFFICE: Duncan, Ind. Ter.

Choctaw Nation

Choctaw Roll
(Not Including Freedmen)

CARD NO.
FIELD NO. **413**

Dawes' Roll No.	NAME	Relationship to Person First Named	AGE	SEX	BLOOD	TRIBAL ENROLLMENT		
						Year	County	No.
791	1 Rector, Ozious James P [24]	First Named	20	M	1/16		Choctaw residing in Chickasaw Dist	CCR #2 417
IW1088	2 Boggess, Eliza Barbara [22]	wife	18	F	I.W.			
792	3 Rector, Mary Delilah [4]	Dau	3mo	"	1/32			
IW1204	4 " , Eliza Ellen	Wife	20	"	I.W.			
	5					No 1	1896	Chickasaw Dist	11087
	6	ENROLLMENT						
	7	OF NOS. 1 and 3 HEREON APPROVED BY THE SECRETARY						
	8	OF INTERIOR Dec 12 1902	No 1 full name is Ozious James Pushmataha Rector					
	9		No 1 on Choctaw roll as Pushmasaha					
	10		No 1 also known as Otis Rector					
	11	ENROLLMENT						
	12	OF NOS. ~ 2 ~ HEREON APPROVED BY THE SECRETARY						
	13	OF INTERIOR Nov 16 1904						
	14	ENROLLMENT						
	15	OF NOS. ~ 4 ~ HEREON APPROVED BY THE SECRETARY						
	16	OF INTERIOR Dec 13 1904						
	17							

TRIBAL ENROLLMENT OF PARENTS

Name of Father	Year	County	Name of Mother	Year	County
1 James H. Rector (I.W.)		Choctaw residing in Chickasaw District	Emma F. Rector		Choctaw residing in Chickasaw Dist
2 I. H. Boggess		non citizen	Eliza B. Boggess		non citizen
3 No 1			No 2		
4 Joe Hodges		non citizen	Eliza Hodges	dead	non citizen
5					
6					
7					
8					
9					
10	No2 not on Choctaw roll				
11	No1 is the husband of Ellen Eliza Rector on Choctaw card #D814, Oct. 16, 1902.				
12	~~Evidence of marriage of Nos 1 and 4 filed Oct. 16, 1902~~ No4 originally listed for enrollment on Choctaw card #D814 Oct. 16, 1902.				
13	transferred to this card Nov. 26, 1904 See decision of Nov. 9, 1904.				
14					
15				Date of Application for Enrollment.	Oct 17/98
16					1 to 3
17					

Choctaw By Blood Enrollment Cards 1898-1914

RESIDENCE: Chickasaw Nation ~~COUNTY~~.
POST OFFICE: Duncan, Ind. Ter.

Choctaw Nation

Choctaw Roll
(Not Including Freedmen)

CARD NO.
FIELD NO. 414

Dawes' Roll No.	NAME	Relationship to Person First Named	AGE	SEX	BLOOD	TRIBAL ENROLLMENT		
						Year	County	No.
793	1 Rector, Emma F. ⁵⁶	First Named	52	F	1/8		Choctaw residing in Chickasaw Dist	CCR #2 417
	2							
	3	ENROLLMENT OF NOS. 1 HEREON APPROVED BY THE SECRETARY OF INTERIOR DEC 12 1902						
	4							
	5							
	6						No 1 1896 Chickasaw Dist 11086 as Emma Rector.	
	7							
	8							
	9							
	10							
	11							
	12							
	13							
	14							
	15							
	16							
	17							

TRIBAL ENROLLMENT OF PARENTS

Name of Father	Year	County	Name of Mother	Year	County
1 Charles W. Flint	Dead	non citizen	Delilah J. Flint		Choctaw residing in Chickasaw Dist
2					
3					
4					
5					
6					
7					
8					
9					
10					
11					
12					
13					
14					
15				Date of Application for Enrollment.		Oct 17/98
16					
17					

114

Choctaw By Blood Enrollment Cards 1898-1914

RESIDENCE: Chickasaw Nation ~~COUNTY~~. **Choctaw Nation**   Choctaw Roll   CARD NO.
POST OFFICE: Bailey, Ind. Ter.   *(Not Including Freedmen)*   FIELD NO.   415

Dawes' Roll No.	NAME	Relationship to Person First Named	AGE	SEX	BLOOD	TRIBAL ENROLLMENT		
						Year	County	No.
I.W. 1089	1 Bullard, Elijah G. ³⁵	First Named	31	M	I.W.		Choctaw residing in Chickasaw Dist	C.I. Roll 11
	2							
	3					1896	Chickasaw Dist	14360
	4							
	5							
	6							
	7							
	8	ENROLLMENT OF NOS. ~~~ 1 ~~~ HEREON						
	9	APPROVED BY THE SECRETARY OF INTERIOR NOV 16 1904						
	10							
	11							
	12	On Choctaw roll as E.E. Bullard						
	13							
	14	Admitted by Dawes Com, Case No. 911, and no appeal taken.						
	15	Marriage license and certificate on file in office of Dawes Com, Muskogee, I.T.						
	16							
	17							

TRIBAL ENROLLMENT OF PARENTS

	Name of Father	Year	County	Name of Mother	Year	County
1	Elijah G. Bullard	Dead	non citizen	Martha Ann Bullard	Dead	non citizen
2						
3						
4						
5						
6						
7						
8						
9						
10						
11						
12						
13						
14						
15				Date of Application for Enrollment.		Oct 18/98
16						
17	P.O. is now Chickasha I.T. Oct 12, 1903					

Choctaw By Blood Enrollment Cards 1898-1914

RESIDENCE: Chickasaw Nation ~~COUNTY~~. POST OFFICE: Bailey, Ind. Ter. **Choctaw Nation** Choctaw Roll (Not Including Freedmen) CARD NO. FIELD NO. **416**

Dawes' Roll No.	NAME	Relationship to Person First Named	AGE	SEX	BLOOD	Year	County	No.
IW963	1 Lyle, Robert Thomas 55	First Named	50	M	I.W.		Choctaw residing in Chickasaw District	CCR#0 246
794	2 " , Lula 31	Wife	27	F	1/8		" "	CCR#2 344
795	3 " , Ada 12	Dau	8	"	1/16		" "	"
796	4 " , Daisy 10	"	6	"	1/16		" "	"
797	5 " , Mabel 9	"	5	"	1/16		" "	"
798	6 " , Cleo 7	"	3	"	1/16		" "	"
799	7 " , Robert Clifford 2	Son	17da	M	1/16			
8								
9	ENROLLMENT OF NOS. 2,3,4,5,6 and 7 HEREON APPROVED BY THE SECRETARY OF INTERIOR Dec 12 1902				No 2 on Choctaw roll as Fuller Lyle			
10								
11								
12	ENROLLMENT OF NOS. 1 HEREON APPROVED BY THE SECRETARY OF INTERIOR Sep 22, 1904							
13								
14								
15								
16								
17								

TRIBAL ENROLLMENT OF PARENTS

	Name of Father	Year	County	Name of Mother	Year	County
1	Wᵐ H. Lyle	Dead	non citizen	Lucinda Lyle	Dead	non citizen
2	Charlie Alexander	"	" "	Sarah Wood		Blue
3	No 1			No 2		
4	No 1			No 2		
5	No 1			No 2		
6	No 1			No 2		
7	No 1			No 2		
8						
9			No1 See Decision of July 19 '04			
10			For child of No2 see N.B. (Mar 3, 1905) #661			
			No2 1896 Chickasaw Dist 8389			
11			No3 1896 " 8393 as Eda Lyle			
12			No4 1896 " 8390			
13			No5 1896 " 8391			
14			No6 1896 " 8392		Date of Application for Enrollment.	
15			No7 Enrolled Oct 9ᵗʰ 1900		Oct 18/98	
16						
17	P.O. Marlow I.T. 3/30/05					

116

Choctaw By Blood Enrollment Cards 1898-1914

RESIDENCE: Chickasaw Nation COUNTY.
POST OFFICE: Petersburg, Ind. Ter.

Choctaw Nation

Choctaw Roll
(Not Including Freedmen)

CARD NO.
FIELD NO. **417**

Dawes' Roll No.	NAME	Relationship to Person First Named	AGE	SEX	BLOOD	TRIBAL ENROLLMENT		
						Year	County	No.
DEAD.	1 Bourland, Lorinda Melvina DEAD.	First Named	46	F	1/2	1896	Choctaw residing in Chickasaw District	1990
VOID.	2 " , William Franklin	Son	25	M	1/4			
VOID.	3 " , James Patrick	"	21	"	1/4			
VOID.	4 " , Lulu Catherine	Dau	16	F	1/4			
VOID.	5 " , Lorinda Melvina Jr.	"	12	"	1/4			
VOID.	6 " , Robert Love	Son	8	M	1/4			
VOID.	7 " , Michael Frazier	"	5	"	1/4			
	8 No. 1 HEREON DISMISSED UNDER							
	9 ORDER OF THE COMMISSION TO THE FIVE							
	10 CIVILIZED TRIBES OF MARCH 31, 1905.							
	11 No1 on Choctaw roll as Mrs. Lorinda Bourland							
	12 No1 wife of William Howard Bourland on Chickasaw roll, Card No. 1290							
	13 No1 also on Chickasaw roll Pickens Co. Page 21							
	All others " " " " " 21, transferred to Choctaw							
	14 roll by Dawes Com.							
	15							
	16 No1 Died Aug. 26, 1899 proof of							
	death filed June 5, 1902							
	17							

TRIBAL ENROLLMENT OF PARENTS

	Name of Father	Year	County	Name of Mother	Year	County
1	David Harkins	Dead	Choctaw roll	Isabella Harkins	Dead	Choctaw roll
2	William Howard Bourland		Chickasaw roll	No 1		
3	" " "	"	"	No 1		
4	" " "	"	"	No 1		
5	" " "	"	"	No 1		
6	" " "	"	"	No 1		
7	" "	"	"	No 1		
8						
9			No 1 on Chickasaw roll as L. M. Bourland			
10			No 2 " " " " W. F. "			
11			No 3 " " " " J. D. "			
12			No 4 " " " " L. C. "			
13			No 5 " " " " L. M. "			
14			No 6 " " " " R. L. "			
15	Nos 2,3,4,5,6 and 7 transferred		No 7 " " " " M. T. "	Date of Application for Enrollment		Oct 18, 1898
16	to Chickasaw Card No. 1636	Oct. 14, 1902				
17	P.O. No2 is Tishomingo I.T.					

117

Choctaw By Blood Enrollment Cards 1898-1914

RESIDENCE: Chickasaw Nation ~~COUNTY~~. **Choctaw Nation** **Choctaw Roll** CARD NO.
POST OFFICE: Petersburg, Ind. Ter. *(Not Including Freedmen)* FIELD NO. 418

Dawes' Roll No.	NAME	Relationship to Person First Named	AGE	SEX	BLOOD	TRIBAL ENROLLMENT		
						Year	County	No.
800	1 Harkins, John G. 17	First Named	13	M	1/4		Choctaw residing in Chickasaw District	CCR #2 258
	2							
	3	ENROLLMENT OF NOS. 1 HEREON						
	4	APPROVED BY THE SECRETARY OF INTERIOR DEC 12 1902						
	5							
	6							
	7	1896 Chickasaw Dist 6144 as John Harkins						
	8							
	9							
	10							
	11							
	12	Ward of William Howard Bourland, Chickasaw roll, Card No. 1290.						
	13							
	14							
	15							
	16							
	17							

TRIBAL ENROLLMENT OF PARENTS

Name of Father	Year	County	Name of Mother	Year	County
1 Albert P. Harkins	Dead	Choctaw residing in Chickasaw Dist	Ellen Harkins		non citizen
2					
3					
4					
5					
6					
7					
8					
9					
10					
11					
12					
13					
14					
15			Date of Application for Enrollment.		Oct 18/98
16					
17					

Choctaw By Blood Enrollment Cards 1898-1914

RESIDENCE: Chickasaw Nation ~~COUNTY.~~
POST OFFICE: Petersburg, Ind. Ter.

Choctaw Nation

Choctaw Roll *(Not Including Freedmen)*

CARD NO.
FIELD NO. 419

Dawes' Roll No.	NAME	Relationship to Person First Named	AGE	SEX	BLOOD	TRIBAL ENROLLMENT		
						Year	County	No.
801	₁ Parrish, Lillie Josephine		15	F	1/4		Choctaw residing in Chickasaw Dist	CCR #2 258
~~802~~	DIED PRIOR TO SEPTEMBER 25, 1902 ₂ Martin V.	Son	1mo	M	1/8			
803	₃ " Jewel Lorena	Dau	2wks	F	1/8			
	₄							
	₅ ENROLLMENT OF NOS. 1, 2 and 3 HEREON		No1	1896	Chickasaw Dist 6143 as Lilie Harkins			
	₆ APPROVED BY THE SECRETARY							
	₇ OF INTERIOR DEC 12 1902							
	₈							
	₉							
	₁₀	Wife of J.B. Parrish, U.S. citizen						
	₁₁	No3 Enrolled August 1, 1901.						
	₁₂	No2 died Nov. 5, 1900: proof of death filed December 6, 1902						
	₁₃	For child of No1 see NB (March 3, 1905) #1015.						
	₁₄							
	₁₅							
	₁₆							
	₁₇							

TRIBAL ENROLLMENT OF PARENTS

	Name of Father	Year	County	Name of Mother	Year	County
₁	Albert P. Harkins	Dead	Choctaw residing in Chickasaw Dist	Ellen Harkins		non citizen
₂	J. B. Parrish		Non Citz	No1		
₃	" " "		" "	No1		
₄						
₅						
₆						
₇						
₈						
₉						
₁₀						
₁₁						
₁₂						
₁₃						
₁₄						
₁₅					Date of Application for Enrollment. Oct 18/98	
₁₆					No 2 enrolled Oct 6/99	
₁₇	Weaverton I.T.					

119

RESIDENCE: Chickasaw Nation ~~COUNTY~~.
POST OFFICE: Rush Springs, Ind. Ter.

Choctaw Nation
(Not Including Freedmen)

Choctaw Roll

CARD NO.
FIELD NO. 420

Dawes' Roll No.	NAME		Relationship to Person First Named	AGE	SEX	BLOOD	TRIBAL ENROLLMENT		
							Year	County	No.
14296	1 Blakely, Perry H	23	First Named	19	M	1/16		Choctaw residing in Chickasaw Dist	CCR #2 82
14297	2 " Emmet	1	Sin	3wks	M	1/32			
I.W. 1285	3 " Anne	19	Wife	19	F	I.W.	1896	Chickasaw Dist No. 1	2048
	4								
	5	ENROLLMENT							
	6	OF NOS. 1 and 2 HEREON APPROVED BY THE SECRETARY							
	7	OF INTERIOR APR 11 1903							
	8	Admitted by Dawes Com. Case No. 865, as Perry H. Blakely, and no							
	9	appeal taken.							
	10								
	11								
	12								
	13								
	14	ENROLLMENT							
	15	OF NOS. 3 HEREON APPROVED BY THE SECRETARY							
	16	OF INTERIOR MAR 14 1905							
	17								

TRIBAL ENROLLMENT OF PARENTS

	Name of Father	Year	County	Name of Mother	Year	County
1	F. C. Blakely		white man	Martha M Blakely	Dead	Choctaw residing in Chickasaw Dist
2	Nº 1			Anna[sic] Blakely		white woman
3	John R Davis		noncitizen	Mary Davis		noncitizen
4						
5						
6						
7						
8						
9	June 20, 1900, Wife of No. 1 on Choctaw R #666. Marriage license					
10	and certificate between Perry H Blakely and Annie Davis filed					
11	this date. See Choc. R. #666					
12	~~Nº2 Born May 6, 1902; enrolled May 27, 1902.~~					
13	No3 transferred from Choctaw Card R #666					
						Date of Application for Enrollment.
14						
15						
16					No. 1	1898
17	For child of Nos 1 & 3 see NB (Mar 3-1905) Card #90				No.3	6-20-1900

Choctaw By Blood Enrollment Cards 1898-1914

RESIDENCE: Chickasaw Nation ~~COUNTY~~. **Choctaw Nation** Choctaw Roll CARD NO.
POST OFFICE: Marlow, Ind Ter (Not Including Freedmen) FIELD NO. **421**

Dawes' Roll No.	NAME	Relationship to Person First Named	AGE	SEX	BLOOD	TRIBAL ENROLLMENT		
						Year	County	No.
14546	1 West, Josephine Percella	First Named	55	F	1/8		Choctaw residing in Chickasaw Dist	CCR #2 22
	2							
	3					1896	Chickasaw Dist	560
	4							
	5							
	6							
	7							
	8							
	9							
	10 On Choctaw roll as Josephine Anderson							
	11 Divorced Feb. 11-99, and her original name Josephine P. West, restored.							
	12 On 1896 Census roll page 14, No 560 as Josephine Anderson							
	13 See additional testimony taken Dec 2, 1902.							
	14							
	15							
	16							
	17							

ENROLLMENT
OF NOS. 1 HEREON
APPROVED BY THE SECRETARY
OF INTERIOR MAY 20 1903

TRIBAL ENROLLMENT OF PARENTS

Name of Father	Year	County	Name of Mother	Year	County
1 Wm Laflore	Dead	Choctaw roll	Martha Laflore	Dead	non citizen
2					
3					
4					
5					
6					
7					
8					
9					
10					
11					
12					
13					
14				Date of Application for Enrollment.	Oct 18/98
15					
16					
17 Antler, I.T.					

Choctaw By Blood Enrollment Cards 1898-1914

RESIDENCE: Chickasaw Nation ~~COUNTY.~~

POST OFFICE: Bailey, Ind. Ter.

Choctaw Nation

Choctaw Roll
(Not Including Freedmen)

CARD No.

FIELD NO. 422

Dawes' Roll No.	NAME		Relationship to Person First Named	AGE	SEX	BLOOD	TRIBAL ENROLLMENT		
							Year	County	No.
15164	1 Holt, Carrie M	47	First Named	43	F	1/16		Choctaw residing in Chickasaw Dist	CCR #2 260
15165	2 " , Alice	13	Dau	9	"	1/32		" "	"
15166	3 " , Collomer	12	"	8	"	1/32		" "	"
15167	4 " , Charley	10	Son	6	M	1/32		" "	"
15168	5 " , Lee	6	"	4	"	1/32		" "	"
	6								
	7								
	8	No3 on Choctaw roll as Colesa.							
	9	No.1 was admitted by act of Choctaw council approved Nov. 3, 1879.							
	10								
	11								
	12								
	13								
	14	ENROLLMENT OF NOS. 1,2,3,4 and 5 HEREON							
	15	APPROVED BY THE SECRETARY OF INTERIOR MAR 26 1904							
	16								
	17								

TRIBAL ENROLLMENT OF PARENTS

	Name of Father	Year	County	Name of Mother	Year	County
1	Charlie Moran	Dead	non citizen	Elizabeth M. Moran		Blue
2	J. F. Holt		" "	No 1		
3	" " "		" "	No 1		
4	" " "		" "	No 1		
5	" " "		" "	No 1		
6						
7						
8						
9	No1 1896 Chickasaw Dist 6230 as Cora M. Holt					
10	No2 1896 Chickasaw Dist 6231					
11	No3 1896 Chickasaw Dist 6232 as Colena Holt					
12	No4 1896 Chickasaw Dist 6233 " Charlie "					
13	No5 1896 Chickasaw Dist 6234					
14						
15				Date of Application for Enrollment.		Oct 18/98
16	P.O. Marlow I.T.					
17						

122

Choctaw By Blood Enrollment Cards 1898-1914

Choctaw Nation

Choctaw Roll (Not Including Freedmen)

CARD NO. FIELD NO. 423

Dawes' Roll No.	NAME	Relationship to Person First Named	AGE	SEX	BLOOD	TRIBAL ENROLLMENT		
						Year	County	No.
804	1 Cochran, Viola ⁴⁶	First Named	42	F	1/16		Choctaw residing in Chickasaw Dist	CCR #2 126
805	2 " , Lula Inez ¹⁸	Dau	14	"	1/32		" "	"
806	3 " , Joseph John ¹³	Son	9	M	1/32		" "	"
807	4 " , Dan Bailey ¹¹	"	7	"	1/32		" "	"
808	5 " , Grover ⁸	"	4	"	1/32		" "	"
809	6 " , Nellie Viola ⁴	Dau	6wks	F	1/32			
	7							
	8	ENROLLMENT OF NOS. 1,2,3,4,5, and 6 HEREON						
	9	APPROVED BY THE SECRETARY OF INTERIOR DEC 12 1902						
	10							
	11							
	12	No2 on Choctaw roll as Lula Cochran						
	13	No3 " " " " Jeapt "						
	14	No4 " " " " Dan G "						
	15	No1 wife of Lynch Bailey Cochran, Chickasaw roll, Card No 1292						
	16							
	17							

TRIBAL ENROLLMENT OF PARENTS

	Name of Father	Year	County	Name of Mother	Year	County
1	Alfred Toole (I.W.)	Dead	Tobucksy	Malinda Toole	Dead	Tobucksy
2	Lynch Bailey Cochran (I.W.)		Pickens County Choctaw roll	No 1		
3	" " "		" "	No 1		
4	" " "		" "	No 1		
5	" " "		" "	No 1		
6	" " "		" "	No 1		
7						
8	No 1 1896 Chickasaw Dist 3140					
9	No 2 1896 " " 3141 as Lula Cochran					
10	No 3 1896 " " 3142 " Jeapt "					
11	No 4 1896 " " 3143 " David G. "					
	No 5 1896 " " 3144					
12						
13						
14					Date of Application for Enrollment.	
15					Oct 18/98	
16					No 6 enrolled Mar. 6/99	
17						

Choctaw By Blood Enrollment Cards 1898-1914

RESIDENCE: Chickasaw Nation ~~COUNTY~~.
POST OFFICE: Elk, Ind. Ter.

Choctaw Nation

Choctaw Roll
(Not Including Freedmen)

CARD NO.
FIELD NO. **424**

Dawes' Roll No.	NAME	Relationship to Person First Named	AGE	SEX	BLOOD	TRIBAL ENROLLMENT		
						Year	County	No.
810	1 Howze, Sophronia 21	First Named	17	F	1/8		Choctaw residing in Chickasaw Dist	CCR #0 30
811	2 Howze, Bessie 2	Dau	4mo	F	1/16			
812	3 " Jeff 1	Son	1mo	M	1/16			
I.W. 1520	4 Rainey, Jackline[sic]	Mother	50	F	I.W.			
	5							
	6	ENROLLMENT OF NOS. 1, 2 and 3 HEREON APPROVED BY THE SECRETARY OF INTERIOR Dec 12 1902						
	7							
	8							
	9 No4 Granted Nov 4 1905							
	10							
	11	ENROLLMENT OF NOS. ~~4~~ HEREON APPROVED BY THE SECRETARY OF INTERIOR Mar 14 1906						
	12							
	13							
	14 No4 was formerly wife of Tom McDaniel a duly recognized Choctaw							
	15 who died in 1882							
	16 On Choctaw Census Record No O, Page 30, No 189 as Froney McDaniel							
	17							

TRIBAL ENROLLMENT OF PARENTS

	Name of Father	Year	County	Name of Mother	Year	County
1	Tom McDaniel	Dead	Sugar Loaf	Jackaline McDaniel(IW)		Choctaw residing in Chickasaw Dist
2	Morris L. Howze		non-citizen	No 1		
3	" " "		" "	No 1		
4						
5	No1 is now the wife of Morris L. Howze a non-citizen					
6	No2 Enrolled Oct. 13th, 1900.					
7	No3 Born Sept 16 1901 and enrolled Oct 18, 1901.					
	No1 identified from No 3, 1893 pay roll page 44 No 429 as Froney McDaniel					
8	For children of No1 see NB March 3, 1905) #1192.					
9	No4 placed hereon under an order of the Commissioner to the Five Civilized Tribes of					
10	July 24, 1905 holding that application was made for her enrollment within the time					
11	provided by the Act of Congress approved July 1, 1902 (32 Stat. 641)					
12						
13						
14						
15				Date of Application for Enrollment.	Oct 19/98	
16	Rush Springs I.T.					
17	10/16/02					

P.O. Atoka I.T. 4/20/05

RESIDENCE: Chickasaw Nation ~~COUNTY.~~ **Choctaw Nation**   **Choctaw Roll**   CARD NO.
POST OFFICE: Rush Springs, Ind. Ter.   *(Not Including Freedmen)*   FIELD NO. **425**

Dawes' Roll No.	NAME	Relationship to Person First Named	AGE	SEX	BLOOD	TRIBAL ENROLLMENT Year	County	No.
813	1 Nale, Robert 25	First Named	21	M	1/4		Tobucksy	CCR #2 378
IW 879	2 " , Luann 30	wife	26	F	I.W.		"	C.I. Roll 80
814	3 " , Joel 5	son	1	M	1/8			
~~815~~	DIED PRIOR TO SEPTEMBER 25, 1902 4 ~~, Josie~~	~~Dau~~	~~1~~	~~F~~	~~1/8~~			
816	5 " , Ella Toil	Dau	3mo	F	1/8			
14547	6 " , Willie George	Son	4mo	M	1/8			
	7							
	8 ~~ENROLLMENT~~ ~~OF NOS. 1,3,4 and 5 HEREON~~							
	9 APPROVED BY THE SECRETARY OF INTERIOR Dec 12 1902		No1 on Choctaw roll as Robert Nale					
	10		No2 " " " " " Loan "					
	11 ENROLLMENT							
	12 OF NOS. 6 HEREON APPROVED BY THE SECRETARY							
	13 OF INTERIOR May 20 1903							
	14 ~~ENROLLMENT~~							
	15 OF NOS. 2 HEREON							
	16 APPROVED BY THE SECRETARY OF INTERIOR Aug 3 1904							
	17							

TRIBAL ENROLLMENT OF PARENTS

	Name of Father	Year	County	Name of Mother	Year	County
1	Dick Nale		San[sic] Bois	Ellen Gray		Choctaw residing in Chickasaw Dist
2	Newt Fulton		non citizen	Mary Fulton	Dead	non citizen
3	No 1			No 2		
4	~~No 1~~			~~No 2~~		
5	No 1			No 2		
6	No 1			No 2		Born June 19, 1902
7						
8	No1 1896 Tobucksy 9602 as Robert Nail					
9	No2 1896 " 14900 " Loen Nale					
10	No.5 Enrolled July 2d 1900					
11	N°4 Died November 1900 proof of death filed Oct. 20, 1902					
12	N°6 Enrolled October 25, 1902					
	See testimony of No1 and others as to Status of No2 on Sept 25, 1902 taken Oct 16 1902					
13						
14						Date of Application for Enrollment.
15						Oct 20/98
16						
17	No.4 died Nov-1900. Enrollment cancelled by Department July 8, 1904.					

For child of Nos 1&2 see ~~N.B.~~ Minor (Apr 26 '06) Card No 199

125

Choctaw By Blood Enrollment Cards 1898-1914

RESIDENCE: Chickasaw Nation ~~COUNTY~~.
POST OFFICE: Chickasha, Ind. Ter.

Choctaw Nation

Choctaw Roll
(Not Including Freedmen)

CARD NO.
FIELD NO. **426**

Dawes' Roll No.	NAME	Relationship to Person First Named	AGE	SEX	BLOOD	TRIBAL ENROLLMENT		
						Year	County	No.
817	1 James, Rogers[sic] 35		31	M	3/4		Choctaw residing in Chickasaw Dist	CCR #2 309
I.W. 1286	2 " , Gertha 22	Wife	18	F	I.W.			
818	3 " , Sarah A 9	Dau	3mos	"	3/8			
819	4 " , Jesse Earnest 3	Son	5mos	M	3/8			
820	5 " , Estie Lee 1	Dau	9mo	F	3/8			
	6							
	7	ENROLLMENT OF NOS 1,3,4 and 5 HEREON APPROVED BY THE SECRETARY						
	8	OF INTERIOR Dec 12 1902						
	9							
	10	No 1 1896 Chickasaw Dist 7407 as Roggers James						
	11	No 2 see U.S. License						
	12	No.4 Died January 21, 1900. Proof of Death Filed Oct 18, 1902						
	13	See testimony of No 2 taken Oct 15, 1902						
	14	For children of Nos 1 and 2 see NB (Mar 3 1905) #513						
	15	No 4 "Died prior to September 25, 1902; not entitled to land or money"						
	16	ENROLLMENT OF NOS. 2 HEREON APPROVED BY THE SECRETARY OF INTERIOR Mar 14 1905			See Indian Office letter May 13, 1910 D.C. #665-1910				
	17							

TRIBAL ENROLLMENT OF PARENTS

	Name of Father	Year	County	Name of Mother	Year	County
1	Asa W. James	Dead	Choctaw roll	Elzira Hunter	Dead	Choctaw roll
2	J.B. Moody		non citizen	Martina Moody		non citizen
3	No 1			No 2		
4	No 1			No 2		
5	No 1			No 2		
6						
7						
8						
9						
10						
11						
12						
13						
14				#1 to 3		
15				Date of Application for Enrollment Oct 20/98		
16	No.4 Enrolled May 24, 1900					
17	No.5 Born July 27, 1902; Enrolled April 4, 1902.					

126

RESIDENCE: Chickasaw Nation ~~COUNTY.~~
POST OFFICE: Chickasha, Ind. Ter.

Choctaw Nation

Choctaw Roll (Not Including Freedmen)

CARD NO.
FIELD NO. **427**

Dawes' Roll No.	NAME	Relationship to Person	AGE	SEX	BLOOD	TRIBAL ENROLLMENT		
						Year	County	No.
880	1 Bailey, William Duncan 53	First Named	51	M	I.W.		Choctaw residing in Chickasaw Dist	C.I Roll 12
15220	2 " , Clementine M 46	Wife	41	F	1/16		" "	CCR #2 82
15221	3 " , Emma 27	Dau	23	"	1/32		" "	"
15222	4 " , Boone 22	Son	18	M	1/32		" "	"
15223	5 " , Gould 21	"	17	"	1/32		" "	"
15224	6 Plato, Clementine 8	Ward	4	F	1/32		" "	CCR #2 405

See opinion of Atty Genl of Feb. 18'04 and letter of Secy of Interior of Feby 24'04 in case of James M Buckholts et al 7-5738

9
10 ENROLLMENT OF NOS. 2-3-4-5-6 HEREON APPROVED BY THE SECRETARY OF INTERIOR May 9 1904
No2 on Choctaw roll as Clementine F. Bailey
No4 " " " " Brown "
No2 Daughter of Wm Buckholts who was admitted by Supreme Court Choctaw Nation Oct '72

13
14 ENROLLMENT OF NOS. 1 HEREON APPROVED BY THE SECRETARY OF INTERIOR Aug 3 1904
16
17

TRIBAL ENROLLMENT OF PARENTS

	Name of Father	Year	County	Name of Mother	Year	County
1	W.S. Bailey	Dead	non citizen	Christianna Bailey	Dead	non citizen
2	Wm Buckholts		Blue	Matilda Buckholts	"	" "
3	No 1			No 2		
4	No 1			No 2		
5	No 1			No 2		
6	Frank Plato (I.W.)		Choctaw residing in Chickasaw Dist	Parry Plato	Dead	Choctaw residing in Chickasaw Dist
7						
8	but No6					
9	All ∧ admitted by Dawes Com Case No 626 and no appeal taken					
10	No6 " " " " " 565 Appeal dismissed					
11						
12						
13	No1 1896 Chickasaw Dist 4366 as W.D Bailey					
14	No2 1896 " " 2044 For child of No.3 see N.B. (Apr 26, 1906) Card No. 27					
15	No3 1896 " " 2045				Date of Application for Enrollment. Oct 20/98
16	No4 1896 " " 2046					
	No5 1896 " " 2047					
17	No6 1896 " " 10635 as Clametine T Platoe					

See additional testimony of No.1 taken Oct. 15, 1902

RESIDENCE: Chickasaw Nation ~~COUNTY~~.
POST OFFICE: Ireton, Ind. Ter.

Choctaw Nation

Choctaw Roll
(Not Including Freedmen)

CARD No.
FIELD No. **428**

Dawes' Roll No.	NAME	Relationship to Person First Named	AGE	SEX	BLOOD	TRIBAL ENROLLMENT		
						Year	County	No.
I.W. 499	1 Ireton, John 47	First Named	43	M	I.W.	1896	Choctaw residing in Chickasaw District	14681
821	2 " , Mary J. 44	Wife	40	F	1/4	1896	" "	6348
822	3 " , David R. 22	Son	18	M	1/8	1896	" "	6350
~~823~~	DIED PRIOR TO SEPTEMBER 25, 1902 20 ~~4 " , Amanda Elizabeth~~	~~Dau~~	~~16~~	~~F~~	~~1/8~~	~~1896~~	~~" "~~	~~6351~~
824	5 " , Ben 16	Son	12	M	1/8	1896	" "	6352
825	6 " , Joel 14	"	10	"	1/8	1896	" "	6353
~~826~~	DIED PRIOR TO SEPTEMBER 25, 1902 12 ~~7 " , George~~	"	~~8~~	"	~~1/8~~	~~1896~~	~~" "~~	~~6354~~
827	8 " , Mamie 9	Dau	5	F	1/8	1896	" "	6355
828	9 " , Joseph Francis 7	Son	3	M	1/8	1896	" "	6456
829	10 " , Juley 5	Dau	1½	F	1/8	Nos 2 to 8 incl on 1896		
830	11 " , Thomas V. 2	Son	1mo	M	1/8	Choctaw Census roll		
831	12 " , Hattie E. 1	Grand dau	2mo	F	1/16	as Iraton		

Nº7 Died Feby 25, 1899 proof of death filed Oct 21 1902
Nº4 Died May 25, 1902 proof of death filed Oct 21 1902
No.3 is the husband of Minnie Ann Ireton on Choctaw Card #D627. 4/6/01
No 12 born Sept 26,1901: Enrolled Nov. 22d, 1901
No 11 Enrolled Oct 9th 1900

No1 Marriage license and certificate to be supplied
No4 on Choctaw roll as Amanda E Iraton
No8 " " " " Sallie "
No9 " " " " Joseph "
No2 " " " " May J. "

TRIBAL ENROLLMENT OF PARENTS

	Name of Father	Year	County	Name of Mother	Year	County
1	John Ireton	Dead	non citizen	Elizabeth Ireton	Dead	non citizen
2	Young Johnson	"	" "	Amanda Johnson	"	Choctaw Roll
3	No 1	ENROLLMENT OF NOS. 2,3,4,5,6,7,8,9,10,11 and 12 HEREON APPROVED BY THE SECRETARY OF INTERIOR Dec 12 1902		No 2		
4	~~No 1~~			~~No 2~~		
5	No 1			No 2		
6	No 1			No 2		
7	~~No 1~~			~~No 2~~		
8	No 1	ENROLLMENT OF NOS. ~~ ~~ 1 ~~ ~~ HEREON APPROVED BY THE SECRETARY OF INTERIOR Dec 24 1903		No 2	For child of Nos 1&2 see N.B. (Mar 3-1905) Card No 48. For child of No.3 see NB (Mar 4 '05) 1159	
9	No 1			No 2		
10	No 1			No 2		
11	No 1			No 2		
12	No. 3			Minnie A. Ireton		non citizen
13						
14					Date of Application for Enrollment. Oct 20/98	

No1 was admitted by Dawes Commission in 1896 as an intermarried citizen: Choctaw Case #1045. No appeal
See testimony of Nº1 taken October 17, 1902

No.4 died May 25-1902: No.7 died Feb. 25-1899
Enrollment cancelled by Department July 8-1904.

Evidence of marriage of No.3 and Minnie A. Ireton filed with Choctaw #D627

128

Choctaw By Blood Enrollment Cards 1898-1914

RESIDENCE: Chickasaw District ~~COUNTY~~.   **Choctaw Nation**   Choctaw Roll   CARD NO.
POST OFFICE: *(Not Including Freedmen)*   FIELD NO. **429**

Dawes' Roll No.	NAME		Relationship to Person First Named	AGE	SEX	BLOOD	TRIBAL ENROLLMENT		
							Year	County	No.
~~Dead~~	1 Henderson, Joe C.		~~43~~	~~43~~	~~M~~	~~I.W.~~		Choctaw residing in Chickasaw Dist	C.I. Roll 47
14298	2 " , Emily	43	Wife	39	F	1/4		" "	CCR#2 259
14299	3 " , Mollie	21	Dau	17	"	1/8		" "	"
14300	4 " , Rosa	16	"	12	"	1/8		" "	"
14301	5 " , Ashley	13	Son	9	M	1/8		" "	"
14302	6 " , Floyd	10	"	6	"	1/8		" "	"
	7 ENROLLMENT								
	8 OF NOS. 2,3,4,5 and 6 HEREON APPROVED BY THE SECRETARY								
	9 OF INTERIOR Apr 11 1903								
	10								
	11 No 1 hereon dismissed under order								
	12 of the Commissioner to the Five								
	13 Civilized Tribes of July 18, 1905								
	14 No1 1896 Chickasaw Dist 14673 as J. Henderson								
	15 No1 marriage license and certificate on file in office of Dawes Com Muskogee Ind Ter								
	16 No1 died October 28, 1899 Proof of death filed March 10, 1906.								
	17 All admitted by Dawes Com Case No. 1340 and no appeal taken.								

TRIBAL ENROLLMENT OF PARENTS

Name of Father	Year	County	Name of Mother	Year	County
1 Wm Henderson	Dead	non citizen	Susan D. Henderson	Dead	non citizen
2 Walker Martin	"	" "	Adeline Martin	"	Choctaw Roll
3 No 1			No 2		
4 No 1			No 2		
5 No 1			No 2		
6 No 1			No 2		
7					
8					
9					
10 No4 on Choctaw roll as Rose Henderson					
11 No 2 1896 Chickasaw Dist 6220 as Emma Henderson					
12 No 3 1896 " " 6221					
13 No 4 1896 " " 6222 as Rose Henderson					
14 No 5 1896 " " 6223					
15 No 6 1896 " " 6224 as Claude Henderson			Date of Application for Enrollment.		Oct 20/98
16					
17 For child of No4 see N.B. (Mar 3-05) Card #89					

RESIDENCE: Chickasaw Nation COUNTY. **Choctaw Nation**   **Choctaw Roll** CARD NO.
POST OFFICE: Purcell, I.T.   *(Not Including Freedmen)* FIELD NO. 430

Dawes' Roll No.	NAME	Relationship to Person First Named	AGE	SEX	BLOOD	TRIBAL ENROLLMENT		
						Year	County	No.
1	Turner, Neiram G.	Named	40	M	I.W.			
2	" Daisy	Wife	21	F	1/8		Choctaw residing in Chickasaw Dist	CCR #2 462
3	" Ludie	Step Dau	8mo	"	1/16			
4	Turner Mary	Dau	6mo	F	1/16			
5								
6								
7								

No2 1896 Towson [Number illegible]
No4 Enrolled August 2, 1901
Nº3 has been legally adopted by Nºs 1 and 2 and her named indexed as Ludie Turner
June 10, 1902.
Nº1 enrolled at Calvin, I.T. 8/8/99 as Daisy Willis; This notation should read Nº2.
Nos 2 and 3 enrolled October 20th, 1898.

Testimony of Nº1 as to his status as an intermarried citizen Sept 25 1902 taken at Parks Valley IT Oct 21 1902

14								
15								
16								
17								

TRIBAL ENROLLMENT OF PARENTS

	Name of Father	Year	County	Name of Mother	Year	County
1	Richard Turner		Non Citz	Josephine Turner		Non Citz
2	Hamp Willie	Dead	Chickasaw Roll	Delila Davis		Towson
3	T.E. Sanborn		Towson	No. 2		
4	No 1			No 2		
5						
6						
7	No2 also on 1896 roll Page 320 No 12953 as Daisie Willis, Gaines Co.					
8						
9						
10	No2 also on 1897 Chickasaw roll page 97 as Daisy Willis. Transferred to Choctaw roll by Dawes Com					
11						
12						
13						
14						
15						Date of Application for Enrollment.
16						8/8/99
17						

Choctaw By Blood Enrollment Cards 1898-1914

RESIDENCE: Chickasaw Nation ~~COUNTY.~~ **Choctaw Nation**   Choctaw Roll   CARD NO.

POST OFFICE: Rush Springs, Ind Ter.   *(Not Including Freedmen)*   FIELD NO.   431

Dawes' Roll No.	NAME	Relationship to Person First Named	AGE	SEX	BLOOD	TRIBAL ENROLLMENT		
						Year	County	No.
14548	1 Moncrief, Margaret ⁷⁴	First Named	70	F	3/8		Choctaw residing in Chickasaw District	CCR #2 359
	2							
	3	ENROLLMENT OF NOS. 1 HEREON						
	4	APPROVED BY THE SECRETARY OF INTERIOR MAY 20 1903						
	5							
	6							
	7							
	8							
	9	No 1 on 1893 Choctaw roll Chick Dist No. 370						
	10							
	11							
	12							
	13							
	14							
	15							
	16							
	17							

TRIBAL ENROLLMENT OF PARENTS

	Name of Father	Year	County	Name of Mother	Year	County
1	William Hall	Dead	Choctaw roll	Susan Hall	Dead	Choctaw roll
2						
3						
4						
5						
6						
7						
8						
9						
10						
11						
12						
13						
14						
15				Date of Application for Enrollment.	Oct 20/98	
16						
17						

Choctaw By Blood Enrollment Cards 1898-1914

RESIDENCE: Chickasaw Nation ~~COUNTY~~.
POST OFFICE: Rush Springs, Ind Ter.

Choctaw Nation

Choctaw Roll
(Not Including Freedmen)

CARD NO.
FIELD NO. 432

Dawes' Roll No.	NAME	Relationship to Person First Named	AGE	SEX	BLOOD	TRIBAL ENROLLMENT		
						Year	County	No.
I.W.881	1 Slaton, James A. 41	First Named	37	M	I.W.			
832	2 " , Mary Jane 44	Wife	40	F	3/16		Choctaw residing in Chickasaw Dist	CCR #2 375
833	3 McDonald, Conales 10	Step Son	15	M	3/32		" "	"
834	4 " , Muir 8	" "	4	"	3/32		" "	"
	5							
	6	ENROLLMENT OF NOS. 2, 3 and 4 HEREON APPROVED BY THE SECRETARY OF INTERIOR DEC 12 1902						
	7							
	8							
	9							
	10	No2 on Choctaw roll as Mary J. McDonald						
	11	No3 " " " " Cornelius "						
	12							
	13							
	14	ENROLLMENT OF NOS. 1 HEREON APPROVED BY THE SECRETARY OF INTERIOR AUG 3 1904						
	15							
	16							
	17							

TRIBAL ENROLLMENT OF PARENTS

	Name of Father	Year	County	Name of Mother	Year	County
1	Wm Slaton	Dead	non citizen	Georgia Slaton	Dead	non citizen
2	Wm Moncrief	"	Choctaw roll	Margaret Moncrief		Choctaw residing in Chickasaw Dist
3	Muir McDonald	"	non citizen	No 2		
4	" "	"	" " "	No 2		
5						
6						
7	No2 1896 Chickasaw Dist 953 as Mary McDowel					
8	No3 1896 " " 9532 " Cornelia "					
	No4 1896 " " 9533 " Myra "					
9						
10						
11						
12						
13						
14						
15			Date of Application for Enrollment. Oct 20/98			
16						
17						

Choctaw By Blood Enrollment Cards 1898-1914

RESIDENCE: Chickasaw Nation ~~COUNTY~~.
POST OFFICE: Chickasha, Ind. Ter.

Choctaw Nation

Choctaw Roll (Not Including Freedmen)

CARD NO.

FIELD NO. 433

Dawes' Roll No.	NAME	Relationship to Person First Named	AGE	SEX	BLOOD	TRIBAL ENROLLMENT		
						Year	County	No.
835	1 Moncrief, William 56	First Named	52	M	3/16	1896	Choctaw residing in Chickasaw District	8962
IW 882	2 " , Lina 45	Wife	41	F	I.W.	"	"	CCR #2 54
836	3 " , Jeff 23	Son	19	M	3/32	1896	"	8963
837	4 " , James 20	"	16	"	3/32	1896	"	8964
838	5 " , Wallace 17	"	13	"	3/32	1896	"	8965
839	6 " , Lulu 15	Dau	11	F	3/32	1896	"	8966
840	7 " , John 13	Son	9	M	3/32	1896	"	8967
841	8 " , William, Jr. 10	"	6	"	3/32	1896	"	8968
842	9 " , Tolbert 6	"	2	"	3/32	1896	"	8969
843	10 " , Mary M 3	Dau	2mo	F	3/32			
	11	ENROLLMENT						
	12	OF NOS. 1,3,4,5,6,7,8,9 and 10 HEREON APPROVED BY THE SECRETARY						
	13	OF INTERIOR DEC 12 1902						
	14							
	15	ENROLLMENT OF NOS. 2 HEREON						
	16	APPROVED BY THE SECRETARY OF INTERIOR AUG 3 1904						
	17							

TRIBAL ENROLLMENT OF PARENTS

	Name of Father	Year	County	Name of Mother	Year	County
1	Wm Moncrief	Dead	Choctaw roll	Margaret Moncrief		Choctaw residing in Chickasaw Dist
2	John Maupin		non citizen	Mary J Maupin	Dead	non citizen
3	No 1			No 2		
4	No 1			No 2		
5	No 1			No 2		
6	No 1			No 2		
7	No 1			No 2		
8	No 1			No 2		
9	No 1			No 2		
10	No 1			No 2		
11	No2 - Marriage license and certificate to be supplied - Received Nov. 28/98					
12	No2 - On Choctaw Census Record No O, Page 54, No 114.					
13	No2 On 1896 roll as Giney Moncrief Page 395					
14	No1 4849 Chick Dist					Date of Application for Enrollment
15	No6 on Choctaw roll as Lula Moncrief					Oct 20/98
16	" 8 " " " W^m " Jr					No 10 enrolled Dec 19/99
	~~10/16/02 James is living in Texas~~					
17						

Choctaw By Blood Enrollment Cards 1898-1914

RESIDENCE: Chickasaw Nation ~~COUNTY.~~
POST OFFICE: Chickasha I.T.

Choctaw Nation

Choctaw Roll
(Not Including Freedmen)

CARD NO.
FIELD NO. 434

Dawes' Roll No.	NAME	Relationship to Person First Named	AGE	SEX	BLOOD	TRIBAL ENROLLMENT		
						Year	County	No.
16201	1 Terrell, Louanna Smith	First Named	26	F	1/16		Choctaw residing in Chickasaw Dist	CCR #2 423
I.W. 1658	2 " Elmer	Hus	32	M	I.W.			
	3							
	4 REFUSED OCT 15 1904			1896 Tobucksy 11315 as Laura A. Smith				
	5 DECISION RENDERED OCT 15 1904							
	6 COPY OF DECISION FORWARDED		On Choctaw roll as Laura Ann Terrell					
	7 APPLICANT OCT 15 1904							
	8 NOTICE OF DECISION	No1 is the wife of Elmer Terrell on Choctaw Card #D-296						
	9 FORWARDED ATTORNEY FOR APPLICANTS.							
	10	Some question as to residence. See testimony attached to her parents						
	11 Card No D-87.	ACTION APPROVED BY						
	12 COPY OF DECISION FORWARDED ATTORNEYS FOR CHOCTAW AND	SECRETARY OF INTERIOR.						
	13 CHICKASAW NATIONS. OCT 15 1904	JUL 19 1905						
	14 RECORD FORWARDED DEPARTMENT. OCT 15 1904	NOTICE OF DEPARTMENTAL ACTION FORWARDED ATTORNEYS FOR CHOCTAW AND CHICKASAW NATIONS. AUG 4 - 1905						
	15							
	16 NOTICE OF DEPARTMENTAL ACTION MAILED APPLICANT AUG 4 - 1905	NOTICE OF DEPARTMENTAL ACTION FORWARDED ATTORNEY FOR APPLICANT. AUG 4 - 1905						
	17							

TRIBAL ENROLLMENT OF PARENTS

	Name of Father	Year	County	Name of Mother	Year	County
1	Dr G.W. Smith		Tobucksy	Mary Smith		Tobucksy
2	J.G. Terrell		non citz	Nancy P. Terrell dead non citz		
3	See Choctaw cards #D-86 and #D-296 and D-87					
4	March 15-1906. Remanded by Department for rehearing and readjudication as to question of					
5	residence.					
6	For child of No1 see NB (Apr 26-06) #1031					
7	[All information below on back of card.]					
8	DECISION RENDERED JUN 5 - 1906					
9						
10	REFUSED JUN 5 - 1906					
11	COPY OF DECISION FORWARDED ATTORNEY FOR APPLICANT. JUN 5 - 1906					
12						
13	COPY OF DECISION FORWARDED ATTORNEYS FOR CHOCTAW AND					
14	CHICKASAW NATIONS. JUN 5 - 1906					
15						
16	COPY OF DECISION FORWARDED APPLICANT JUN 5 - 1906					
17						

ENROLLMENT
OF NOS. ~~~ 1 ~~~ HEREON
APPROVED BY THE SECRETARY
OF INTERIOR Mar 4 - 1907

ENROLLMENT
OF NOS. ~~~ 2 ~~~ HEREON
APPROVED BY THE SECRETARY
OF INTERIOR Mar 4 - 1907

Date of Application for Enrollment.
Oct 20/98

RECORD FORWARDED DEPARTMENT JUN 5 - 1906

Nos 1&2 GRANTED FEB 15 1907

No2 transferred from Choctaw Card No D-296 under Dept instructions of Feby 15-1907

(See reverse side for additional information.)

134

Choctaw By Blood Enrollment Cards 1898-1914

RESIDENCE: Chickasaw Nation ~~COUNTY~~.
POST OFFICE: Chickasha, Ind. Ter.

Choctaw Nation

Choctaw Roll
(Not Including Freedmen)

CARD NO.
FIELD NO. **435**

Dawes' Roll No.	NAME	Relationship to Person First Named	AGE	SEX	BLOOD	TRIBAL ENROLLMENT		
						Year	County	No.
15225	1 Plato, Waity Lee		16	M	1/32		Choctaw residing in Chickasaw Dist	CCR #2 405
15226	2 " , William Ward	Bro	12	"	1/32		"	"
15227	3 " , Pearl Myrtle	Sister	10	F	1/32		"	"
15228	4 " , Arthur Herbert	Bro	6	M	1/32		"	"
I.W. 883	5 " , Frank W. (50)	Father	46	"	I.W.			
	6	No1 on Choctaw roll as Waitie Plato						
	7	No2 " " " " Ward "						
	8	No3 " " " " Myrtle "						
		No4 " " " " Arthur "						
	9	No.5 transferred from Choctaw card #D.88 July 7-'04. See decision of June 21 - 1904						
	10	All admitted by Dawes Com, Case No. 565, and no appeal taken.						
	11							
	12	ENROLLMENT OF NOS. 1-2-3-4 HEREON APPROVED BY THE SECRETARY OF INTERIOR MAY 9 1904						
	13							
	14							
	15	ENROLLMENT OF NOS. 5 HEREON APPROVED BY THE SECRETARY OF INTERIOR AUG 3 1904						
	16							
	17							

TRIBAL ENROLLMENT OF PARENTS

	Name of Father	Year	County	Name of Mother	Year	County
1	Frank W. Plato		non citizen	M.P. Buckholts Plato	Dead	Choctaw residing in Chickasaw Dist
2	" " "		" "	" " " "	"	" "
3	" " "		" "	" " " "	"	" "
4	" " "		" "	" " " "	"	" "
5	J.W Plato	Dead	" "	Harriet C. Plato		non citizen
6						
7	No1 1896 Chickasaw Dist 10637 as Wattie Platoe					
8	No2 1896 " " 10639 " Ward "					
9	No3 1896 " " 10640 " Myrtle "					
10	No4 1896 " " 10641 " Arthur "					
11	For children of No5 see NB (Apr 26 '06) #1130					
12						
13						
14					#1 to 4	
15		Date of application for enrollment			Oct 20/98	
16					Date of Application for Enrollment.	
17						

Choctaw By Blood Enrollment Cards 1898-1914

RESIDENCE: Chickasaw Nation ~~COUNTY~~.   **Choctaw Nation**   Choctaw Roll   CARD NO.
POST OFFICE: Chickasha, Ind. Ter.   (Not Including Freedmen)   FIELD NO. 436

Dawes' Roll No.	NAME	Relationship to Person First Named	AGE	SEX	BLOOD	TRIBAL ENROLLMENT		
						Year	County	No.
I.W. 500	₁ Garland, Daniel N. ³⁸		34	M	I.W.		Choctaw residing in Chickasaw Dist	C.I. Roll 39
14549	₂ " , Inez ³⁸	Wife	34	F	1/8		" "	CCR #2 216
14550	₃ " , Ollie Lou ¹⁴	Dau	10	"	1/16		" "	"
DEAD.	₄ " , Mildred	"	~~5~~	"	~~1/16~~		" "	"
14551	₅ " , Allison Nelson ⁷	Son	3	M	1/16		" "	"
14552	₆ " , Mary ³	Dau	2mo	F	1/16			
	₇ See testimony of Nº1 taken Oct. 16, 1902.							
	₈ No1 admitted by Dawes Com, Case No. 992, and no appeal taken							
	₉ No3 on Choctaw roll as Ollie Lee Garland							
	₁₀ ENROLLMENT	No4 "	"	" " Willard	"			
	₁₁ OF NOS. ~~1~~ HEREON APPROVED BY THE SECRETARY	No5 "	"	" " Allison L "				
	₁₂ OF INTERIOR DEC 24 1903							
	₁₃ Nº4 Died Oct. 2, 1901; proof of death filed Oct. 20, 1902							
	₁₄ ENROLLMENT OF NOS. 2,3,5 & 6 HEREON	No. 4 HEREON DISMISSED UNDER						
	₁₅ APPROVED BY THE SECRETARY	ORDER OF THE COMMISSION TO THE FIVE						
	OF INTERIOR MAY 20 1903	CIVILIZED TRIBES OF MARCH 31, 1905.						
	₁₆							
	₁₇							

TRIBAL ENROLLMENT OF PARENTS

Name of Father	Year	County	Name of Mother	Year	County
₁ Peter Garland	Dead	non citizen	Louisa Garland		non citizen
₂ Alfred Toole	"	" "	Belinda Toole	Dead	Tobucksy
₃	No 1		No 2		
₄	~~No 1~~		~~No 2~~		
₅	No 1		No 2		
₆	No 1		No 2		
₇					
₈	No1 1896 Chickasaw Dist 14590 as D. N. Garland				
₉	No2 1896 " " 5049		For child of Nos 1&2 see NB (Mar 3 '05) #659		
₁₀	No3 1896 " " 5050				
	~~No4 1896 " " 5051~~				
₁₁	No5 1896 " " 5052				
₁₂					
₁₃			Date of Application for Enrollment.		
₁₄					
₁₅			Oct 20/98		
₁₆			No6 enrolled Nov 24/99		
₁₇					

136

Choctaw By Blood Enrollment Cards 1898-1914

RESIDENCE: Chickasaw Nation ~~COUNTY.~~
POST OFFICE: Chickasha, Ind. Ter.

Choctaw Nation

Choctaw Roll
(Not Including Freedmen)

CARD NO.
FIELD NO. **437**

Dawes' Roll No.	NAME	Relationship to Person First Named	AGE	SEX	BLOOD	TRIBAL ENROLLMENT		
						Year	County	No.
I.W. 501	1 Anderson, Joseph 50	First Named	46	M	I.W.	1896	Choctaw residing in Chickasaw Dist	14270
14303	2 " , Margaret 42	Wife	38	F	1/8	1896	" "	552
14304	3 " , Albert Loray 19	Son	15	M	1/16	1896	" "	553
14305	4 " , Willis Elyot 18	"	14	"	1/16	1896	" "	554
14306	5 " , Burney Etta 15	Dau	11	F	1/16	1896	" "	555
14307	6 " , Manly Marlin 13	Son	9	M	1/16	1896	" "	556
14308	7 " , Joseph Kyle 12	"	8	"	1/16	1896	" "	557
14309	8 " , Cynthia Payne 10	Dau	6	F	1/16	1896	" "	558
14310	9 " , Maxey Overton 8	Son	4	M	1/16	1896	" "	559
14311	10 " , Hazel 5	Dau	1	F	1/16			
	11							
	12 See testimony of Nº 1 taken October 16, 1902							
	13 No8 on Choctaw roll as Cynthia Anderson							
	No9 " " Marcleo							
	14 No2 is mother of Walter Lee Bennett on							
	15 Choctaw card #5640	ENROLLMENT						
	16	OF NOS. 2 3 4 5 6 7 8 9 and 10 HEREON APPROVED BY THE SECRETARY						
	17	OF INTERIOR Apr 11 1903						

TRIBAL ENROLLMENT OF PARENTS

Name of Father	Year	County	Name of Mother	Year	County
1 James Anderson	Dead	non citizen	Lucinda Anderson		non citizen
2 Wᵐ Muncrief	"	Choctaw roll	Margaret Muncrief		Choctaw residing in Chickasaw Dist
3 No 1			No 2		
4 No 1			No 2		
5 No 1			No 2		
6 No 1			No 2		
7 No 1			No 2		
8 No 1			No 2		
9 No 1			No 2		
10 No 1			No 2		
11 ~~All except No.10 admitted by Dawes Com. Case No.491 and no appeal taken~~					
12 No1 - Marriage papers on file in office of Dawes Com Muskogee Ind. Ter.					
13 No3 on Choctaw roll as Ray Anderson					
14 No4 " " " Elliott			ENROLLMENT		Date of Application for Enrollment.
~~No5 " " " Burnice "~~			OF NOS. ---- ---- HEREON		
15 No6 " " " Manly "			APPROVED BY THE SECRETARY		Oct 20/98
16 No7 " " " Joe			OF INTERIOR Dec 24 1903		
17					

For child of No.5 see NB (March 3, 1905) #716

RESIDENCE: Chickasaw Nation ~~COUNTY~~.
POST OFFICE: Ryan, Ind Ter.

Choctaw Nation

Choctaw Roll
(Not Including Freedmen)

CARD NO.

FIELD NO. 438

Dawes' Roll No.	NAME	Relationship to Person First Named	AGE	SEX	BLOOD	TRIBAL ENROLLMENT		
						Year	County	No.
VOID.	1 ~~Ryan, Thomas Walker~~		18	M	1/8			
VOID.	2 ~~", Ada Pearl~~	Sister	16	F	1/8			
VOID.	3 ~~", Gussie VanBuren~~	"	14	"	1/8			
VOID.	4 ~~", Elbert Llewellyn~~	Bro	9	M	1/8			
VOID.	5 ~~Campbell, William G~~	Son of No2	5mo	M	1/16			
	6							
	7 All on Chickasaw roll, Pickens Co., Page 20; transferred to Choctaw roll by Dawes Com.							
	8							
	9 No1 on Chickasaw roll as Tom Ryan							
	10 No2 " " " " Ada "							
	11 No3 " " " " Gussie "							
	12 No4 " " " " Elbert "							
	No2 is now the wife of John E Campbell a noncitizen. Evidence marriage filed Sept 24 1901							
	13 No5 Enrolled Sept 24, 1901							
	14							
	15							
	16							
	17							

TRIBAL ENROLLMENT OF PARENTS

	Name of Father	Year	County	Name of Mother	Year	County
1	~~Steven Walker Ryan~~		white man	~~Carrie Cheadle Ryan~~	Dead	Choctaw roll
2	" " "		"	" " "	"	" "
3	" " "		"	" " "	"	" "
4	" " "		"	" " "	"	" "
5	~~John E Campbell~~		"	No 2		
6						
7						
8						
9						
10						
11						
12						
13						
14						
15				Date of Application for Enrollment.		Oct 20/98
16						
17						

Choctaw By Blood Enrollment Cards 1898-1914

RESIDENCE: Chickasaw Nation ~~COUNTY~~. **Choctaw Nation** **Choctaw Roll** CARD NO.
POST OFFICE: Norman. Okl. Ter. *(Not Including Freedmen)* FIELD NO. **439**

Dawes' Roll No.	NAME	Relationship to Person First Named	AGE	SEX	BLOOD	TRIBAL ENROLLMENT			
						Year	County		No.
844	1 Kelly, Joe J. 31	First Named	27	M	1/32		Atoka		CCR #2 323
	2								
	3 ENROLLMENT					1896	Atoka		7648
	4 OF NOS. 1 HEREON APPROVED BY THE SECRETARY								
	5 OF INTERIOR DEC 12 1902								
	6								
	7								
	8 For child of No1 see NB (Mar 3rd 1905) Card #91.								
	9								
	10								
	11								
	12								
	13								
	14								
	15								
	16								
	17								

TRIBAL ENROLLMENT OF PARENTS

	Name of Father	Year	County	Name of Mother	Year	County
1	W. W. Kelly	Dead	non citizen	S. A. Bell		Atoka
2						
3						
4						
5						
6						
7						
8						
9						
10						
11						
12						
13						
14						
15					Date of Application for Enrollment.	Oct 20/98
16						
17	P.O. Herbert I.T. 3/22/05					

Choctaw By Blood Enrollment Cards 1898-1914

RESIDENCE: Chickasaw Nation ~~COUNTY.~~
POST OFFICE: Chickasha, Ind. Ter.

Choctaw Nation

Choctaw Roll
(Not Including Freedmen)

CARD NO.
FIELD NO. **440**

Dawes' Roll No.	NAME	Relationship to Person First Named	AGE	SEX	BLOOD	TRIBAL ENROLLMENT		
						Year	County	No.
845	1 Davis, John C. 59	First Named	55	M	1/8		Atoka	CCR #2 149
I.W. 626	2 " , Mollie M 32	Wife	28	F	I.W.		Choctaw residing in Chickasaw Dist	C.I. Roll 24
846	3 " , Theodore H 10	Son	6	M	1/16		" "	CCR #2 149
847	4 " , Roxie G 6	Dau	4	F	1/16		" "	"
848	5 " , Mabel I. 5	"	1	"	1/16		" "	"
849	6 " , Joel Nail 2	Son	1mo	M	1/16			
	7	ENROLLMENT						
	8	OF NOS. 1,3,4,5 and 6 HEREON APPROVED BY THE SECRETARY						
	9	OF INTERIOR Dec 12 1902						
	10							
	11	See testimony of Nº1 taken October 17. 1902		No3 on Choctaw roll as Theodore Davis				
	12			No4 " " " " Roxie			"	
	13							
	14	ENROLLMENT OF NOS. 2 HEREON						
	15	APPROVED BY THE SECRETARY						
	16	OF INTERIOR Mar 26 1904						
	17							

TRIBAL ENROLLMENT OF PARENTS

	Name of Father	Year	County	Name of Mother	Year	County
1	J.D. Davis	Dead	non citizen	Salina Nail Davis	Dead	Choctaw roll
2	E.T. Ferrell	"	" "	Liney Ferrell	"	non citizen
3	No 1			No 2		
4	No 1			No 2		
5	No 1			No 2		
6	No 1			No 2		
7						
8	No2 admitted by Dawes Commission in 1896 as an intermarried					
9	in Choctaw case #309 no appeal					
10	~~No1 1896 Atoka 3594 as John Davis~~			Evidence of birth of No.5 received and		
11	No2 1896 " 14484 " Maud M "			filed March 18, 1902		
12	No3 1896 " 3612 " Theodore "					
13	~~No4 1896 " 3613 " Richie "~~ ~~No6 Enrolled Aug. 22d, 1900.~~					
14	For child of Nos 1&2 see NB (Mar 3-1905) Card #92				#1 to 5 inc	
15					Date of Application for Enrollment. Oct 20/98	
16						
17	Naples I.T. Oct 17/02					

Choctaw By Blood Enrollment Cards 1898-1914

RESIDENCE: Chickasaw Nation <s>COUNTY.</s> **Choctaw Nation** Choctaw Roll CARD NO.
POST OFFICE: Chickasha, Ind. Ter. *(Not Including Freedmen)* FIELD NO. **441**

Dawes' Roll No.	NAME	Relationship to Person First Named	AGE	SEX	BLOOD	TRIBAL ENROLLMENT		
						Year	County	No.
I.W. 1664	1 Mathews, James S. ⁵⁰	First Named	46	M	I.W.	1896	Choctaw residing in Chickasaw Dist	14847
15384	2 " , Fannie A. ⁴³	Wife	39	F	1/16	1896	" "	8951
15385	3 " , Harvey A . ²⁶	Son	22	M	1/32	1896	" "	8952
15386	4 " , Augustus F. ¹⁹	"	15	"	1/32	1896	" "	8953
15387	5 " , Alma Lee ¹⁶	Dau	12	F	1/32	1896	" "	8954
15388	6 " , Aroma B. ⁶	"	2	"	1/32	1896	" "	8955
	7							
	8 ENROLLMENT OF NOS 2-3-4-5-6- HEREON APPROVED BY THE SECRETARY							
	9 OF INTERIOR May 9 1904							
	10							
	11 For child of No.5 see NB (Mar. 3 05) #520							
	12							
	13 No 1 refused Apr 23 1906							
	14 April 23 1906 Record forwarded Department							
	15 Nov 5,1906 Department directs that Atty for Nations be allowed time to file argument.							
	16 Dec. 21, 1906 Report to Department.							
	17							

TRIBAL ENROLLMENT OF PARENTS

Name of Father	Year	County	Name of Mother	Year	County
1 John G. Matthews[sic]		non citizen	Jane Matthews	Dead	non citizen
2 Jackson Lee	Dead	" "	Amanda Lee	"	Choctaw roll
3 No 1			No 2		
4 No 1	ENROLLMENT OF NOS. One HEREON		No 2		
5 No 1	APPROVED BY THE SECRETARY OF INTERIOR Mar 4 - 1907		No 2		
6 No 1			No 2		
7					
8 All admitted by Dawes Com Case No 358, and appeal dismissed.					
9 No 1 also denied in '96 Case #1290					
10 No1 marriage papers on file in office of Dawes Com. Muskogee I.T.					
11 No4 on Choctaw roll as Guess Mathew					
12 No5 " " " " Almer "			March 1, 1907 Department		
13 No6 " " " " Arena "			directed enrollment of No.1		
13 No2 " " " " Annie L "			as intermarried citizen.		
14 No3 " " " " Harvey "					
15				Date of Application for Enrollment. Oct 21/99	
16					
17					

Choctaw By Blood Enrollment Cards 1898-1914

Dawes' Roll No.	NAME	Relationship to Person First Named	AGE	SEX	BLOOD	TRIBAL ENROLLMENT Year	County	No.
850	1 Hampton, Benjamin 50		46	M	1/2		Choctaw residing in Chickasaw Dist	CCR #2 260
I.W. 884	2 " , Fannie 38	Wife	34	F	I.W.		" "	Cpl Roll
851	3 " , Phoebe 17	Dau	13	"	1/4		Choctaw residing in Chickasaw Dist	CCR #2 260
852	4 " , Perry 14	Son	10	M	1/4		" "	"
853	5 " , Howard 11	"	7	"	1/4		" "	"
854	6 " , Edward Ray 8	"	4	"	1/4		" "	"
	7							
	8	ENROLLMENT OF NOS. 1,3,4,5 and 6 HEREON APPROVED BY THE SECRETARY OF INTERIOR Dec 12 1902						
	9					No 3 on Choctaw roll as L.P. Hampton		
	10					No.6 " " " " Edward "		
	11	ENROLLMENT OF NOS. 2 HEREON APPROVED BY THE SECRETARY OF INTERIOR Aug 3 1904						
	12							
	13							
	14							
	15							
	16							
	17							

TRIBAL ENROLLMENT OF PARENTS

	Name of Father	Year	County	Name of Mother	Year	County
1	Nicholas Hampton	Dead	Blue	Phoebe Hampton	Dead	Wade
2	J.M. Sims		non citizen	Julia Sims		non citizen
3	No.1			No.2		
4	No.1			No.2		
5	No.1			No.2		
6	No.1			No.2		
7						
8						
9						
10						
11						
12	No 1 1896 Chickasaw Dist	6225				
13	No.2 1896 " "	4670				
14	No.3 1896 " "	6226			Date of Application for Enrollment.	
15	No.4 1896 " "	6227 as Terry Hampton			Oct 21/98	
16	No.5 1896 " "	6229				
17	No.6 1896 " "	6228 as Edward Hampton				
	See testimony of Nº 1 taken	October 17, 1902				

Cards 3590-3649-4642

Choctaw By Blood Enrollment Cards 1898-1914

RESIDENCE: Chickasaw Nation ~~COUNTY.~~ **Choctaw Nation** **Choctaw Roll** CARD No.
POST OFFICE: Waldon, Ind. Ter. *(Not Including Freedmen)* FIELD No. 443

Dawes' Roll No.	NAME	Relationship to Person First Named	AGE	SEX	BLOOD	TRIBAL ENROLLMENT		
						Year	County	No.
855	1 Anderson, Ebel 25	First Named	21	M	Full		Atoka	CCR #2 18
	2							
	3 ENROLLMENT					1896	Atoka	445
	4 OF NOS. 1 HEREON APPROVED BY THE SECRETARY							
	5 OF INTERIOR DEC 12 1902							
	6							
	7							
	8							
	9	On Choctaw roll as Abel Anderson						
	10							
	11							
	12							
	13							
	14							
	15							
	16							
	17							

TRIBAL ENROLLMENT OF PARENTS

	Name of Father	Year	County	Name of Mother	Year	County
1	Anderson	Dead	Choctaw roll	Hettie Anderson	Dead	Choctaw roll
2						
3						
4						
5						
6						
7						
8						
9						
10						
11						
12						
13						
14						
15				Date of Application for Enrollment.		Oct 24/98
16						
17						

RESIDENCE: Chickasaw Nation COUNTY.
POST OFFICE: Minco Ind Ter

Choctaw Nation

Choctaw Roll
(Not Including Freedmen)

CARD No.
FIELD No. 444

Dawes' Roll No.	NAME	Relationship to Person First Named	AGE	SEX	BLOOD	TRIBAL ENROLLMENT		
						Year	County	No.
✓	1 McBride, Hiram Young	Named	40	M	I.W.	1896	Chick Dist	148870
✓	2 ", Lovica Colbert	Wife	30	F	1/4	1896	" "	9523
✓	3 ", Hettie A	Dau	10	"	1/8	1896	" "	9525
✓	4 ", Corrinne	"	7	"	1/8	1896	" "	9524
✓	5 ", Hiram Hadyn	Son	5	M	1/8	1896	" "	9526
✓	6 ", Lovica Czarius	dau	3	F	1/8	1896	" "	9527
✓	7 ", Colbert M	Son	1	M	1/8			
	8 Williams, Frances	Ward	19	F			Choctaw residing in Chickasaw Dist	CCR #Q 771
✓	9 McBride, Walter C Ben	Son	6wks	M	1/8			
✓	10 ", Mildred Mahota	Dau	2mo	F	1/8			

No1 admitted by Dawes Com Case No 1272 and no appeal taken
Marriage license and certificate on file in office of Dawes Com, Muskogee, I.T.
No1 on Chickasaw roll, Pontotoc Co, Page 81; transferred to Choctaw roll by Dawes Com
Nos2,3,4,5 &6 " " " " " " 66
11 No1 " " " " as H.Y.McBride - No7 affidavit of attending physician to be supplied
No4 " " " " Corrine No8 Choctaw roll as Frances Rec'd Nov 14/98
No5 " " " " Hiram H Williams
16 No6 " " " " Dora C No9 enrolled Dec 14/99
No10 born Oct 15, 1901, Enrolled Dec 23rd 1901

TRIBAL ENROLLMENT OF PARENTS

	Name of Father	Year	County	Name of Mother	No	County
1	John McBride	Dead	non citizen	Harriet McBride	Dead	non citizen
2	James Colbert	"	Chickasaw roll	Athenius Colbert		Choctaw residing in Chickasaw Dist
3	No 1			No 2		
4	No 1			No 2		
5	No 1			No 2		
6	No 1			No 2		
7	No 1			No 2		
8	James Williams	Dead	Gaines		Dead	Gaines
9	No 1			No 2		
10	No 1			No 2		
11	No1 on 1896 roll as H.G. McBride					
12	No2 " 1896 " " Levisey "					
13	No3 " 1896 " " Hattie "					
14	No4 " 1896 " " Lorena "					
15	No5 " 1896 " " Hiram "					
16	No6 " 1896 " " Levisey "					
	No8 is now the wife of LL Schrock and transferred to Choctaw card #5328					
17	P.O. Tuttle IT.				Date of Application for Enrollment.	Oct 21/98

144

Choctaw By Blood Enrollment Cards 1898-1914

Choctaw Nation

Choctaw Roll *(Not Including Freedmen)*

CARD NO.

FIELD NO. **445**

Dawes' Roll No.	NAME	Relationship to Person First Named	AGE	SEX	BLOOD	TRIBAL ENROLLMENT		
						Year	County	No.
~~856~~	DIED PRIOR TO SEPTEMBER 25, 1902 ³¹ 1 ~~Cook, Sarah E.~~		~~27~~	~~F~~	~~1/8~~		~~Wade~~	CCR #2 98
857	2 Gann, Walter Marion ¹³	Son	9	M	1/16		"	CCR #2 201
858	3 Cook, Myrtle Lee ¹¹	Dau	7	F	1/16		"	CCR #2 98
4553	4 " , Jennie Donnie ⁶	"	2	F	1/16			
859	5 " , Anna Bessie ³	"	5mo	F	1/16			
	6 ENROLLMENT							
	7 OF NOS. 1,2,3 and 5 HEREON							
	8 APPROVED BY THE SECRETARY OF INTERIOR Dec 12, 1902							
	9							
	10	No2 on Choctaw roll as Walter N. Gann.						
	11	No3 "	"	"	" Martha Cook.			
	12							
	13							
	14 ENROLLMENT							
	15 ~~OF NOS. 4 HEREON~~ APPROVED BY THE SECRETARY							
	16 OF INTERIOR May 20, 1903							
	17							

TRIBAL ENROLLMENT OF PARENTS

Name of Father	Year	County	Name of Mother	Year	County
1 ~~Henry Stidham~~	~~Dead~~	~~Non-Citizen~~	~~Maria Ady~~		Choctaw residing in Chickasaw Dist
2 Wᵐ N. Gann		" "	No.1		
3 Jim Cook		" "	No.1		
4 " "		" "	No.1		
5 " "		" "	No.1		
6					
7 No1 1896 Wade 2403					
8 No2 1896 " 4719 as Walter M. Garvin					
9 No3 1896 " 2404					
~~No5 Enrolled June 5, 1900.~~					
10 No4 - Proof of birth filed Dec 23, 1902 - Born Nov. 22, 1896 Additional affidavits filed 3/20/03.					
11 No1 - Died Nov. 28, 1900: Proof of death filed Dec 23, 1902.					
12					
13				ꞁ1 to 4	
14				Date of Application for Enrollment.	
15 P.O. Durant, Ok 12/14/08				Oct 21/98	
16 No1 died Nov 28, 1900: Enrollment					
17 Department July 8, 1904					

Choctaw By Blood Enrollment Cards 1898-1914

RESIDENCE: Chickasaw Nation ~~COUNTY.~~
POST OFFICE: Chickasha, Ind. Ter.

Choctaw Nation

Choctaw Roll
(Not Including Freedmen)

CARD NO.
FIELD NO. 446

Dawes' Roll No.	NAME	Relationship to Person First Named	AGE	SEX	BLOOD	TRIBAL ENROLLMENT		
						Year	County	No.
860	1 Kirkland, Rebecca 31	First Named	27	F	1/4		Choctaw residing in Chickasaw District	CCR #2 325
861	2 " , Lulu May 12	Dau	8	"	1/8		" "	"
	3							
	4	ENROLLMENT OF NOS. 1 and 2 HEREON						
	5	APPROVED BY THE SECRETARY OF INTERIOR Dec 12 1902						
	6							
	7	No.1 1896 Chickasaw Dist 7670						
	8	No.2 1896 " " 7671 as Lula Kirkland						
	9							
	10							
	11							
	12							
	13							
	14							
	15							
	16							
	17							

TRIBAL ENROLLMENT OF PARENTS

	Name of Father	Year	County	Name of Mother	Year	County
1	George Gardner	Dead	Choctaw roll	Phoebe Gardner	Dead	Choctaw residing in Chickasaw Dist
2	Chas M. Kirkland		non-citizen	No. 1		
3						
4						
5						
6						
7						
8						
9						
10						
11						
12						
13					Date of Application for Enrollment	
14						
15					Oct 21/98	
16						
17						

146

Choctaw By Blood Enrollment Cards 1898-1914

RESIDENCE: Chickasaw Nation ~~COUNTY.~~ **Choctaw Nation** **Choctaw Roll** CARD NO.
POST OFFICE: Purdy, Ind. Ter.   *(Not Including Freedmen)* FIELD NO. 447

Dawes' Roll No.	NAME	Relationship to Person First Named	AGE	SEX	BLOOD	TRIBAL ENROLLMENT		
						Year	County	No.
862	1 Gibson, Joseph ^34^	First Named	30	M	Full		Choctaw residing in Chickasaw Dist	CCR #2 216
	2							
	3	ENROLLMENT OF NOS. 1 HEREON APPROVED BY THE SECRETARY OF INTERIOR DEC 12 1902				1896	Chickasaw Dist	5042
	4							
	5							
	6							
	7							
	8							
	9	Husband of Emily Gibson, Chickasaw roll, Card No. 1323						
	10							
	11							
	12							
	13							
	14							
	15							
	16							
	17							

TRIBAL ENROLLMENT OF PARENTS

	Name of Father	Year	County	Name of Mother	Year	County
1	Isaac Gibson	Dead	Choctaw roll	Lucinda Gibson	Dead	Choctaw roll
2						
3						
4	Emily Gibson, wife, gives evidence of death of No1 in August 1905 in NB (Apr 26-06) jacket #22					
5	For child of No.1 see NB (March 3 1905) #359					
6	" " " " " " (April 26, 1906) #221					
7						
8						
9						
10						
11						
12						
13						
14						
15				Date of Application for Enrollment.		Oct 21/98
16						
17	Foster, I.T.					

147

Choctaw By Blood Enrollment Cards 1898-1914

RESIDENCE: Chickasaw Nation ~~COUNTY~~.
POST OFFICE: Hope, Ind Tery

Choctaw Nation

Choctaw Roll
(Not Including Freedmen)

CARD NO.
FIELD NO. 448

Dawes' Roll No.	NAME		Relationship to Person	AGE	SEX	BLOOD	TRIBAL ENROLLMENT		
							Year	County	No.
863	1 Robinson, Alex	40	First Named	38	M	3/8		Blue	CCR #2 414
I.W. 885	2 " Mary E.	40	wife	36	F	I.W.			
864	3 " Emely F.	15	dau	11	"	3/16		Blue	CCR #2 414
865	4 " Ida M.	13	"	9	"	3/16		"	"
866	5 " Birdie E.	11	"	7	"	3/16		"	"
867	6 " James B.	5	son	15mo	M	3/16			
868	7 " Ollie Fay	2	Dau	2W	F	3/16			
	8								
	9	ENROLLMENT OF NOS. 1,3,4,5,6 and 7 HEREON							
	10	APPROVED BY THE SECRETARY							
	11	OF INTERIOR Dec 12 1902							
	12								
	13								
	14	ENROLLMENT OF NOS. 2 HEREON							
	15	APPROVED BY THE SECRETARY							
	16	OF INTERIOR Aug 3 1904							
	17								

TRIBAL ENROLLMENT OF PARENTS

Name of Father	Year	County	Name of Mother	Year	County
1 James Robinson	Dead	Blue	Emeline Robinson		Blue
2 Anderson Riddle	"	Non Citz	Martha Riddle	Dead	Non citz
3	No.1		No.2		
4	No.1		No.2		
5	No.1		No.2		
6	No.1		No.2		
7	No.1		No.2		
8					
9					
10					
11	No.1 1896 Blue 10949				
12	No.3 1896 " 10950				
13	No.4 1896 " 10951				
	No.5 1896 " 10952				
14	No. 7 Enrolled February 1, 1901		#1 to 6 Date of Application for Enrollment		
15				On White Card Oct. 13, 1898	
16	12/18/02			On this Card Nov. 17, 1898	
17	Dovle I.T.		See additional testimony of No.1, taken Oct 15, 1902		

148

RESIDENCE: **Blue** COUNTY.
POST OFFICE: Caddo, Ind. Ter.

Choctaw Nation

Choctaw Roll
(Not Including Freedmen)

CARD NO.
FIELD NO. 449

Dawes' Roll No.	NAME	Relationship to Person First Named	AGE	SEX	BLOOD	TRIBAL ENROLLMENT		
						Year	County	No.
VOID. 1	Goforth, Levi P.		27	M	1/4			
2								
3								
4								
5								
6								
7	No.1 on Chickasaw roll as L.P. Goforth							
8								
9	On Chickasaw roll 1897, Page 74; transferred to Choctaw roll by Dawes Com							
10								
11								
12								
13								
14								
15								
16								
17								

TRIBAL ENROLLMENT OF PARENTS

	Name of Father	Year	County	Name of Mother	Year	County
1	Solomon Goforth		Chick residing in Choctaw N. 3rd Dist	Caroline Goforth	Dead	Choctaw roll
2						
3						
4						
5						
6						
7						
8						
9						
10						
11						
12						
13						
14						
15				Date of Application for Enrollment.		Nov. 21/98
16						
17						

Transferred to Chickasaw Card No. 1658, Oct. 14, 1902

CANCELLED

Choctaw By Blood Enrollment Cards 1898-1914

RESIDENCE:	Blue	COUNTY.								
POST OFFICE:	Caddo, Ind. Ter.								FIELD NO.	450

Choctaw Nation — **Choctaw Roll** *(Not Including Freedmen)* — CARD NO.

Dawes' Roll No.	NAME	Relationship to Person First Named	AGE	SEX	BLOOD	TRIBAL ENROLLMENT		
						Year	County	No.
VOID. 1	Goforth, Joe H.		25	M	1/4			
2								
3								
4								
5								
6	On Chickasaw roll 1897, Page 74; transferred to Choctaw roll by Dawes Com.							
7								
8								
9								
10								
11								
12								
13								
14								
15								
16								
17								

TRIBAL ENROLLMENT OF PARENTS

	Name of Father	Year	County	Name of Mother	Year	County
1	Solomon Goforth		Chick residing in Choctaw N. 3rd Dist	Caroline Goforth	Dead	Choctaw roll
2						
3						
4						
5						
6						
7						
8						
9						
10						
11						
12						
13						
14						
15					Date of Application for Enrollment.	Nov 21/98
16						
17						

CANCELLED

Transferred to Chickasaw Card No. 1639 Oct 14, 1902

Choctaw By Blood Enrollment Cards 1898-1914

RESIDENCE: Chickasaw Nation ~~COUNTY.~~ **Choctaw Nation**   Choctaw Roll   CARD No.
POST OFFICE: Arthur, Ind Ter.   (Not Including Freedmen)   FIELD No. 451

Dawes' Roll No.	NAME	Relationship to Person First Named	AGE	SEX	BLOOD	TRIBAL ENROLLMENT		
						Year	County	No.
1	~~Copeland, John Forster~~	~~Named~~	64	M	I.W.			
2								
3								
4								
5								
6								
7								
8								
9								
10								
11								
12								
13								
14								
15								
16								
17								

DISMISSED
FEB 4 1907

TRIBAL ENROLLMENT OF PARENTS

	Name of Father	Year	County	Name of Mother	Year	County
1	~~Wilkerson Copeland~~	~~Dead~~	~~non-citizen~~	~~Nancy Copeland~~	~~Dead~~	~~non-citizen~~
2						
3						
4						
5						
6						
7						
8						
9						
10						
11						
12						
13						
14						
15				Date of Application for Enrollment.	Nov 21/98	
16						
17						

Choctaw By Blood Enrollment Cards 1898-1914

RESIDENCE:	Atoka	COUNTY.						CARD NO.	
POST OFFICE:	Kiowa, Ind Ter.							FIELD NO. 452	

Choctaw Nation

Choctaw Roll (Not Including Freedmen)

Dawes' Roll No.	NAME	Relationship to Person First Named	AGE	SEX	BLOOD	TRIBAL ENROLLMENT Year	County	No.
869	1 Folsom, Wade ²⁹	First Named	25	M	1/2		Tobucksy	CCR #2 172
870	2 " , Guy Vann ⁹	Son	5	"	1/4		"	"
871	3 " , Ellina ⁷	Dau	3	F	1/4		"	"
872	4 DIED PRIOR TO SEPTEMBER 25, 1902 , Myrtle Marie	"	5mo	"	1/4			
IW 558	5 " , Maud A. ²⁹	Wife	26	"	I.W.	1896	Chick Dist	14526
873	6 " , Bertha Bell ²	Dau	1mo	F	1/4			
	7							
	8 ENROLLMENT OF NOS. 1,2,3,4 and 5 HEREON							
	9 APPROVED BY THE SECRETARY							
	10 OF INTERIOR DEC 12 1902							
	11 No3 on Choctaw roll as Ellen Folsom.							
	12 No4 affidavit of attending physician to be supplied-Received Dec 17/98							
	13							
	14 ENROLLMENT OF NOS. 5 HEREON							
	15 APPROVED BY THE SECRETARY							
	16 OF INTERIOR FEB -8 1904							
	17							

TRIBAL ENROLLMENT OF PARENTS

	Name of Father	Year	County	Name of Mother	Year	County
1	Rufus Folsom	Dead	Choctaw roll	Sallie Folsom	Dead	Choctaw roll
2	No 1			No 5		
3	No 1			No 5		
4	No 1			No 5		
5	Stephen Poe		Non citz	Liddie Poe	Dead	Non Citz
6	No 1			No 5		
7						
8	For children of Nos 1&5 see NB (March 3, 1905) #874					
9	No.4 died Aug 15-1901; Enrollment cancelled by Department [remainder illegible]					
10	No1 1896 Tobucksy 4053 as Wade Fulsom					
11	No2 1896 " 4054 " Guy V. "					
12	No3 1896 " 4055 " Ellen "					
13	No.6 Enrolled Oct. 8th, 1900					
14	N°4 Died Aug. 15, 1901; Proof of death filed Nov. 10, 1902				Date of Application for Enrollment.	
15						
16					Nov 21/98	
17	11/6/02 P.O. Linn I.T.			No5 enrolled Aug 7/99		

152

Choctaw By Blood Enrollment Cards 1898-1914

RESIDENCE: Chickasaw Nation ~~COUNTY.~~ **Choctaw Nation** **Choctaw Roll** CARD No.
POST OFFICE: Purcell, Ind. Ter.   *(Not Including Freedmen)* FIELD No. 453

Dawes' Roll No.	NAME	Relationship to Person First Named	AGE	SEX	BLOOD	TRIBAL ENROLLMENT		
						Year	County	No.
I.W. 502	1 Sacra, R.C. 41	First Named	44	M	I.W.			
	2							
	3							
	4							
	5							
	6							
	7							
	8 ENROLLMENT OF NOS. ~~ 1 ~~ HEREON							
	9 APPROVED BY THE SECRETARY							
	10 OF INTERIOR DEC 24 1903							
	11 No1 is the husband of Clemmie G. Sacra, and father of the children,							
	12 on Choctaw Card #123							
	13							
	14 In prison at Leavenworth. Sentence will expire in about 1 year							
	15							
	16 No1 was admitted as an intermarried citizen by Dawes Commission							
	17 Choctaw Case #830: no appeal.							

TRIBAL ENROLLMENT OF PARENTS

	Name of Father	Year	County	Name of Mother	Year	County
1	Ed Sacra		non citizen			non citizen
2						
3						
4						
5						
6						
7						
8						
9						
10						
11						
12						
13						
14						
15				Date of Application for Enrollment.		Nov 22/98
16						
17						

Choctaw By Blood Enrollment Cards 1898-1914

RESIDENCE:	Cedar	COUNTY.	**Choctaw Nation**			**Choctaw Roll** *(Not Including Freedmen)*	CARD NO.	
POST OFFICE:	Kosonia, Ind. Ter.						FIELD NO.	454

Dawes' Roll No.	NAME	Relationship to Person First Named	AGE	SEX	BLOOD	TRIBAL ENROLLMENT		
						Year	County	No. COR #2
VOID. 1	Davenport, Betsey		38	F	1/2		Cedar	137
VOID. 2	" , Becky	Dau	18	"	1/2		"	"
VOID. 3	" , George	Son	11	M	1/2		"	"
VOID. 4	" , Eliza	Dau	9	F	1/2		"	"
VOID. 5	" , Pearlie	"	7	"	1/2		"	"
VOID. 6	" , Joe	Son	5	M	1/2		"	"
VOID. 7	" , Vena	Dau	3	F	1/2		"	"
VOID. 8	" , Ivy	"	1	"	1/2		"	"
9					No1	96	Cedar	3361
10					No2	1896	"	3366
11								
12	May 16/99. All above parties, except 2-6							
13	have been transferred to Card No 1766.							
14	Nos 2-6 are on Card No 1767.							
15	No1 wife of George Davenport, Chickasaw roll, Card No. 1334							
16	No5 on Choctaw roll as Polly Davenport							
17	No7 " " " " Emily "							

TRIBAL ENROLLMENT OF PARENTS

	Name of Father	Year	County	Name of Mother	Year	County
1	Ah Kom bey	Dead	Chickasaw roll Liza			Jack Fork
2	George Davenport		Chick residing in Choctaw N. 2nd Dist	No 1		
3	" "		" " "	No 1		
4	" "		" " "	No 1		
5	" "		" " "	No 1		
6	" "		" " "	No 1		
7	" "		" " "	No 1		
8	" "		" " "	No 1		
9						
10						
11			No3 1896 Cedar 3362			
12			No4 1896 " 3363			
13			No5 1896 " 3364			
14			No6 1896 " 3367			
			No7 1896 " 3365			
15				Date of Application for Enrollment.	Nov 22/98	
16						
17						

CANCELLED

Choctaw By Blood Enrollment Cards 1898-1914

RESIDENCE: Chickasaw Nation ~~COUNTY.~~
POST OFFICE: Marlow Ind Ter.

Choctaw Nation

Choctaw Roll
(Not Including Freedmen)

CARD NO.
FIELD NO. **455**

Dawes' Roll No.	NAME	Relationship to Person First Named	AGE	SEX	BLOOD	TRIBAL ENROLLMENT		
						Year	County	No.
I.W. 1552	1 Morris, John 50	First Named	46	M	I.W.		Choctaw residing in Chickasaw District	C.I. Roll 72
	2							
	3					1896	Chickasaw Dist	14851
	4							
	5	ENROLLMENT OF NOS. ~~ 1 ~~ HEREON APPROVED BY THE SECRETARY OF INTERIOR Aug 2 1906						
	6							
	7							
	8							
	9							
	10							
	11	Take no further action relative to enrollment for No1						
	12	Protest of Attys for Choctaw and Chickasaw Nations						
	13	Jan. 25, 04						
	14							
	15							
	16							
	17							

TRIBAL ENROLLMENT OF PARENTS

	Name of Father	Year	County	Name of Mother	Year	County
1	Charley Morris	Dead	non citizen	Mary Morris	Dead	non citizen
2						
3						
4						
5						
6						
7						
8						
9						
10	Evidence as to seperation[sic] from Choctaw wife taken by stenographer					
11	Wife is Rhoda S. Morris on Choctaw #4950					
12	See testimony of No1 taken October 17, 1902 Married out Notify Chas Von Weise, Ardmore IT of decision 4/26/06					
13	No1 was formerly husband of Rhoda S. Morris, Choctaw roll No 13504.					
14						
15					Date of Application for Enrollment.	Nov. 22/98
16				Granted Jun. 13 1906		
17						

155

Choctaw By Blood Enrollment Cards 1898-1914

RESIDENCE: Kiamitia COUNTY.	**Choctaw Nation**	**Choctaw Roll** (Not Including Freedmen)	CARD NO.
POST OFFICE: Nelson, Ind. Ter.			FIELD NO. **456**

Dawes' Roll No.	NAME	Relationship to Person First Named	AGE	SEX	BLOOD	TRIBAL ENROLLMENT Year	County	No.
874	₁ Griggs, Thomas L. ⁵⁴	First Named	50	M	3/8		Kiamitia	CCR #2 207
	₂							
	₃	ENROLLMENT				1896	Kiamitia	4828
	₄	OF NOS. 1 HEREON APPROVED BY THE SECRETARY						
	₅	OF INTERIOR Dec 12 1902						
	₆							
	₇							
	₈							
	₉							
	₁₀	Husband of Dora Griggs, Chickasaw roll Card No. 1335						
	₁₁							
	₁₂							
	₁₃							
	₁₄							
	₁₅							
	₁₆							
	₁₇							

TRIBAL ENROLLMENT OF PARENTS

Name of Father	Year	County	Name of Mother	Year	County
₁ Leroy Griggs	Dead	non citizen	Lizzie Griggs	Dead	Kiamitia
₂					
₃					
₄					
₅					
₆					
₇					
₈					
₉					
₁₀					
₁₁					
₁₂					
₁₃					
₁₄					
₁₅			Date of Application for Enrollment.	Nov 22/98	
₁₆					
₁₇					

156

Choctaw By Blood Enrollment Cards 1898-1914

Lula - Rt. 6, Bx 436 I.T.

RESIDENCE: Chickasaw Nation ~~COUNTY~~.
POST OFFICE: Roff Ind Ter.

10-31-39

Choctaw Nation

Choctaw Roll (Not Including Freedmen)

CARD NO.

FIELD NO. 457

Dawes' Roll No.	NAME	Relationship to Person First Named	AGE	SEX	BLOOD	TRIBAL ENROLLMENT		
						Year	County	No.
875	1 Taylor, Oliver 31	First Named	27	M	1/4		Choctaw residing in Chickasaw Dist	CCR #2 452
876	2 " , Lonnie W. 4	Son	1mo	"	1/8			
877	3 " , Mabel 2	Dau	3wk	F	1/8			
I.W. 1521	4 " , Lula	Wife	35	"	I.W.			
	5 ENROLLMENT					No1	1896 Chickasaw Dist	12552
	6 OF NOS. 1 2 and 3 HEREON APPROVED BY THE SECRETARY							
	7 OF INTERIOR DEC 12 1902							
	8							
	9 GRANTED							
	10 NOV 4- 1905							
	11							
	12							
	13 ENROLLMENT							
	14 OF NOS. ~~~4~~~ HEREON APPROVED BY THE SECRETARY							
	15 OF INTERIOR MAR 14 1906							
	16							
	17							

TRIBAL ENROLLMENT OF PARENTS

Name of Father	Year	County	Name of Mother	Year	County
1 Jack Taylor	Dead	Blue	Rebecca Taylor	Dead	non citizen
2 No 1			Lula "		" "
3 No 1			" "		" "
4 John Hammond		non citizen	Mollie Hammond		" "
5					
6 No3 Enrolled November 8th 1900					
7 Evidence of marriage of No.1 to be supplied					
8 Received and filed, November 21st, 1900.					
9 No4 placed on this card September 28th, 1905, in accordance with order of Commissioner					
10 to the Five Civilized Tribes of that date holding application was made within time prescribed					
11 by act of Congress approved July 1, 1902 (32 Stat 641)					
12 For child of No1 see NB (Mar 3-1905) Card #9B					
13					
14			Date of Application for Enrollment.	#1&2	
15				Nov 24/98	
16					
17					

157

RESIDENCE:	Tobucksy	COUNTY.	**Choctaw Nation**	Choctaw Roll	CARD NO.	
POST OFFICE:	Kiowa, Ind. Ter			*(Not Including Freedmen)*	FIELD NO.	458

Dawes' Roll No.	NAME	Relationship to Person First Named	AGE	SEX	BLOOD	TRIBAL ENROLLMENT		
						Year	County	No.
15389	1 Hewitt, Lelah ²⁴		20	F	1/8		Tobucksy	CCR #2 36
IW886	2 Hewitt, George W. �37							
	3					1896	Tobucksy 862 as Lelah Bohren	
	4							
	5	ENROLLMENT						
	6	OF NOS. ~~~~1~~~~ HEREON APPROVED BY THE SECRETARY						
	7	OF INTERIOR MAY 9 1904						
	8	ENROLLMENT						
	9	OF NOS. 2 HEREON APPROVED BY THE SECRETARY						
	10	OF INTERIOR AUG 3 1904						
	11							
	12	Wife of Geo. W. Hewitt, a non citizen, on Choc. Card D.477						
	13							
	14	On Choctaw roll as Lula Bohren						
	15	No1 Admitted by Dawes Com 1896 Case No 617 - No appeal						
	16							
	17							

TRIBAL ENROLLMENT OF PARENTS

	Name of Father	Year	County	Name of Mother	Year	County
1	John Bohren		non citizen	Susie Bohren		Tobucksy
2	J B Hewitt		noncitizen	May Hewitt		noncitizen
3						
4						
5						
6						
7	See testimony of Oct 24 '02 & Oct 29-02 in jacket of husband					
8						
9						
10						
11						
12						
13						
14	No2 transferred from Choctaw card D 477, April 13, 1904					
15	See decision of March 15, 1904.			Date of Application for Enrollment.		Nov 24/98
16						
17	P.O. Hugo I.T 6/18/04					

Choctaw By Blood Enrollment Cards 1898-1914

RESIDENCE:		COUNTY.	**Choctaw Nation**	**Choctaw Roll**	CARD NO.
POST OFFICE:	Wilburton, Ind. Ter.			*(Not Including Freedmen)*	FIELD NO. **459**

Dawes' Roll No.	NAME	Relationship to Person First Named	AGE	SEX	BLOOD	TRIBAL ENROLLMENT		
						Year	County	No.
14554	1 Ward, Plenna ⁸	First Named	4	F	1/2	1896	Gaines	12982
	2							
	3	ENROLLMENT						
	4	OF NOS. 1 HEREON APPROVED BY THE SECRETARY						
	5	OF INTERIOR May 20 1903						
	6							
	7	Father Henry Ward, on Chickasaw Card No 1389						
	8	Mother, Judie " " Choctaw roll as Jennie Ward.						
	9							
	10	Oct 25/99 Duplicate of 4847 Card.						
	11	4847 cancelled						
	12							
	13							
	14							
	15							
	16							
	17							

TRIBAL ENROLLMENT OF PARENTS

Name of Father	Year	County	Name of Mother	Year	County	
1 Henry Ward		Chick residing in Choctaw N. 1ˢᵗ Dist	Judie Ward	Dead	Gaines	No 12980
2						
3						
4						
5						
6						
7						
8						
9						
10						
11						
12						
13						
14					Date of Application for Enrollment.	
15					Mar 20/99	
16						
17						

Choctaw By Blood Enrollment Cards 1898-1914

RESIDENCE:	COUNTY.							CARD NO.	
POST OFFICE: Savannah, Ind. Ter.	**Choctaw Nation**					Choctaw Roll *(Not Including Freedmen)*		FIELD NO. **460**	

Dawes' Roll No.	NAME		Relationship to Person First Named	AGE	SEX	BLOOD	TRIBAL ENROLLMENT		
							Year	County	No.
14555	1 Carney, Lucy Ann	35	First Named	31	F	Full	1896	Atoka	2946
878	2 " , Allen	13	Son	9	M	1/2	1896	"	2945
15390	3 " , Sampson	7	"	3	"	1/2			
14556	4 " , Levison	2	Son	19mo	M	1/2			
	5								
	6	ENROLLMENT							
	7	OF NOS. 2 HEREON							
		APPROVED BY THE SECRETARY							
	8	OF INTERIOR Dec 12 1902							
	9					No			
	10	ENROLLMENT							
	11	OF NOS. 1 and 4 HEREON APPROVED BY THE SECRETARY							
	12	OF INTERIOR May 20 1903							
	13								
	14	ENROLLMENT							
	15	OF NOS. 3 HEREON							
	16	APPROVED BY THE SECRETARY OF INTERIOR May 9 1904							
	17								

TRIBAL ENROLLMENT OF PARENTS

	Name of Father	Year	County	Name of Mother	Year	County
1	Sampson Bushbo	Dead	Choctaw roll	Sophie Bushbo		Tobucksy
2	Norris Carney		Chick residing in Choctaw N. 1st Dist	No 1		
3	" "		" " "	No 1		
4	" "		" " "	No 1		
5						
6						
7						
8						
9	Norris Carney husband of No1 on Chickasaw Card No. 1391					
10	No1 on 1896 Roll No. 2946 as Lucy Ann Carney?					
11	N°4 Born Feby. 1, 1901; enrolled Sept. 10, 1902.					No 15834
	N°1 on 1893 Leased district payment roll Tobucksy Co as Louisianna Cobb					1902 GOF.
12	No3 See letter of explanation why not on Roll by Norris Carney Decr. 26 '03					See copy of
13						letter from R.B. Coleman
14	For child of No1 see NB (Mar 3-1903) Card #96.					filed Sept. 29, 1902
15						Date of Application for Enrollment.
16						Mar 20/99
17						1to3

160

RESIDENCE: COUNTY.

POST OFFICE: Alderson, Ind. Ter.   **Choctaw Nation**   **Choctaw Roll** _(Not Including Freedmen)_   CARD NO. / FIELD NO. **461**

Dawes' Roll No.	NAME	Relationship to Person First Named	AGE	SEX	BLOOD	TRIBAL ENROLLMENT		
						Year	County	No.
✓ 1	Nail, Jincy	Named						
✓ 2	" , Jimmie		14	M	3/4			
DEAD DEAD 3	" , Joe		3	"	3/4			
✓ 4	Anderson, Malinne		17	F	3/4			
✓ 5	" , Mollie		15	"	3/4			
✓ 6	" , Gipson		10	M	3/4			
✓ 7	" , Lizzie		5	F	3/4			
8	No. 3 hereon dismissed under order							
9	of the Commission to the Five							
10	Civilized Tribes of March 31, 1905							
11								
12								
13	Sept							
14	No3 died July 7 1899. Proof of death filed Aug 22, 1901							
15								
16	No2 on Chickasaw Roll ... transferred to Choctaw Roll by Dawes Com							
17	Nos 3,4,5,6 &7 " " " 10 " " " " "							

For corrected enrollment see card Nos 4736 and 4737

TRIBAL ENROLLMENT OF PARENTS

	Name of Father	Year	County				Name of Mother	Year	County
1			Chick residing in						
2	Alfred Nail		Choctaw N. 1st Dist				Winey Nail	Dead	Tobucksy
3	" "		" " "	"	"		Jincy Nail		"
4	Wesley Anderson	Dead	"	"	"		" "		"
5	" "		"	"	"		" "		"
6	" "		"	"	"		" "		"
7	William McCann		Tobucksy				" "		"
8									
9									
10									
11									
12									
13	Alfred Nail on Chickasaw Card No. 1392								
14									
15	No.7 Is Lizzie Carnes; her father George Carnes.						Date of Application for Enrollment.	Mar 20/99	
16	The name Anderson, is error & name of her								
17	father, William McCann is error								

CANCELLED

Choctaw By Blood Enrollment Cards 1898-1914

RESIDENCE: Chickasaw Nation ~~COUNTY~~.　**Choctaw Nation**　Choctaw Roll　CARD NO.
POST OFFICE: Fitzhugh, Ind. Ter.　　　　　　　　　(Not Including Freedmen)　FIELD NO. 462

Dawes' Roll No.	NAME	Relationship to Person First Named	AGE	SEX	BLOOD	TRIBAL ENROLLMENT		
						Year	County	No.
879	₁ Cope, John B. ¹⁴	First Named	10	M	3/8	1896	Tobucksy	2328
880	₂ " , Harry A ¹³	Bro	9	"	3/8	1896	"	2329
881	₃ " , Mamie ¹¹	Sister	7	F	3/8	1896	"	2330
882	₄ " , Pearl ¹¹	"	7	"	3/8	1896	"	2331
	₅							
	₆	ENROLLMENT						
	₇	OF NOS. 1,2,3 and 4 HEREON APPROVED BY THE SECRETARY						
	₈	OF INTERIOR DEC 12 1902						
	₉							
	₁₀	Father A.W. Cope on Choctaw card No D.115						
	₁₁	No1 on Choctaw Census Roll as John Cope						
	₁₂	No2 " " " " " Henry "						
		No3 " " " " " " Maria "						
	₁₃							
	₁₄							
	₁₅							
	₁₆							
	₁₇							

TRIBAL ENROLLMENT OF PARENTS

Name of Father	Year	County	Name of Mother	Year	County
₁ A.W. Cope		White man	Collice Cope	Dead	Tobucksy
₂ " " "		" "	" "	"	"
₃ " " "		" "	" "	"	"
₄ " " "		" "	" "	"	"
₅					
₆					
₇					
₈					
₉					
₁₀					
₁₁					
₁₂					
₁₃				Date of Application for Enrollment.	
₁₄					
₁₅				Mar 20/99	
₁₆					
₁₇					

162

Choctaw By Blood Enrollment Cards 1898-1914

RESIDENCE:	COUNTY.	**Choctaw Nation**	**Choctaw Roll**	CARD NO.
POST OFFICE: Kosome[sic], Ind. Ter.			*(Not Including Freedmen)*	FIELD NO. 463

Dawes' Roll No.	NAME	Relationship to Person First Named	AGE	SEX	BLOOD	TRIBAL ENROLLMENT Year	County	No.
883	1 Impson, Isaac J ⁴⁴	First Named	40	M	1/2	1896	Jacks Fork	6333
	2							
	3	ENROLLMENT OF NOS. 1 HEREON						
	4	APPROVED BY THE SECRETARY OF INTERIOR DEC 12 1902						
	5							
	6							
	7							
	8							
	9	Wife and children on Chickasaw card No. 1393						
	10							
	11							
	12							
	13							
	14							
	15							
	16							
	17							

TRIBAL ENROLLMENT OF PARENTS

	Name of Father	Year	County	Name of Mother	Year	County
1	Josiah Impson	Dead	Jacks Fork	Jane Impson	Dead	Jacks Fork
2						
3						
4						
5						
6						
7						
8						
9						
10						
11						
12						
13						
14						
15					Date of Application for Enrollment.	Mar 20/99
16						
17	Antlers I.T. 12/11/02					

RESIDENCE:	COUNTY.		Choctaw Nation		Choctaw Roll	CARD NO.
POST OFFICE: Tuskahoma, Ind Ter					(Not Including Freedmen)	FIELD NO. 464

Dawes' Roll No.	NAME	Relationship to Person First Named	AGE	SEX	BLOOD	TRIBAL ENROLLMENT		
						Year	County	No.
884	1 Jones, Sim ³¹		27	M	Full	1896	Jacks Fork	7350
	2							
	3	ENROLLMENT						
	4	OF NOS. 1 HEREON APPROVED BY THE SECRETARY						
	5	OF INTERIOR DEC 12 1902						
	6							
	7							
	8							
	9							
	10	Some intimation that his mother's mother may have been a Chickasaw. If						
	11	no evidence to substantiate this intimation, however, is presented by the Commissioners of the Choctaw and Chickasaw Nations, party to remain on this card.						
	12	No 1 is now husband of Nancy Sexton on Choctaw card #4286; evidence of						
	13	marriage filed December 15, 1902.						
	14							
	15							
	16							
	17							

TRIBAL ENROLLMENT OF PARENTS

	Name of Father	Year	County	Name of Mother	Year	County
1	Jones Hokatubby	Dead	Jacks Fork	Peggy	Dead	Jacks Fork
2						
3						
4						
5						
6						
7						
8						
9						
10						
11						
12						
13						
14						
15						
16						
17						

Date of Application for Enrollment.

Mar 21/99

Choctaw By Blood Enrollment Cards 1898-1914

RESIDENCE:		COUNTY.	**Choctaw Nation**				**Choctaw Roll** *(Not Including Freedmen)*	CARD NO.	
POST OFFICE: Goodland, Ind. Ter.								FIELD NO. 465	

Dawes' Roll No.	NAME	Relationship to Person First Named	AGE	SEX	BLOOD	TRIBAL ENROLLMENT		
						Year	County	No.
885	1 Locke, Josie 12	First Named	8	F	1/4	1896	Kiamitia	8089
886	2 " , Jimmie Susan 7	Sister	3	"	1/4	1896	"	8090
	3							
	4 ENROLLMENT OF NOS. 1 and 2 HEREON APPROVED BY THE SECRETARY							
	5 OF INTERIOR DEC 12 1902							
	6							
	7							
	8							
	9 No2 on Choctaw roll as Ginnie Locke							
	10							
	11							
	12							
	13							
	14							
	15							
	16							
	17							

TRIBAL ENROLLMENT OF PARENTS

	Name of Father	Year	County	Name of Mother	Year	County
1	Benj. F. Locke		White man	Susan Locke	Dead	Kiamitia
2	" " "		" "	" "	"	"
3						
4						
5						
6						
7						
8						
9						
10						
11						
12						
13						
14						
15				Date of Application for Enrollment.	Mar 21/99	
16						
17						

Choctaw By Blood Enrollment Cards 1898-1914

RESIDENCE: Chickasaw Nation ~~COUNTY~~.
POST OFFICE: Dixie, Ind. Ter.

Choctaw Nation

Choctaw Roll
(Not Including Freedmen)

CARD NO.
FIELD NO. **466**

Dawes' Roll No.	NAME	Relationship to Person First Named	AGE	SEX	BLOOD	TRIBAL ENROLLMENT Year	County	No.
14557	1 Stidham, Frank R. 28		24	M	1/8	1896	Tobucksy	11255
16202	2 " , Pearl	Dau	7	F	1/16	"	"	11256
	3	ENROLLMENT						
	4	OF NOS. ~~1~~ HEREON APPROVED BY THE SECRETARY						
	5	OF INTERIOR May 20, 1903						
	6							
	7	~~See Pearl Stidham on C.C. Roll page 290 #11256 - can she be enrolled?~~						
	8	see testimony of Maria J. Aday Dec. 24, 1902						
	9	Affid as to amount of Choctaw blood filed Oct 18, 1902						
	10							
	11	No2 transferred from Choctaw card No D-995 Feby 12-1907 -						
	12	see decision of same date.						
	13 #2	For child of No1 see N.B. (March 3, 1905) #1108						
	14 Granted Feb. 12, 1907							
	15	ENROLLMENT OF NOS. 2 HEREON						
	16	APPROVED BY THE SECRETARY OF INTERIOR Mar. 4-1907						
	17							

TRIBAL ENROLLMENT OF PARENTS

	Name of Father	Year	County	Name of Mother	Year	County
1	Henry Stidham	Dead	Non citizen	Jennie Ady	1896	Sugar Loaf
2	No 1			Pearlee Baker		non citz
3						
4						
5						
6						
7						
8						
9						
10						
11						
12						
13						
14					Date of Application for Enrollment.	Mar. 21/99
15						
16					No.2 enrolled Dec. 24, 1902	
17	P.O. Berwyn I.T. 8/14/05					

166

Choctaw By Blood Enrollment Cards 1898-1914

RESIDENCE: Chickasaw Nation ~~COUNTY.~~
POST OFFICE: Fitzhugh, Ind. Ter.

Choctaw Nation

Choctaw Roll (Not Including Freedmen)

CARD NO.
FIELD NO. 467

Dawes' Roll No.	NAME	Relationship to Person First Named	AGE	SEX	BLOOD	TRIBAL ENROLLMENT Year	County	No.
I.W.887	1 Steward, Samuel P ㊴	First Named	36	M	I.W.	1896	Tobucksy	15039
887	2 " , Vicey	Wife	34	F	3/4	1896	"	11302
888	3 " , Carrie B.	Dau	3	"	3/8	1896	"	11303
VOID.	4 " , ~~Robert~~	~~Son~~	~~1~~	~~M~~	~~3/8~~			
889	5 Nail, Saphronia E ¹²	StepDau	8	F	3/4	1896	Tobucksy	9604
890	6 Steward, Robert Lee ²	Son	11mo	M	3/8			
891	7 " , Benjamin Layfett	Son	5m	M	3/8			
	8							
	9	ENROLLMENT						
	10	OF NOS. 2,3,5,6 and 7 HEREON APPROVED BY THE SECRETARY						
	11	OF INTERIOR DEC 12 1902						
	12							
	13							
	14	ENROLLMENT OF NOS. 1 HEREON						
	15	APPROVED BY THE SECRETARY						
	16	OF INTERIOR AUG 3 1904						
	17							

TRIBAL ENROLLMENT OF PARENTS

	Name of Father	Year	County	Name of Mother	Year	County
1	Jessie Steward	Dead	Non-citizen	Caroline Steward	Dead	Non citizen
2	Solomon Smith	"	Choctaw roll	Siney Smith	"	
3	No 1			No 2		
4	~~No 1~~			~~No 2~~		
5	Joe Nail	Dead	Tobucksy	No 2		
6	No 1			No 2		
7	No 1			No 2		
8						
9	No4 Affidavit as to birth to be supplied.					
10	For child of Nos. 1&2 see N.B. (Apr 26, 1906) Card No. 108.					
11	~~No1 on 1896 roll as Samane P. Stewart~~					
12	No5 on Choctaw roll as Sophony Nail.					
13	No.7 Enrolled February 4, 1901.					
14	Nº5 is duplication of Nº1 on Choctaw card 4890		No.6 Proof of birth filed Nov. 18-1902			#1 to 5
15	For child of Nos 1&2 see NB (Mar 3-1905) Card No 27.			Date of Application for Enrollment.		
16				Mar 21/99		
17				Nº6 April 27/99		

167

Choctaw By Blood Enrollment Cards 1898-1914

Dawes' Roll No.	NAME	Relationship to Person First Named	AGE	SEX	BLOOD	TRIBAL ENROLLMENT Year	County	No.
892	1 Wachubbe, Willie		40	M	Full	1893	Kiamitia	#863
	2							
	3 ENROLLMENT							
	4 OF NOS. 1 HEREON APPROVED BY THE SECRETARY							
	5 OF INTERIOR Dec 12 1902							
	6							
	7							
	8							
	9 On Kiamitia 1893 Pay roll (Choctaw Pay Roll No4), Page 105 No 863 as Willie							
	10 Wechubbie Chickasaw							
	11 Husband of Rhoda Wachubbe ^Card No. 1337							
	12							
	13							
	14							
	15							
	16							
	17							

TRIBAL ENROLLMENT OF PARENTS

	Name of Father	Year	County	Name of Mother	Year	County
1	Wachubbe	Dead	Choctaw Roll	Vicey Wachubbe	Dead	Choctaw roll
2						
3						
4						
5						
6						
7						
8						
9						
10						
11						
12						
13						
14						Date of Application for Enrollment.
15						Mar 21/99
16						
17						

168

Choctaw By Blood Enrollment Cards 1898-1914

RESIDENCE: Chickasaw Nation ~~COUNTY~~. **Choctaw Nation** Choctaw Roll CARD No.
POST OFFICE: Mill Creek, Ind. Ter. *(Not Including Freedmen)* FIELD No. 469

Dawes' Roll No.	NAME	Relationship to Person First Named	AGE	SEX	BLOOD	TRIBAL ENROLLMENT		
						Year	County	No.
IW 888	1 Keltner, William H.H. 48	First Named	44	M	I.W.			
893	2 " , Mattie A. 26	Wife	22	F	3/8	1893	Sugar Loaf	#63
894	3 " , Sylvester G. 3	Son	3mo	M	3/16			
895	4 " , Neroli 1	Dau	2wks	F	3/16			
	5							
	6 ENROLLMENT							
	7 OF NOS. 2, 3 and 4 HEREON APPROVED BY THE SECRETARY							
	8 OF INTERIOR DEC 12 1902							
	9							
	10							
	11							
	12							
	13							
	14 ENROLLMENT							
	15 OF NOS. 1 HEREON APPROVED BY THE SECRETARY							
	16 OF INTERIOR AUG 3 1904							
	17							

TRIBAL ENROLLMENT OF PARENTS

	Name of Father	Year	County	Name of Mother	Year	County
1	J.C.C. Keltner		Non citizen	M.E.E. Keltner	Dead	Non citizen
2	Buckner Burns		white man	Isabel Burns	"	Sugar Loaf
3	No 1			No 2		
4	No 1			No 2		
5						
6	No2 on 1893 Sugar Loaf Pay Roll, Page 7, No. 63, as M.A. Burns					
7	No.4 Born Oct. 31, 1901; Enrolled Nov. 13, 1901					
8	For child of Nos 1&2, see N.B. (Apr. 26, 1906) Card No. 147					
9	" " " " " " (Mar 3 1905) " No 22.					
10						
11						
12						
13						
14					Date of Application for Enrollment.	
15					Mar 22/99	
16				No3 enrolled Oct. 6/99		
17	Leon I.T.					

Choctaw By Blood Enrollment Cards 1898-1914

RESIDENCE: Eagle   COUNTY.   **Choctaw Nation**   **Choctaw Roll**   CARD No.
POST OFFICE: Eagletown, Ind. Ter.   *(Not Including Freedmen)*   FIELD No.   470

Dawes' Roll No.	NAME	Relationship to Person First Named	AGE	SEX	BLOOD	TRIBAL ENROLLMENT		
						Year	County	No.
896	1 Howell, Calvin ^59		56	M	1/4	1896	Eagle	5610
	2							
	3	ENROLLMENT						
	4	OF NOS. 1 HEREON APPROVED BY THE SECRETARY						
	5	OF INTERIOR DEC 12 1902						
	6							
	7							
	8							
	9	No 1 is husband of Leuvina[sic] Hudson on Choctaw card #732						
	10	Evidence filed 12/10/02						
	11							
	12							
	13							
	14							
	15							
	16							
	17							

TRIBAL ENROLLMENT OF PARENTS

	Name of Father	Year	County	Name of Mother	Year	County
1	Calvin Howell	Dead	Non Citz.	Rhoda Howell	1896	Choc residing in Chick Nation
2						
3						
4						
5						
6						
7						
8						
9						
10						
11						
12						
13						
14						
15						
16				Date of Application for Enrollment		April 18/99
17	Wapanucka 1/19/03					

170

Choctaw By Blood Enrollment Cards 1898-1914

RESIDENCE: Red River COUNTY. **Choctaw Nation** Choctaw Roll CARD NO.
POST OFFICE: Shawneetown, Ind. Ter. *(Not Including Freedmen)* FIELD NO. **481**

Dawes' Roll No.	NAME	Relationship to Person First Named	AGE	SEX	BLOOD	TRIBAL ENROLLMENT Year	County	No.
897	1 Taylor, John 59	First Named	56	M	Full	1896	Red River	12257
898	2 " Catherine 39	Wife	36	F	"	1896	" "	12258
899	3 " Mary 5	Dau	2	"	"	1896	" "	12295
900	4 " Joseph 3	Son	1mo	M	"			
	5							
	6 ENROLLMENT							
	7 OF NOS. 1, 2, 3 and 4 HEREON APPROVED BY THE SECRETARY							
	8 OF INTERIOR DEC 12 1902							
	9							
	10							
	11 No3 Affidavit of birth to be supplied Recd May 2/99							
	12 Nº1 identified from 1893 pay roll Red River County page 74 #649							
	13 For child of No1 see NB (March 3 1905) #938							
	14							
	15							
	16							
	17							

TRIBAL ENROLLMENT OF PARENTS

	Name of Father	Year	County	Name of Mother	Year	County
1	Wa-ha-la	Dead	Red River	Fannie Taylor	Dead	Red River
2	Simon Clay	"	" "	Betsey Clay	1896	" "
3	No 1			No 2		
4	No 1			No 2		
5						
6						
7						
8						
9						
10						
11						
12						
13						
14						
15					No4 enrolled Nov 24/99	
16				Date of Application for Enrollment.	April 18/99	
17	P.O. Idabel IT 4/10/05				1 to 3	

171

Choctaw By Blood Enrollment Cards 1898-1914

RESIDENCE: Red River   COUNTY. **Choctaw Nation**   **Choctaw Roll**   CARD No.
POST OFFICE: Shawneetown, Ind. Ter.   *(Not Including Freedmen)*   FIELD No. **472**

Dawes' Roll No.	NAME	Relationship to Person First Named	AGE	SEX	BLOOD	TRIBAL ENROLLMENT		
						Year	County	No.
901	₁ Taylor, Jonas ²⁸	First Named	25	M	Full	1896	Red River	12260
902	₂ "　Johnson ⁹	Nephew	6	"	"	1896	"　　"	12261
	3							
	4	ENROLLMENT OF NOS. 1 and 2 HEREON						
	5	APPROVED BY THE SECRETARY OF INTERIOR Dec 12 1902						
	6							
	7							
	8							
	9							
	10	No1 has been appointed guardian of No2 by the Court.						
	11	No1 is now husband of Betsy Clay on Choctaw card #478; evidence						
	12	of marriage filed December 3, 1902.						
	13							
	14							
	15							
	16							
	17							

TRIBAL ENROLLMENT OF PARENTS						
Name of Father	Year	County	Name of Mother	Year	County	
₁ John Taylor	1896	Red River	Sallie Taylor	Dead	Red River	
₂ Williams Willie	1896	"　　"	Francis Willie	"	"　　"	
3						
4						
5						
6						
7						
8						
9						
10						
11						
12						
13						
14						
15						
16			Date of Application for Enrollment		April 18/99	
17						

172

Choctaw By Blood Enrollment Cards 1898-1914

RESIDENCE: Towson COUNTY. **Choctaw Nation** Choctaw Roll CARD NO.
POST OFFICE: Garvin, Ind. Ter. (Not Including Freedmen) FIELD NO. **473**

Dawes' Roll No.	NAME	Relationship to Person First Named	AGE	SEX	BLOOD	TRIBAL ENROLLMENT		
						Year	County	No.
903	1 Morrison, Charles W 70	Named	67	M	Full	1896	Towson	8602
904	2 " Sarah 41	Wife	42	F	"	1896	"	8603
	3							
	4	ENROLLMENT OF NOS. 1 and 2 HEREON						
	5	APPROVED BY THE SECRETARY OF INTERIOR Dec 12 1902						
	6							
	7							
	8							
	9							
	10	No 1 on 1896 roll as Chas. W. Morrison						
	11							
	12							
	13							
	14							
	15							
	16							
	17							

TRIBAL ENROLLMENT OF PARENTS

	Name of Father	Year	County	Name of Mother	Year	County
1	Watkin	Dead	Red River	le-ma-huna	Dead	Red River
2	A-cha-fa-ta-by	"	Gaines		"	Gaines
3						
4						
5						
6						
7						
8						
9						
10						
11						
12						
13						
14						
15						
16				Date of Application for Enrollment.		April 18/99
17						

Choctaw By Blood Enrollment Cards 1898-1914

RESIDENCE: Red River COUNTY.
POST OFFICE: Kully Tuklo[sic], Ind. Ter. **Choctaw Nation**

Choctaw Roll CARD NO.
(Not Including Freedmen) FIELD NO. **474**

Dawes' Roll No.	NAME	Relationship to Person First Named	AGE	SEX	BLOOD	TRIBAL ENROLLMENT		
						Year	County	No.
905	1 Lemon, John 43	First Named	40	M	Full	1896	Red River	8044
906	2 " , Salina 39	wife	36	F	"	1896	" "	8045
907	3 " , Sarah 13	dau	10	"	"	1896	" "	8046
908	4 " , Hudson 10	son	7	M	"	1896	" "	8047
909	5 " , Adaline 4	dau	6mo	dau	"			
	6							
	7	ENROLLMENT						
	8	OF NOS. 1,2,3,4 and 5 HEREON APPROVED BY THE SECRETARY						
	9	OF INTERIOR Dec 12 1902						
	10	No5 Affidavit of birth to be supplied - Recd. May 9/99						
	11	No2 on 1896 roll as Selina Lemmon						
	12	Sirnamen[sic] on 1896 roll as Lemmon						
	13							
	14							
	15							
	16							
	17							

TRIBAL ENROLLMENT OF PARENTS

	Name of Father	Year	County	Name of Mother	Year	County
1	Little John	dead	Red River	Falina John	Dead	Red River
2	Robison Jimahaka	"	" "	Amy Robison	1896	" "
3	No.1			No.2		
4	No.1			No.2		
5	No.1			No.2		
6						
7						
8						
9						
10						
11	No 1 now husband of Ida Fowler on Choc. card 5637 evidence of marriage filed Dec. 11, 1902.					
12	This notation is in error. See letter of Ida Lemon of[sic]					
13	in which she states that her husband John R. Lemon is a non citizen.					
14						Date of Application for Enrollment.
15						
16	P.O. Leon I.T. 4/5/05					April 18/99
17	Nelson I.T.					

174

Choctaw By Blood Enrollment Cards 1898-1914

RESIDENCE: Red River COUNTY. **Choctaw Nation** **Choctaw Roll** CARD No.
POST OFFICE: Shawneetown, Ind. Ter. *(Not Including Freedmen)* FIELD No. 475

Dawes' Roll No.	NAME		Relationship to Person First Named	AGE	SEX	BLOOD	TRIBAL ENROLLMENT		
							Year	County	No.
910	1 Taylor, Alex	58	First Named	55	M	Full	1896	Red River	12304
911	2 " Yimmihona	63	wife	60	F	"	1896	" "	P. R 625
~~DEAD~~	3 " Samuel ~~DEAD~~		~~son~~	~~20~~	~~M~~	~~"~~	~~1896~~	~~" "~~	~~12305~~
912	4 " Sibby	19	dau	16	F	"	1896	" "	12306
913	5 " Salina	15	"	12	"	"	1896	" "	12307
914	6 " Emma	12	"	9	"	"	1896	" "	12308
915	7 " David	11	son	8	M	"	1896	" "	12309
916	8 " Robert	7	"	4	"	"	1896	" "	12310
	9	ENROLLMENT							
	10	OF NOS. 1,2,4,5,6,7 and 8 HEREON							
	11	APPROVED BY THE SECRETARY OF INTERIOR Dec 12 1902							
	12								
	13								
	14	No 3 hereon dismissed under order							
	15	of the Commission to the Five Civilized Tribes of March 31, 1905							
	16								
	17								

TRIBAL ENROLLMENT OF PARENTS

	Name of Father	Year	County	Name of Mother	Year	County
1	Ima-ha-la	Dead	Red River	Fannie Taylor	dead	Red River
2	Bob Shaw	"	" "	Hul-ba-tu-na	"	" "
3	~~No 1~~			~~No 2~~		
4	No 1			No 2		
5	No 1			No 2		
6	No 1			No 2		
7	No 1			No 2		
8	No 1			No 2		
9						
10			No2 on 1893 Pay roll as Yim-mi-ttahona Page 72.			
11			No4 " 1896 roll as Zibby			
12			No3 died January 19, 1901 Evidence of death filed March 23, 1901.			
13			No2 also on 1896 Choctaw census roll page 373 #14230 as Yimmehona			
14						
15					Date of Application for Enrollment.	
16					April 18/99	
17						

Choctaw By Blood Enrollment Cards 1898-1914

RESIDENCE: Red River COUNTY.
POST OFFICE: Shawneetown, Ind. Ter.
Choctaw Nation
Choctaw Roll
(Not Including Freedmen)
CARD NO.
FIELD NO. **476**

Dawes' Roll No.	NAME	Relationship to Person First Named	AGE	SEX	BLOOD	TRIBAL ENROLLMENT		
						Year	County	No.
917	1 Peter, Sina 25	First Named	22	F	Full	1896	Red River	10415
918	2 " Hodges 8	son	5	M	"	1896	" "	10416
	3							
	4	ENROLLMENT						
	5	OF NOS. 1 and 2 HEREON APPROVED BY THE SECRETARY						
	6	OF INTERIOR Dec 12, 1902						
	7							
	8							
	9	No2 is an illegitimate child by full blood Choctaw name could not						
	10	be ascertained.						
	11							
	12							
	13							
	14							
	15							
	16							
	17							

TRIBAL ENROLLMENT OF PARENTS

	Name of Father	Year	County	Name of Mother	Year	County
1	Peter	dead	Red River	Yimmihona	1896	Red River
2				No 1		
3						
4						
5						
6						
7						
8						
9						
10						
11						
12						
13						
14						
15				Date of Application for Enrollment. April 18/99		
16						
17						

176

Choctaw By Blood Enrollment Cards 1898-1914

DIED PRIOR TO SEPTEMBER 25, 1902

RESIDENCE: Neshoba[sic] COUNTY.
POST OFFICE: Alikchi, Ind. Ter.

Choctaw Nation

Choctaw Roll
(Not Including Freedmen)

CARD NO.
FIELD NO. **477**

Dawes' Roll No.	NAME	Relationship to Person First Named	AGE	SEX	BLOOD	TRIBAL ENROLLMENT Year	County	No.
919	₁ Watson, Thomas	First Named	39	M	full	1896	Nashoba	13255
~~920~~	₂ " ~~Lizzie~~	~~wife~~	~~29~~	~~F~~	"	~~1896~~	"	~~13256~~
921	₃ " George	son	16	M	"	1896	"	13257
922	₄ " Sam	"	14	"	"	1896	"	13258
923	₅ " Silas	"	12	"	"	1896	"	13259
924	₆ " Insie	dau	4	F	"	1896	"	13263
925	₇ " Caston	son	2	M	"			
926	₈ " Agnes	dau	15mo	F	"			
	₉							
	₁₀	ENROLLMENT OF NOS.1,2,3,4,5,6,7 and 8 HEREON						
	₁₁	APPROVED BY THE SECRETARY OF INTERIOR Dec 12 1902						
	₁₂							
	₁₃							
	₁₄	No2 died July 12-1900: Enrollment cancelled by Department July 8-1904						
	₁₅	No8 Enrolled July 25, 1901						
	₁₆							
	₁₇							

TRIBAL ENROLLMENT OF PARENTS

Name of Father	Year	County	Name of Mother	Year	County
₁ George Watson	Dead	Nashoba	Nancy Watson	Dead	Nasahoba
₂ ~~Robert James~~	"	"	~~Martha James~~	1896	"
₃ No 1			No 2		
₄ No 1			No 2		
₅ No 1			No 2		
₆ No 1			No 2		
₇ No 1			No 2		
₈ No 1			No 2		
₉					
₁₀ No1 is now husband of Margaret W. Jefferson on Choctaw card #497					
₁₁ No2 died July 12, 1900, proof of death filed Jany 28, 1903					
₁₂ For child of No.4 see N.B. (March 3, 1905) #906					
₁₃					#1 to 7
₁₄					Date of Application for Enrollment.
₁₅					April 18/99
₁₆					
₁₇ P.O. Smithville, I.T. 9/5/06					

Choctaw By Blood Enrollment Cards 1898-1914

RESIDENCE: Red River COUNTY. **Choctaw Nation** **Choctaw Roll** CARD No.
POST OFFICE: Shawneetown, Ind. Ter *(Not Including Freedmen)* FIELD No. 478

Dawes' Roll No.	NAME	Relationship to Person First Named	AGE	SEX	BLOOD	TRIBAL ENROLLMENT		
						Year	County	No.
927	1 Clay, Simpson 76	First Named	73	M	Full	1896	Red River	2659
928	2 " Wysa 43	Dau	40	F	"	1896	" "	2660
929	3 " Lizzie 41	"	38	"	"	1896	" "	2661
930	4 " Betsy 39	"	36	"	"	1896	" "	2662
	5							
	6	ENROLLMENT						
	7	OF NOS. 1,2,3 and 4 HEREON APPROVED BY THE SECRETARY						
	8	OF INTERIOR DEC 12 1902						
	9							
	10							
	11							
	12	No4 is now wife of Jonas Taylor on Choctaw card #472						
	13	Evidence of marriage filed December 3, 1902.						
	14							
	15							
	16							
	17							

TRIBAL ENROLLMENT OF PARENTS

	Name of Father	Year	County	Name of Mother	Year	County
1	Ka-ych-ta-by	Dead	Red River	A-cha-ya-huna	Dead	Red River
2	No 1			La-pu-na	"	" "
3	No 1			La-pu-na	"	" "
4	No 1			La-pu-na	"	" "
5						
6						
7						
8						
9						
10						
11						
12						
13						
14						
15						
16				Date of Application for Enrollment.		April 18/99
17						

178

Choctaw By Blood Enrollment Cards 1898-1914

RESIDENCE: Red River COUNTY.
POST OFFICE: Shawneetown, Ind. Ter.

Choctaw Nation

Choctaw Roll
(Not Including Freedmen)

CARD NO.
FIELD NO. **479**

Dawes' Roll No.	NAME		Relationship to Person First Named	AGE	SEX	BLOOD	TRIBAL ENROLLMENT		
							Year	County	No.
931	1 Lewis, Lucy	63	First Named	60	F	Full	1896	Red River	8026
932	2 " David	21	son	18	M	"	1896	" "	8029
933	3 " James	16	"	13	"	"	1896	" "	8030
934	4 " James[sic]	14	"	11	"	"	1896	" "	8031
935	5 " Wattis	12	"	9	"	"	1896	" "	8032
936	6 " Listie	10	dau	7	F	"	1896	" "	8033
✱16203	7 " Kitsy		dau of No.3	1	F	"			
	8								
	9	ENROLLMENT							
	10	OF NOS. 1,2,3,4,5 and 6 HEREON APPROVED BY THE SECRETARY							
	11	OF INTERIOR Dec 12 1902							
	12								
	13	ENROLLMENT							
	14	OF NOS. ~~~ 7 ~~~ HEREON APPROVED BY THE SECRETARY							
	15	OF INTERIOR Mar 4-1907							
	16								
	17								

TRIBAL ENROLLMENT OF PARENTS

	Name of Father	Year	County	Name of Mother	Year	County
1	James Homby	dead	Red River	Clu-im-yo-ra	dead	Bok Fuklo
2	Lewis	"	" "	No.1		
3	"	"	" "	No.1		
4	"	"	" "	No.1		
5	"	"	" "	No.1		
6	"	"	" "	No.1		
7	No 3			Isabelle Ishcomer		
8						
9	No7 transferred from Choctaw N.B. #1531(Act of Mch 3, 1905) February 19, 19067.					
10	See decision of that date					
11	For child of No.2 see N.B. (March 3, 1905) #897					
12						
13	2-11-30✱ - "Double enrollment of No. 2470, not entitled to land					
14	or money under this number " (Letter #516-30)					
15					1/24/30	#1 to 6 inc
16					Date of Application for Enrollment.	
17						April 18/99

179

Choctaw By Blood Enrollment Cards 1898-1914

RESIDENCE: Red River COUNTY.								
POST OFFICE: Shawneetown, Ind. Ter.	**Choctaw Nation**				**Choctaw Roll** *(Not Including Freedmen)*		CARD NO. FIELD NO.	**480**

Dawes' Roll No.	NAME		Relationship to Person First Named	AGE	SEX	BLOOD	TRIBAL ENROLLMENT		
							Year	County	No.
937	1 Parker, Dixon	33	First Named	30	M	full	1896	Red River	10411
938	2 " Betsy	32	wife	29	F	"	1896	" "	10412
14558	3 " Simeon	6	son	2	M	"			
939	4 " Hafin	1	dau	2mo	F	"			
	5	ENROLLMENT							
	6	OF NOS. 1, 2 and 4 HEREON APPROVED BY THE SECRETARY							
	7	OF INTERIOR Dec 12 1904							
	8								
	9								
	10								
	11								
	12								
	13	ENROLLMENT OF NOS. 3 HEREON APPROVED BY THE SECRETARY OF INTERIOR May 20 1903							
	14								
	15								
	16								
	17								

TRIBAL ENROLLMENT OF PARENTS						
Name of Father	Year	County	Name of Mother	Year	County	
1 James Parker	dead	Bok Fuklo	Tibbie Parker	dead	Bob Fuklo	
2 Lewis	"	Red River	Lucy Lewis	1896	Red River	
3 No 1			No 2			
4 No 1			No 2			
5						
6		No3 affidavit as to birth to be supplied - Recd May 2/99				
7		No2 on 1896 roll as Betsey Parker				
8		No 4 Born Sept 14, 1901, Enrolled Nov. 7, 1901				
9		No3 Proof of birth received and filed Of. 13, 1902				
10						
11		For child of Nos 1&2 see N.B. (Apr 20-06) card #649				
12						
13					#1 to 3 inc	
14					Date of Application for Enrollment.	
15						
16					April 18/99	
17						

180

Choctaw By Blood Enrollment Cards 1898-1914

RESIDENCE: Red River COUNTY.	**Choctaw Nation**	Choctaw Roll (Not Including Freedmen)	CARD NO.
POST OFFICE: Shawneetown, I.T.			FIELD NO. 481

Dawes' Roll No.	NAME	Relationship to Person First Named	AGE	SEX	BLOOD	TRIBAL ENROLLMENT		
						Year	County	No.
940	1 Lewis, Wilson 28	First Named	25	M	Full	1896	Red River	8027
941	2 " Cissy 26	Wife	23	F	"	1896	" "	8028
	3							
	4 ENROLLMENT OF NOS. 1 and 2 HEREON							
	5 APPROVED BY THE SECRETARY OF INTERIOR DEC 12 1902							
	6							
	7							
	8							
	9							
	10							
	11							
	12							
	13							
	14							
	15							
	16							
	17							

TRIBAL ENROLLMENT OF PARENTS

	Name of Father	Year	County	Name of Mother	Year	County
1	Lewis	Dead	Red River	Lucy Lewis	1896	Red River
2	Sampson Williams	1896	" "	Betsy Williams	Dead	" "
3						
4						
5						
6						
7						
8						
9						
10						
11						
12						
13						
14				Date of Application for Enrollment.		
15						
16				April 18/99		
17						

Choctaw By Blood Enrollment Cards 1898-1914

RESIDENCE: Red River   COUNTY.   **Choctaw Nation**   Choctaw Roll   CARD NO.
POST OFFICE: Harris, Ind. Ter.   (Not Including Freedmen)   FIELD NO. 482

Dawes' Roll No.	NAME	Relationship to Person First Named	AGE	SEX	BLOOD	TRIBAL ENROLLMENT Year	County	No.
942	1 Robinson, Betsy DIED PRIOR TO SEPTEMBER 25, 1902		65	F	Full	1896	Red River	10811
	2							
	3							
	4							
	5							
	6							
	7							
	8							
	9							
	10							
	11							
	12							
	13							
	14							
	15							
	16							
	17							

ENROLLMENT
OF NOS. 1 HEREON
APPROVED BY THE SECRETARY
OF INTERIOR DEC 12 1902

TRIBAL ENROLLMENT OF PARENTS

	Name of Father	Year	County	Name of Mother	Year	County
1	Moses Frazier	Dead	Red River	A-tuk-la-huna	Dead	Red River
2						
3						
4						
5						
6						
7						
8						
9						
10						
11						
12						
13						
14						
15						
16				Date of Application for Enrollment.	April 18/99	
17						

Choctaw By Blood Enrollment Cards 1898-1914

RESIDENCE: Red River COUNTY. **Choctaw Nation** Choctaw Roll CARD NO.
POST OFFICE: Kullituklo, Ind. Ter. *(Not Including Freedmen)* FIELD NO. 483

Dawes' Roll No.	NAME	Relationship to Person First Named	AGE	SEX	BLOOD	TRIBAL ENROLLMENT		
						Year	County	No.
943	1 Robinson, Amy 73		70	F	Full	1896	Red River	10810
	2							
	3	ENROLLMENT						
	4	OF NOS. 1 HEREON APPROVED BY THE SECRETARY						
	5	OF INTERIOR DEC 12 1902						
	6							
	7							
	8							
	9							
	10							
	11							
	12							
	13							
	14							
	15							
	16							
	17							

TRIBAL ENROLLMENT OF PARENTS

	Name of Father	Year	County	Name of Mother	Year	County
1	Moses Frazier	Dead	Red River	A-tuk-la-huna	Dead	Red River
2						
3						
4						
5						
6						
7						
8						
9						
10						
11						
12						
13						
14				Date of Application for Enrollment.		
15						
16				April 18/99		
17						

183

Choctaw By Blood Enrollment Cards 1898-1914

<table>
<tr><td>RESIDENCE:</td><td>Neshoba</td><td>COUNTY.</td><td rowspan="2">Choctaw Nation</td><td>Choctaw Roll</td><td>CARD NO.</td></tr>
<tr><td>POST OFFICE:</td><td>Alikchi, Ind. Ter.</td><td></td><td>(Not Including Freedmen)</td><td>FIELD NO. 484</td></tr>
</table>

Dawes' Roll No.	NAME	Relationship to Person First Named	AGE	SEX	BLOOD	TRIBAL ENROLLMENT Year	County	No.
944	1 Jefferson, Hickson 48	First Named	45	M	Full	1896	Neshoba	6866
945	2 " Adeline 43	Wife	40	F	"	1896	"	6867
946	3 " Samuel 18	Son	15	M	"	1896	"	6868
947	4 " Alliston 16	"	13	"	"	1896	"	6869
948	5 " Lenie 13	Dau	10	F	"	1896	"	6870
949	6 " Simeon 11	Son	8	M	"	1896	"	6871
950	7 " Saikon 9	"	6	"	"	1896	"	6872
	8							
	9	ENROLLMENT OF NOS. 1,2,3,4,5,6 and 7 HEREON						
	10	APPROVED BY THE SECRETARY OF INTERIOR Dec. 12 1902						
	11							
	12							
	13	No 2 on 1896 roll as Adaline Jefferson.						
	14							
	15							
	16							
	17							

TRIBAL ENROLLMENT OF PARENTS

Name of Father	Year	County	Name of Mother	Year	County
1 John Sofers	Dead	Neshoba	Me-che-huna	Dead	Neshoba
2 Ok-lo-tom-by	"	"	Ma-ka-haw-tema	"	"
3 No 1			No 2		
4 No 1			No 2		
5 No 1			No 2		
6 No 1			No 2		
7 No 1			No 2		
8					
9					
10 For child of No5 see N.B. (Apr. 26-06) card #634					
11 " " " No3 " " (Mar 3-05) " #940					
12 " " " " " (Apr. 26-06) " #637				Date of Application for Enrollment.	
13 " " " Nos1&2 " (Mar 3-05) " #941					
14					
15				April 18/99	
16					
17 P.O. Bethel I.T. 4/6/05					

Choctaw By Blood Enrollment Cards 1898-1914

RESIDENCE: Neshoba COUNTY. **Choctaw Nation** Choctaw Roll *(Not Including Freedmen)* CARD NO.
POST OFFICE: Alikchi, Ind. Ter FIELD NO. **485**

Dawes' Roll No.	NAME	Relationship to Person First Named	AGE	SEX	BLOOD	TRIBAL ENROLLMENT		
						Year	County	No.
951	1 Wade, Kosom *DIED PRIOR TO SEPTEMBER 25, 1902*		52	M	Full	1896	Neshoba	13332
952	2 " Susanna 48	wife	45	F	"	1896	"	13333
953	3 " Maggie 9	dau	6	"	"	1896	"	13334
954	4 " Mistwright 6	son	3	M	"	1896	"	13335
955	5 " Fana *DIED PRIOR TO SEPTEMBER 25, 1902*	dau	6mo	F	"			
	6							
	7 ENROLLMENT							
	8 OF NOS. 1,2,3,4 and 5 HEREON APPROVED BY THE SECRETARY							
	9 OF INTERIOR Dec. 12, 1902							
	10							
	11 No1 died March 7-1901; No5 died July 16-1900 Enrollment cancelled by Department							
	12 July 8-1904							
	13 No4 on roll as Muster W. Wade							
	14 No5 Affidavit of birth to be supplied; Recd April 21/99							
	15							
	16							
	17							

TRIBAL ENROLLMENT OF PARENTS

	Name of Father	Year	County	Name of Mother	Year	County
1	We-ke-te-bee	Dead	Neshoba	Amy	Dead	Neshoba
2	Charles Noah	"	"	E-ma-tona	"	"
3	No 1			No 2		
4	No 1			No 2		
5	No 1			No 2		
6						
7						
8						
9						
10						
11						
12						
13						
14						
15	No1 died March 7, 1901, proof of death filed Dec. 13, 1902				Date of Application for Enrollment.	
16	No5 " July 16, 1900 " " " " " " "				April 18/99	
17						

185

Choctaw By Blood Enrollment Cards 1898-1914

RESIDENCE: Neshoba COUNTY.
POST OFFICE: Smithville, Ind. Ter
Choctaw Nation
Choctaw Roll (Not Including Freedmen)
CARD NO.
FIELD NO. **486**

Dawes' Roll No.	NAME	Relationship to Person First Named	AGE	SEX	BLOOD	TRIBAL ENROLLMENT Year	County	No.
DEAD	1 Watson, Washington DEAD		33	M	Full	1896	Neshoba	13244
956	2 Johnson, Frances 31	wife	28	F	"	1896	Red River	11439
957	3 Watson, Borris 15	dau	12	"	"	1896	Neshoba	13246
958	4 " Jincy 13	"	10	"	"	1896	"	13247
959	5 " Ann 7	"	7	"	"	1896	"	13249
960	6 Johnson, Cora 1	dau of No 2	3mo	"	"			
	7							
	8							
	9	ENROLLMENT OF NOS. 2,3,4,5 and 6 HEREON APPROVED BY THE SECRETARY						
	10	OF INTERIOR Dec. 12 1902						
	11	No. 1 hereon dismissed under order of						
	12	the Commission to the Five Civilized Tribes of March 31, 1905.						
	13	No.5 Died prior to September 25, 1902						
	14	not entitled to land or money. See						
	15	Indian office letter of July 15, 1910.						
	16	D.C. File #1012-1910						
	17							

TRIBAL ENROLLMENT OF PARENTS

Name of Father	Year	County	Name of Mother	Year	County
1 George Watson	dead	Neshoba	Nancy Watson	dead	Neshoba
2	"	Red River		"	Red River
3 No 1			Betsy Watson	"	" "
4 No 1			" "	"	" "
5 No 1			" "	"	" "
6 Elam J Johnson	1896	Neshoba	No 2		
7					
8					
9	No1 died April 23,1899; proof of death filed December 15, 1902				
10	No2 on 1896 roll as Frances Short				
11	No3 " 1896 " " Burris Watson				
	No5 " 1896 " " Annie "				
12	No1 was killed shortly after being enrolled				
13	No2 is now the wife of Elam J. Johnson on Choc. card #667, Nov. 29, 1901				
14	No6 born August 31, 1901; Enrolled Nov. 29, 1901				
15				Date of Application for Enrollment.	
16				April 18/99	
17					

Choctaw By Blood Enrollment Cards 1898-1914

RESIDENCE: Neshoba COUNTY. **Choctaw Nation** Choctaw Roll CARD NO.
POST OFFICE: Alikchi, Ind. Ter. *(Not Including Freedmen)* FIELD NO. 487

Dawes' Roll No.	NAME	Relationship to Person First Named	AGE	SEX	BLOOD	TRIBAL ENROLLMENT Year	County	No.
961	1 Watkins, Joseph	First Named	28	M	Full	1896	Neshoba	13366
962	2 " Eliza	Wife	20	F	"	1896	"	13367
~~963~~	~~DIED PRIOR TO SEPTEMBER 25, 1902~~ ~~Silvey~~	~~Dau~~	~~4~~	"	"	~~1896~~	"	~~13368~~
964	4 " Louisiana	"	6mos	"	"			
965	5 " Johnson	Son	2	M	"			
966	6 " Mealey	Dau	9mo	F	"			
	7							
	8	ENROLLMENT ~~OF NOS. 1,2,3,4,5 and 6~~ HEREON APPROVED BY THE SECRETARY OF INTERIOR DEC 12 1902						
	9							
	10							
	11							
	12	No4 – Affidavit of birth to be supplied – Recd April 19/99						
	13	No5 - " " " " " " " " 19/99						
	14	No6 Enrolled Aug 27 1901						
	15	N°3 Died Dec. 5, 1900. Proof of death filed Dec. 24, 1902						
	16							
	17							

TRIBAL ENROLLMENT OF PARENTS

	Name of Father	Year	County	Name of Mother	Year	County
1	Eastman Watkins	1896	Neshoba	Winey Watkins	1896	Neshoba
2	Joseph James	Dead	Cedar	Metsey[sic] James	1896	"
3	~~No 1~~			~~No 2~~		
4	No 1			No 2		
5	No 1			No 2		
6	No 1			No 2		
7						
8						
9						
10						
11						
12						
13	For child of Nos 1&2 see NB (Apr 26 06) Card #865					
14	" " " " " " " (Mar 3-05) " #1084					
15				Date of Application for Enrollment.		
16				April 18/99		
17						

Choctaw By Blood Enrollment Cards 1898-1914

RESIDENCE: Towson COUNTY.
POST OFFICE: Fowlerville, Ind. Ter.

Choctaw Nation

Choctaw Roll
(Not Including Freedmen)

CARD NO.
FIELD NO. 488

Dawes' Roll No.	NAME	Relationship to Person First Named	AGE	SEX	BLOOD	TRIBAL ENROLLMENT		
						Year	County	No.
967	1 Jones, Joseph 24		21	M	Full	1896	Kiamitia	7072
	2							
	3 ENROLLMENT							
	4 OF NOS. 1 HEREON APPROVED BY THE SECRETARY							
	5 OF INTERIOR Dec. 12 1902							
	6							
	7							
	8							
	9							
	10 On 1896 roll as Joseph G. Jones							
	11							
	12							
	13							
	14							
	15							
	16							
	17							

TRIBAL ENROLLMENT OF PARENTS

	Name of Father	Year	County	Name of Mother	Year	County
1	James Jones	1896	Nashoba	Rhodie Jones	Dead	Nashoba
2						
3						
4						
5						
6						
7						
8						
9						
10						
11						
12						
13						
14						
15						
16				Date of Application for Enrollment.		April 18/99
17						

188

Choctaw By Blood Enrollment Cards 1898-1914

RESIDENCE:	Nashoba	COUNTY.	**Choctaw Nation**			**Choctaw Roll** *(Not Including Freedmen)*		CARD NO.	
POST OFFICE:	Alikchi, I.T.							FIELD NO.	489

Dawes' Roll No.	NAME		Relationship to Person First Named	AGE	SEX	BLOOD	TRIBAL ENROLLMENT		
							Year	County	No.
968	1 Watkins, Eastman	66	First Named	63	M	Full	1896	Nashoba	13375
969	2 " Wynie	62	Wife	59	F	"	1896	"	13376
970	3 " Austin	11	G. Son	8	M	"	1896	"	13377
	4								
	5	ENROLLMENT OF NOS. 1 2 and 3 HEREON APPROVED BY THE SECRETARY OF INTERIOR DEC 12 1902							
	6								
	7								
	8								
	9								
	10	No3 on 1896 roll as Austen Watkins							
	11								
	12								
	13								
	14								
	15								
	16								
	17								

TRIBAL ENROLLMENT OF PARENTS

Name of Father	Year	County	Name of Mother	Year	County
1 To-sho-ya	Dead	Nashoba	Pi-sa-he-ma	Dead	Nashoba
2	"	Eagle		"	Eagle
3 Elum Watkins		Nashoba	Lisbet Watkins	"	Nashoba
4					
5					
6					
7					
8					
9					
10					
11					
12					
13					
14				Date of Application for Enrollment.	April 18/99
15					
16					
17					

Choctaw By Blood Enrollment Cards 1898-1914

RESIDENCE: Nashoba COUNTY. **Choctaw Nation** Choctaw Roll CARD NO.
POST OFFICE: Alikchi, Ind. Ter. *(Not Including Freedmen)* FIELD NO. 490

Dawes' Roll No.	NAME	Relationship to Person First Named	AGE	SEX	BLOOD	TRIBAL ENROLLMENT Year	County	No.
971	1 Samis, Lyman 32		29	M	Full	1896	Nashoba	11405
972	2 " Susan 28	Wife	25	F	"	1896	"	11406
973	3 " Frank 8	Son	5	M	"	1896	"	11407
974	4 " Annie 6	Dau	3	F	"	1896	"	11408
975	5 " Lyda 5	"	1	F	"			
976	6 " Noah 3	Son	19mo	M	"			
	7							
	8 ENROLLMENT							
	9 OF NOS. 1,2,3,4,5 and 6 HEREON APPROVED BY THE SECRETARY							
	10 OF INTERIOR DEC 12 1902							
	11							
	12							
	13 No4 on 1896 roll as Annie Samis							
	14 No5 – Affidavit of birth to be supplied. Rec'd Apr 21-1899							
	15 No1 on 1896 roll as Lymon Samis							
	No.6 Enrolled Aug 27, 1902.							
	16 For child of Nos 1&2 see NB (Apr 26-06) Card #729							
	17							

TRIBAL ENROLLMENT OF PARENTS

	Name of Father	Year	County	Name of Mother	Year	County
1	He-me-a-by	1896	Nashoba	Amy	Dead	Nashoba
2	Edmund LeFlore	1896	Cedar		"	Cedar
3	No 1			No 2		
4	No 1			No 2		
5	No 1			No 2		
6	No 1			No 2		
7						
8						
9						
10						
11						
12						
13						
14					#1 to 5	
15				Date of Application for Enrollment.		
16				April 18/99		
17	P.O. Noah I.T. 10/30/06					

190

Choctaw By Blood Enrollment Cards 1898-1914

RESIDENCE: Nashoba COUNTY. **Choctaw Nation** **Choctaw Roll** CARD NO.
POST OFFICE: Alikchi, Ind. Ter. *(Not Including Freedmen)* FIELD NO. **491**

Dawes' Roll No.	NAME		Relationship to Person First Named	AGE	SEX	BLOOD	TRIBAL ENROLLMENT		
							Year	County	No.
977	1 Noah, Wilmon	68	First Named	65	M	Full	1896	Nashoba	9690
978	2 " Salenna	59	Wife	56	F	"	1896	"	9691
989	3 " Marcus	22	Son	19	M	"	1896	"	9693
980	4 " Reed	20	"	17	"	"	1896	"	9694
981	5 " Agnes	13	Dau	10	F	"	1896	"	9695
	6								
	7	ENROLLMENT OF NOS. 1,2,3,4 and 5 HEREON APPROVED BY THE SECRETARY OF INTERIOR Dec 12 1902							
	8								
	9								
	10								
	11	No 3 on 1896 roll as Morgan Noah							
	12								
	13								
	14								
	15								
	16								
	17								

TRIBAL ENROLLMENT OF PARENTS

	Name of Father	Year	County	Name of Mother	Year	County
1	Nashoba Noah	Dead	Nashoba	Sophie Noah	Dead	Nashoba
2	Jack Battiest	1896	Cedar	Ema-to-na	"	"
3	No 1			No 2		
4	No 1			No 2		
5	No 1			No 2		
6						
7						
8						
9						
10						
11						
12						
13						
14						
15				Date of Application for Enrollment		
16				April 18/99		
17						

Choctaw By Blood Enrollment Cards 1898-1914

Choctaw Nation

Choctaw Roll (Not Including Freedmen)

CARD NO.
FIELD NO. 492

Dawes' Roll No.	NAME	Relationship to Person First Named	AGE	SEX	BLOOD	TRIBAL ENROLLMENT		
						Year	County	No.
982	1 Emeyabbi DIED PRIOR TO SEPTEMBER 25, 1902		76	M	Full	1896	Nashoba	3736
	2							
	3	ENROLLMENT						
	4	OF NOS. 1 HEREON APPROVED BY THE SECRETARY						
	5	OF INTERIOR DEC 12 1902						
	6							
	7							
	8	No1 died May 18, 1902; proof of death filed Dec 13, 1902						
	9							
	10							
	11							
	12							
	13							
	14							
	15							
	16							
	17							

TRIBAL ENROLLMENT OF PARENTS

	Name of Father	Year	County	Name of Mother	Year	County
1	Hak-lo-lambee	Dead	Nashoba		Dead	In Mississippi
2						
3						
4						
5						
6						
7						
8						
9						
10						
11						
12						
13						
14						
15						
16				Date of Application for Enrollment.		April 18/99
17						

Choctaw By Blood Enrollment Cards 1898-1914

RESIDENCE: Nashoba COUNTY.
POST OFFICE: Alikchi, Ind. Ter.

Choctaw Nation

Choctaw Roll (Not Including Freedmen)

CARD NO.
FIELD NO. **493**

Dawes' Roll No.	NAME		Relationship to Person First Named	AGE	SEX	BLOOD	TRIBAL ENROLLMENT		
							Year	County	No.
983	1 Noah, Newman	31	First Named	28	M	Full	1896	Nashoba	9696
984	2 " Sis	7	Dau	4	F	1/2	1896	"	9698
985	3 " William	6	Son	2	M	1/2			
986	4 " Binsey	4	Dau	3mo	F	1/2			
987	5 " Lila	1	Dau	2mo	F	1/2			
15974	6 " Emma	28	Wife	28	F	1/2	1896	Nashoba	9697
	7								
	8	ENROLLMENT OF NOS. 1,2,3,4 and 5 HEREON APPROVED BY THE SECRETARY							
	9	OF INTERIOR Dec 12 1902							
	10								
	11								
	12	ENROLLMENT							
	13	OF NOS. ~~~ 6 ~~~ HEREON APPROVED BY THE SECRETARY							
	14	OF INTERIOR June 16 1906							
	15								
	16								
	17								

TRIBAL ENROLLMENT OF PARENTS

	Name of Father	Year	County	Name of Mother	Year	County
1	Wilmon Noah	1896	Nashoba	Salama Noah	1896	Nashoba
2	No 1			Emma Noah		Non Citz
3	No 1			" "		" "
4	No 1			" "		" "
5	No 1			" "		" "
6	Tobias Windship	Dead	Choctaw	Mary Miashintube		Choctaw Roll LW.1504
7	No3 – Affidavit of birth to be supplied. Rec'd April 22/99					
8	No4 " " " " " " " 22/99					
9	For child of Nos 1&6 see NB (March 3, 1905) #1195					
10	No2 on 1896 roll as Saies Noah — No6 Granted Apr 24 1906.					
11	Nº5 Born March 25, 1902, enrolled May 31, 1902. Returned for correction May 31, 1902					
12	Received and filed June 16, 1902.					
13	No6 placed hereon under order of the Commissioner to the Five Civilized Tribes of March 14, 1906.					
14	holding application was made for her enrollment within the time provided				— 1 to 4	
15	by act of Congress of July 1, 1902 (32 Stat 641.)					
16						April 18/99
17	P.O. Bethel - 1902			Date of Application to Enrollment		

193

Choctaw By Blood Enrollment Cards 1898-1914

RESIDENCE: Nashoba COUNTY.
POST OFFICE: Alikchi, Ind. Ter.

Choctaw Nation

Choctaw Roll
(Not Including Freedmen)

CARD NO.
FIELD NO. 494

Dawes' Roll No.	NAME	Relationship to Person First Named	AGE	SEX	BLOOD	TRIBAL ENROLLMENT		
						Year	County	No.
988	1 Bond, Wachit 48	First Named	45	M	Full	1896	Nashoba	1172
989	2 " Martha 28	Wife	25	F	"	1896	"	1173
	3							
	4 ENROLLMENT							
	OF NOS. 1 and 2 HEREON							
	5 APPROVED BY THE SECRETARY							
	OF INTERIOR DEC 12 1902							
	6							
	7							
	8							
	9							
	10							
	11							
	12							
	13							
	14							
	15							
	16							
	17							

TRIBAL ENROLLMENT OF PARENTS

	Name of Father	Year	County	Name of Mother	Year	County
1	Wachit Bond	Dead	Nashoba	Bicey Bond	Dead	Nashoba
2	Chalata King	"	"	Wisey King	"	"
3						
4						
5						
6						
7						
8						
9						
10						
11						
12						
13						
14						
15				Date of Application for Enrollment.		
16				April 18/99		
17						

194

Choctaw By Blood Enrollment Cards 1898-1914

RESIDENCE: Nashoba COUNTY. **Choctaw Nation** Choctaw Roll CARD NO.
POST OFFICE: Alikchi, I.T. *(Not Including Freedmen)* FIELD NO. 495

Dawes' Roll No.	NAME	Relationship to Person First Named	AGE	SEX	BLOOD	TRIBAL ENROLLMENT		
						Year	County	No.
990	Emey abbi, Forbis ⁴⁸ ~~DIED PRIOR TO SEPTEMBER 25, 1902~~	First Named	45	M	Full	1896	Nashoba	3733
~~991~~	~~" Elizabeth~~ ⁵⁸	~~Wife~~	~~55~~	~~F~~	~~"~~	~~1896~~	~~"~~	~~3734~~
3								
4	ENROLLMENT OF NOS. 1 and 2 HEREON							
5	APPROVED BY THE SECRETARY OF INTERIOR DEC 12 1902							
6								
7								
8	No 2 Died Sept. 2, 1902: Proof of death filed Dec. 30, 1902.							
9								
10	For child of No1 see NB (March 3, 1905) #1452							
11	" " " " " " (April 26, 1906) #838							
12								
13								
14								
15								
16								
17								

TRIBAL ENROLLMENT OF PARENTS

	Name of Father	Year	County	Name of Mother	Year	County
1	Emey abbi		Nashoba	Amy Emey abbi	Dead	Nashoba
2	~~E-la-pin-tubbi~~	~~Dead~~	~~Jacks Fork~~	~~Ma-to-ua~~	~~"~~	~~"~~
3						
4						
5						
6						
7						
8						
9						
10						
11						
12						
13						
14						
15					Date of Application for Enrollment	April 18/99
16						
17						

195

Choctaw By Blood Enrollment Cards 1898-1914

RESIDENCE: Nashoba COUNTY. **Choctaw Nation** Choctaw Roll CARD NO.
POST OFFICE: Alikchi, Ind. Ter. (Not Including Freedmen) FIELD NO. 496

Dawes' Roll No.	NAME	Relationship to Person First Named	AGE	SEX	BLOOD	TRIBAL ENROLLMENT Year	County	No.
992	1 Noah, Pearl 27	First Named	24	M	Full	1896	Nashoba	9692
993	2 " Lizzie 29	Wife	26	F	"	1896	"	3737
994	3 DIED PRIOR TO SEPTEMBER 25, 1902 " Burke	Son	1	M	"			
995	4 " Sillis 2	Dau	20mo	F	"			
	5							
	6	ENROLLMENT						
	7	OF NOS. 1, 2, 3 and 4 HEREON APPROVED BY THE SECRETARY						
	8	OF INTERIOR DEC 12 1902						
	9							
	10	For child of Nos 1&2 see NB (Apr 26-06) Card #683						
	11	No2 on 1896 roll as Lizzie Emey abbi						
	12	No3 – Affidavit of birth to be supplied: Recd April 19/99						
	13							
	14	N⁰4 Born Oct. 10, 1900: enrolled June 2, 1902						
	15	No. 3 died Dec. 18-1899: Enrollment cancelled by Department						
	16							
	17							

TRIBAL ENROLLMENT OF PARENTS

	Name of Father	Year	County	Name of Mother	Year	County
1	Wilmon Noah	1896	Nashoba	Sallena Noah	1896	Nashoba
2	Emey abbi	1896	"	Amy Emey abbi	Dead	"
3	No 1			No 2		
4	N⁰1			N⁰2		
5						
6						
7						
8						
9						
10						
11						
12						
13						
14					#1 to 3	
15				Date of Application for Enrollment.		
16				Nos. 1 and 2 – April 18/99		
17						

196

Choctaw By Blood Enrollment Cards 1898-1914

RESIDENCE: Nashoba COUNTY. **Choctaw Nation** **Choctaw Roll** CARD NO.
POST OFFICE: Alikchi, Ind. Ter *(Not Including Freedmen)* FIELD NO. 497

Dawes' Roll No.	NAME	Relationship to Person First Named	AGE	SEX	BLOOD	TRIBAL ENROLLMENT Year	County	No.
996	1 Jefferson, Austin 26		23	M	Full	1896	Nashoba	6863
997	2 " Margaret W 27	Wife	24	F	"	1896	"	6864
	3							
	4	ENROLLMENT						
	5	OF NOS. 1 and 2 HEREON APPROVED BY THE SECRETARY						
	6	OF INTERIOR DEC 12 1902						
	7							
	8	Nos 1&2 have been divorced. No1 is now husband of Agnes						
	9	Brewer Choc Card #628 12/10/02						
	10	No2 is now wife of Thomas Watson on Choctaw card #477: evidence of divorce from No1 and marriage to second husband filed Dec. 11, 1902						
	11	For child of No.1 see NB (March 3, 1905) #924						
	12							
	13							
	14							
	15							
	16							
	17							

TRIBAL ENROLLMENT OF PARENTS

	Name of Father	Year	County	Name of Mother	Year	County
1	David Jefferson	Dead	Nashoba	Sarah Jefferson	1896	Nashoba
2	Stephen Watkins	1896	"	Nancy Watkins	Dead	
3						
4						
5						
6						
7						
8						
9						
10						
11						
12						
13						
14						
15						
16			Date of Application for Enrollment.	April 18/99		
17						

Choctaw By Blood Enrollment Cards 1898-1914

RESIDENCE: Nashoba   COUNTY.
POST OFFICE: Alikchi, Ind. Ter.

Choctaw Nation

Choctaw Roll
(Not Including Freedmen)

CARD NO.
FIELD NO. 498

Dawes' Roll No.	NAME	Relationship to Person First Named	AGE	SEX	BLOOD	TRIBAL ENROLLMENT Year	County	No.
998	1 Dwight, Levi ⁴¹	First Named	38	M	Full	1896	Nashoba	3386
999	2 " Sarah ⁵³	Wife	50	F	"	1896	"	3387
1000	3 Jefferson, Chisney ²³	S. Dau	20	"	"	1896	"	6814
1001	4 Battiest, Willy ¹⁸	S. Son	15	M	"	1896	"	1127
	5							
	6	ENROLLMENT						
	7	OF NOS. 1 2 3 and 4 HEREON APPROVED BY THE SECRETARY						
	8	OF INTERIOR DEC 12 1902						
	9							
	10							
	11							
	12							
	13							
	14							
	15							
	16							
	17							

TRIBAL ENROLLMENT OF PARENTS

Name of Father	Year	County	Name of Mother	Year	County
1 Moses Dwight	Dead	Bok Tuklo	Sta-hu-na	Dead	Bok Tuklo
2 Ta-bo-ka	"	Nashoba	Ak-chok-montema	"	Nashoba
3 David Jefferson	"	"	No 2		
4 William Battiest	1896	"	No 2		
5					
6					
7					
8					
9					
10					
11					
12					
13					
14					
15					
16			Date of Application for Enrollment.	April 18/99	
17					

198

Choctaw By Blood Enrollment Cards 1898-1914

RESIDENCE: Nashoba COUNTY. **Choctaw Nation** Choctaw Roll CARD No.
POST OFFICE: Alikchi, Ind. Ter. *(Not Including Freedmen)* FIELD No. 499

Dawes' Roll No.	NAME		Relationship to Person First Named	AGE	SEX	BLOOD	TRIBAL ENROLLMENT		
							Year	County	No.
1002	1 Watkins, Hoppen	25	Named	22	M	Full	1896	Nashoba	13386
1003	2 " Sinsie	22	Wife	19	F	"	1896	"	6815
1004	3 " Sealney	5	Dau	6mo	F	"			
	4								
	5								
	6	No2 on 1896 roll as Sinsie Jefferson							
	7	No3 Enrolled Aug 27, 1901							
	8								
	9								
	10	ENROLLMENT							
	11	OF NOS. 1 2 and 3 HEREON APPROVED BY THE SECRETARY							
	12	OF INTERIOR DEC 12 1902							
	13								
	14								
	15								
	16								
	17								

TRIBAL ENROLLMENT OF PARENTS

	Name of Father	Year	County	Name of Mother	Year	County
1	Eastman Watkins	1896	Nashoba	Winey Watkins	1896	Nashoba
2	Levi Dwight	1896	"	Sarah Dwight	1896	"
3	No 1			No 2		
4						
5						
6						
7						
8						
9						
10						
11						
12						
13						
14						
15						
16				Date of Application for Enrollment.		April 18/99
17						

RESIDENCE:	Red River	COUNTY.	Choctaw Nation		Choctaw Roll	CARD No.	
POST OFFICE:	Kullitucklo, Ind. Ter.				(Not Including Freedmen)	FIELD No.	500

Dawes' Roll No.	NAME	Relationship to Person First Named	AGE	SEX	BLOOD	TRIBAL ENROLLMENT		
						Year	County	No.
DEAD	1 Fisher, Wilson DEAD	First Named	28	M	Full	1896	Red River	4210
DEAD	2 " Emiline DEAD	Wife	20	F	"	1896	"	8080
DEAD	3 " Osmon DEAD	Son	2	M	"			
DEAD	4 " Cisty DEAD	Dau	3mo	F	"			
	5							
	6							
	7							
	8							
	9							
	10							
	11 No. 1-2-3-4 Hereon dismissed under order							
	12 of the Commission to the Five Civilized							
	13 Tribes of March 31, 1905.							
	14							
	15							
	16							
	17							

TRIBAL ENROLLMENT OF PARENTS

	Name of Father	Year	County	Name of Mother	Year	County
1	John Fisher	Dead	Red River	Mary Fisher	1896	Red River
2	Ellis Cobb	"	Nashoba	Martha Cobb	Dead	Nashoba
3	No 1			No 2		
4	No 1			No 2		
5						
6						
7						
8						
9	No2 on 1896 roll as Emma Leney.					
10	Affidavits as to birth of Nos 3&4 to be supplied. Recd Mau 6/99					
11	No4 died July 5, 1899. Proof of death filed Aug. 10, 1901					
12	No3 died November 15, 1899 " " " " Aug. 10, 1901					
13	No2 died January 7, 1900 " " " " Aug. 10, 1901					
14	No1 is now husband of Viney Wilson on Choctaw card #1326. See letter					
15	filed Aug 21, 1901, with papers in that case.					
16	No1 died March 17, 1901, proof of death filed Dec 4/02				Date of Application for Enrollment.	
17					April 18/99	

CANCELLED

Died prior to Sept. 25, '02

Choctaw By Blood Enrollment Cards 1898-1914

						TRIBAL ENROLLMENT		
RESIDENCE: Red River COUNTY. POST OFFICE: Kullituklo, Ind. Ter.	**Choctaw Nation**					**Choctaw Roll** *(Not Including Freedmen)*	CARD NO. FIELD NO. **501**	

Dawes' Roll No.	NAME	Relationship to Person First Named	AGE	SEX	BLOOD	Year	County	No.
1005	1 Battiest, Sophia ²³	First Named	20	F	Full	1896	Red River	1369
1006	2 " Annie ⁴	Dau	9mo	"	"			
14559	3 William[sic], Sarah ¹	Dau	1	F	"			
	4							
	5 ENROLLMENT							
	6 OF NOS. 1 and 2 HEREON APPROVED BY THE SECRETARY							
	7 OF INTERIOR Dec 12 1902							
	8							
	9 ENROLLMENT							
	10 OF NOS. 3 HEREON APPROVED BY THE SECRETARY							
	11 OF INTERIOR May 20 1903							
	12							
	13							
	14							
	15							
	16							
	17							

TRIBAL ENROLLMENT OF PARENTS

Name of Father	Year	County	Name of Mother	Year	County
1 Cholina	Dead	Red River	Lyna Cholina	Dead	Red River
2 Watson Fisher	"	" "	No 1		
3 Moses Williams		Choctaw Roll	No 1		
4					
5					
6					
7					
8					
9					
10					
11					

12 No2 is an illegitimate child. Affidavit of birth to be supplied Rec'd May 6/99	
No1 on 1896 roll as Sopha Battiest, Page 33, No 1346	
13 No1 " 1896 " " " "	
14 No3 born Sept. 30, `90`; enrolled Dec. 2, `901	Date of Application for Enrollment.
15 No1 is wife of Moses Williams Choctaw card `743	April 18/99
For child of No1 see NB (March 3, 1905) #1021.	
16	
17 Garvin I.T.	

Choctaw By Blood Enrollment Cards 1898-1914

RESIDENCE: Red River   COUNTY.   **Choctaw Nation**   **Choctaw Roll**   CARD NO.
POST OFFICE: Kullituklo, I.T.   (Not Including Freedmen)   FIELD NO. **502**

Dawes' Roll No.	NAME	Relationship to Person First Named	AGE	SEX	BLOOD	TRIBAL ENROLLMENT		
						Year	County	No.
1007	1 Wilson, Anderson ²⁸	First Named	25	M	Full	1896	Red River	13578
1008	2 " Leus ²⁴	Wife	21	F	"	1896	" "	13579
1009	3 " Dwight ⁶	Son	2	M	"	1896	" "	13701
1010	4 " Alden ⁽?⁾	"	6mo	"	"			
1011	5 " Florence ²	Dau	11mo	F	"			
14560	6 " Nancy ¹	Dau	8mo	F	"			
	7							
	8 ~~ENROLLMENT~~							
	9 ~~OF NOS. 1,2,3,4 and 5 HEREON~~							
	APPROVED BY THE SECRETARY							
	10 OF INTERIOR Dec 12 1902							
	11							
	12 ENROLLMENT							
	OF NOS. 6 HEREON							
	13 APPROVED BY THE SECRETARY							
	14 OF INTERIOR May 20 1903							
	15							
	16							
	17							

TRIBAL ENROLLMENT OF PARENTS

Name of Father	Year	County	Name of Mother	Year	County
1 Daniel Wilson	Dead	Red River	Siney Wilson	Dead	Red River
2 Lewis Konchehomby	"	" "	Lucy Konchehomby	1896	" "
3 No 1			No 2		
4 No 1			No 2		
5 No 1			No 2		
6 No 1			No 2		
7					
8					
9 Affidavits as to birth of Nos 3&4 to be supplied. Rec'd My 6/99.					
10 No5 Enrolled Aug 10, 1901					
11 N°6 Born March 26 1902 Enrolled Dec 24, 1902.					
12					
13					
14					1 to 4 inc
15				Date of Application for Enrollment	
16				April 18/99	
17 P.O. Garvin, Okla.					

Choctaw By Blood Enrollment Cards 1898-1914

RESIDENCE: Red River COUNTY.
POST OFFICE: Garvin, Ind. Ter.

Choctaw Nation

Choctaw Roll
(Not Including Freedmen)

CARD NO.
FIELD NO. **503**

Dawes' Roll No.	NAME		Relationship to Person First Named	AGE	SEX	BLOOD	TRIBAL ENROLLMENT		
							Year	County	No.
1012	1 Peter, Pitman	37	First Named	34	M	Full	1896	Red River	10413
14561	2 Mitchell, Mary	49	Wife	44	F	"	1896	" "	8659
~~1013~~	~~3 Peter, John~~ DIED PRIOR TO SEPTEMBER 25, 1902	~~10~~	~~Son~~	~~7~~	~~M~~	~~"~~	~~1896~~	~~" "~~	~~10414~~
1014	4 Parker, Lizzie	15	Ward	12	F	"	1896	" "	10341
1015	5 " Moses	9	"	6	M	"	1896	" "	10421
	6								
	7	ENROLLMENT OF NOS. 1,3,4 and 5 HEREON							
	8	APPROVED BY THE SECRETARY OF INTERIOR Dec 12 1902							
	9								
	10	ENROLLMENT OF NOS. 2 HEREON							
	11	APPROVED BY THE SECRETARY							
	12	OF INTERIOR May 20 1903							
	13								
	14	No2 on 1896 roll as Mary Mitchell							
	15								
	16								
	17								

TRIBAL ENROLLMENT OF PARENTS

	Name of Father	Year	County	Name of Mother	Year	County
1	Ema-mm-tube	Dead	Eagle	A-shu-lah-ta	Dead	Eagle
2	Hote	"	Red River	Sukey Hote	"	Red River
3	~~No 1~~			~~Nicey Peter~~	"	" "
4	Farlis Parker	Dead	Red River	Sissy Parker	"	" "
5	" "	"	" "	" "	"	" "
6						
7						
8						
9	~~No2 is also on 1893 payroll Red River County page 58 #515 as Mary Mitchell~~					
10	No2 was divorced from No1 July 7, 1900 and assumed her maiden name of Mary Mitchell. See copy of her letter filed Oct. 17, 1902.					
11	No1 is now husband of Tennessee Juzan on Choctaw card #965: evidence of marriage filed Dec 3, 1902					
12	No3 died Aug. 18, 1900: Enrollment cancelled by Department Sept. 16, 1904					
13	No3 died August 18, 1900: proof [sic] death filed Dec. 4, 1902					
14						
15				Date of Application for Enrollment.		
16				April 18/99		
17	Kullitucko I.T. 12/02/02					

Choctaw By Blood Enrollment Cards 1898-1914

RESIDENCE: Bok Tuklo   COUNTY.   **Choctaw Nation**   **Choctaw Roll** *(Not Including Freedmen)*   CARD NO.

POST OFFICE: Lukfata Ind. Ter.   FIELD NO. **504**

Dawes' Roll No.	NAME	Relationship to Person First Named	AGE	SEX	BLOOD	TRIBAL ENROLLMENT		
						Year	County	No.
IW889	1 Costilow, Elijah (31)		28	M	I.W.	1896	Red River	14407
1016	2 " Jennie (23)	Wife	20	F	1/2	1896	" "	2655
1017	3 " Lena (6)	Dau	3	"	1/4	1896	" "	2656
1018	4 " James D	Son	4mo	M	1/4			
1019	5 " Henretta[sic] (3)	Dau	2mo	F	1/4			
	6							
	7	ENROLLMENT						
	8	OF NOS. 2,3,4 and 5 HEREON APPROVED BY THE SECRETARY						
	9	OF INTERIOR Dec 12 1902						
	10							
	11	ENROLLMENT						
	12	OF NOS. 1 HEREON APPROVED BY THE SECRETARY						
	13	OF INTERIOR Aug 3 1904						
	14							
	15							
	16							
	17							

DIED PRIOR TO SEPTEMBER 25, 1902 (on line 4)

TRIBAL ENROLLMENT OF PARENTS

	Name of Father	Year	County	Name of Mother	Year	County
1	Elijah Costilow	Dead	Non Citz	Henrietta Costilow		Non Citz
2	Isom Durant	"	Blue	Phoebe Durant	Dead	Blue
3	No 1			No 2		
4	No 1			No 2		
5	No 1			No 2		
6						
7						
8						
9						
10			No4 Affidavit of birth to be supplied: Recd May 9/99			
11			No.5 Enrolled March 19th, 1901			
12			For child of Nos. 1&2 see NB (March 3 1905) #873			
13			No4 died March 3, 1901: proof of death filed Dec. 6, 1902			
			No4 died March 3, 1901: Enrollment cancelled by Department July 8, 1904			
14						
15						
16					Date of Application for Enrollment	April 18/99
17						

Choctaw By Blood Enrollment Cards 1898-1914

RESIDENCE: **Bok Tuklo**   COUNTY.

POST OFFICE: **Lukfata, Ind. Ter.**

Choctaw Nation

Choctaw Roll *(Not Including Freedmen)*

CARD NO. FIELD NO. **505**

Dawes' Roll No.	NAME	Relationship to Person First Named	AGE	SEX	BLOOD	TRIBAL ENROLLMENT Year	County	No.
1020	1 Costilow, Emma 23 ~~DIED PRIOR TO SEPTEMBER 25, 1902~~		20	F	1/2	1896	Eagle	2602
1021	2 " Laura B. 7	Dau	4	"	1/4	1896	"	2622
1022	3 " Charles G. 6	Son	3	M	1/4	1896	"	2645
1023	4 " Ida Daisy 3	Dau	3wk	F	1/4			
IW 1090	5 " James W. 39	Husband	39	M	I W	1896	Eagle	14406
	6							
	7							
	8							
	9							
	10							
	11							
	12							
	13							
	14							
	15							
	16							
	17							

ENROLLMENT OF NOS. 1 2 3 and 4 HEREON APPROVED BY THE SECRETARY OF INTERIOR Dec. 12, 1902

ENROLLMENT OF NOS. 5 HEREON APPROVED BY THE SECRETARY OF INTERIOR Nov. 16, 1904

TRIBAL ENROLLMENT OF PARENTS

	Name of Father	Year	County	Name of Mother	Year	County
1	Charles Goffner		Non Citz	Wilkie Clay	1896	Bok Tuklo
2	James W. Costilow		" "	No 1		
3	" " "		" "	No 1		
4	" " "		" "	No 1		
5	Elijah Costilow	dead	" "	Henrietta Costilow		Noncitizen
6						
7	Husband of No1 and father of her children is on Card D 116					
8	No.5 on 1896 Choctaw roll as Jas. W Costilow					
9	No3 on 1896 roll as Chas. G. Costilow					
	~~No5 transferred from Choctaw card #D.116, Oct. 31,1904: See decision of Oct. 15, 1904~~					
10	Ida D Costilow born dec. 28/99. On Card No. D-556					
11	No1 died March 22-1901: Enrollment cancelled by Department, July 8-1904.					
12	No4 born December 28, 1899, transferred to this card May 24, 1902					
	~~No1 died March 22, 1901, proof of death filed Dec. 6, 1902~~					
13	For children of No5 see (Apr. 26,06) #1091.					
14	No3 Died prior to September 25, 1902: not entitled to land of money- see Indian office					
15	Letter April 1, 1908 (I.T. 19598 – 1908)				#1 to 3	
16				Date of Application for Enrollment	April 18/99	
17						

205

RESIDENCE: Bok Tuklo	COUNTY.	**Choctaw Nation**		**Choctaw Roll**	CARD No.	
POST OFFICE: Lukfata, Ind. Ter.				(Not Including Freedmen)	FIELD No.	506

Dawes' Roll No.	NAME		Relationship to Person First Named	AGE	SEX	BLOOD	TRIBAL ENROLLMENT		
							Year	County	No.
See 5360	1 Farver, Lula			14	F	1/2	1896	Towson	4132
1024	2 " Peru	15	Bro	12	M	1/2	1893	Eagle	P. R. 278
1025	3 " William	19	Bro	16	M	1/2	1893	Blue	63
	4								
	5								
	6	ENROLLMENT							
	7	OF NOS. 2 and 3 HEREON APPROVED BY THE SECRETARY							
	8	OF INTERIOR DEC 12 1902							
	9								
	10	No2 is a Male sex changed under Departmental instructions							
	11	of August 11, 1904 (D C. #29368-1904)							
	12								
	13	Not on 1896 roll as Lula Farbee							
	14	No3 on 1893 Pay roll as Willie Farber, Page 121 No63 Blue Co							
	15								
	16	Not transferred to Choctaw card #5360 with							
	17	her husband Jany. 3d, 1901.							

	TRIBAL ENROLLMENT OF PARENTS						
	Name of Father	Year	County	Name of Mother	Year	County	
1	Sim Farver	Dead	Eagle	Helen Farver	Dead	Non Citz	
2	" "	"	"	" "	"	" "	
3	" "	"	"	" "	"	" "	
4							
5							
6							
7							
8							
9							
10							
11							
12							
13							
14							
15						#1 &2	
16					Date of Application for Enrollment	April 18/99	
17						No3 enrolled 5/26/99	

Choctaw By Blood Enrollment Cards 1898-1914

RESIDENCE: Bok Tuklo   COUNTY.
POST OFFICE: Lukfata, Ind. Ter.

Choctaw Nation

Choctaw Roll (Not Including Freedmen)

CARD NO. / FIELD NO. **507**

Dawes' Roll No.	NAME	Relationship to Person First Named	AGE	SEX	BLOOD	TRIBAL ENROLLMENT		
						Year	County	No.
1026	1 Clay, Abner H. 30	First Named	27	M	3/4	1896	Bok Tuklo	2574
IW 699	2 " Mattie (32)	wife	26	F	I.W.			
1027	3 " Abner Henry ✓	son	1	M	3/8			
1028	4 " Mattie Lorena 3	dau	1mo	F	3/8			
14562	5 " Myrtle Eugenia 1	"	8mo	F	3/8			
	6					ENROLLMENT		
	7					OF NOS. ~~ 2 ~~ HEREON APPROVED BY THE SECRETARY		
	8					OF INTERIOR May 7 – 1904		
	9	ENROLLMENT						
	10	OF NOS. 1, 3, and 4 HEREON APPROVED BY THE SECRETARY						
	11	OF INTERIOR Dec. 12, 1902						
	12							
	13							
	14	ENROLLMENT				No		
	15	OF NOS. ~~ 5 ~~ HEREON APPROVED BY THE SECRETARY						
	16	OF INTERIOR May 20, 1903						
	17							

TRIBAL ENROLLMENT OF PARENTS

Name of Father	Year	County	Name of Mother	Year	County
1 Henry Clay	Dead	Bok Tuklo	Wilsey Clay	1896	Bok Tuklo
2 Joseph H Denson		Non Citz	Mattie E. Denson		Non citz
3	No 1		No 2		
4	No 1		No 2		
5	No 1		No 2		
6					
7					
8	No2 see Decision of March 2 1904				
9	No1 on 1896 roll as Abner Clay				
10	No3 Affidavit as to birth to be supplied: Recd May 9/99				
11					
12	No5 Born Mar 8, 1902, Enrolled Nov. 4, 1902				
13	No1 and 2 have separated – Oct. 1902 / For child of Nos 1&2 see NB (March 3, 1905) #902				
14					
15				#1 to 3 inc	
16			Date of Application for Enrollment.	April 18/99	
17	P.O. Lockerberg Arkansas Dec 16-02		No4 enrolled Nov 1/99		

Choctaw By Blood Enrollment Cards 1898-1914

RESIDENCE: Nashoba COUNTY.
POST OFFICE: Alikchi, Ind. Ter.

Choctaw Nation

Choctaw Roll CARD NO.
(Not Including Freedmen) FIELD NO. 508

Dawes' Roll No.	NAME	Relationship to Person First Named	AGE	SEX	BLOOD	TRIBAL ENROLLMENT		
						Year	County	No.
1029	1 Bond, Byington		38	M	Full	1896	Nashoba	1177
1030	2 " Moses	Son	8	"	"	1896	"	1179
1031	3 " Simmons	"	6	"	"	1896	"	1180
1032	4 " Allen	"	5	"	"	1896	"	1181
1033	5 " Sikus	DIED PRIOR TO SEPTEMBER 25, 1902 "	2					
	6							
	7							
	8							
	9							
	10							
	11	ENROLLMENT OF NOS. 1 2 3 4 and 5 HEREON						
	12	APPROVED BY THE SECRETARY						
	13	OF INTERIOR Dec 12 1902						
	14							
	15							
	16							
	17							

TRIBAL ENROLLMENT OF PARENTS

	Name of Father	Year	County	Name of Mother	Year	County
1	Colone Bond	Dead	Nashoba	Larkie Bond	Dead	Nashoba
2	No 1			Susan Bond	"	"
3	No 1			" "	"	"
4	No 1			" "	"	"
5	No 1			" "	"	"
6						
7						
8						
9						
10						
11	No5 – Affidavit as to birth to be supplied: Rec'd April 18/99					
12						
13	No5 died Dec - 1901: proof of death filed Dec 16, 1902. Nº1 is husband of Liksie Noahobi Choctaw card #657, Jany 28, 1903					
14	No.5 died Dec. – 1901: Enrollment cancelled by Department July 8 – 1904					
15	For child of No.1 see NB (March 3, 1905) #920				Date of Application for Enrollment.	
16					April 18/99	
17						

Choctaw By Blood Enrollment Cards 1898-1914

RESIDENCE: Nashoba   COUNTY.   **Choctaw Nation**   **Choctaw Roll** CARD NO.
POST OFFICE: Alikchi, I.T.   *(Not Including Freedmen)* FIELD NO. 509

Dawes' Roll No.	NAME	Relationship to Person First Named	AGE	SEX	BLOOD	TRIBAL ENROLLMENT		
						Year	County	No.
1034 1 A-fa-ma-ho-na			76	F	Full	1896	Nashoba	237
2								
3								
4								
5								
6								
7								
8								
9								
10								
11								
12								
13								
14								
15								
16								
17								

DIED PRIOR TO SEPTEMBER 25, 1902

ENROLLMENT
OF NOS. 1 HEREON
APPROVED BY THE SECRETARY
OF INTERIOR DEC 12 1902

TRIBAL ENROLLMENT OF PARENTS

	Name of Father	Year	County	Name of Mother	Year	County
1	Netak-aucha-[illegible]	Dead	Nashoba		Dead	Nashoba
2						
3						
4						
5						
6						
7						
8						
9						
10						
11						
12						
13						
14						
15				Date of Application for Enrollment.	April 18/99	
16						
17						

Choctaw By Blood Enrollment Cards 1898-1914

RESIDENCE: Towson COUNTY.		**Choctaw Nation**	**Choctaw Roll** (*Not Including Freedmen*)	CARD NO.	
POST OFFICE: Alikchi, Ind. Ter.				FIELD NO. 510	

Dawes' Roll No.	NAME	Relationship to Person First Named	AGE	SEX	BLOOD	TRIBAL ENROLLMENT		
						Year	County	No.
1035	1 Tims, James B 39	First Named	36	M	1/2	1896	Towson	12112
1036	2 " Mary J 34	Wife	31	F	Full	1893	"	P.R. 329
1037	3 " Evelyn 10	Dau	8	"	3/4	1896	"	12113
1038	4 " Dixon 8	Son	5	M	3/4	1896	"	12114
1039	5 " Rufus 4	"	5mo	"	3/4			
~~1040~~	6 " ~~Lula~~	~~Dau~~	~~2mo~~	~~F~~	~~3/4~~			
1041	7 " Lowie 1	Son	2mo	M	3/4			
	8							
	9							
	10							
	11							
	12							
	13							
	14							
	15							
	16							
	17							

ENROLLMENT
OF NOS. 1 2 3 4 5 6 and 7 HEREON
APPROVED BY THE SECRETARY
OF INTERIOR DEC 12 1902

TRIBAL ENROLLMENT OF PARENTS

	Name of Father	Year	County	Name of Mother	Year	County
1	Vinson W. Tims	Dead	Towson	Emeline Tims	1896	Towson
2	Dixon Willis	"	"	Elizabeth Willis	Dead	"
3	No 1			No 2		
4	No 1			No 2		
5	No 1			No 2		
6	~~No 1~~			~~No 2~~		
7	No 1			No 2		
8						
9						
10						
11	No5 – Affidavit as to birth to be supplied. Recd May 4/99					
12	No 1 on 1896 roll as Jas. B. Tims					
13	No 2 " 1893 Payroll as Mary Jane Tims					
14	No.6 Enrolled Sept 23 1901					#1 to 5
15	No.7 Enrolled Sept 23 1901					Date of Application for Enrollment.
16	~~No 6 and 7 are twins.~~ N°6 Died Jany 19, 1902, proof of death filed Oct. 29, 1902					April 18/99
17	No6 died Jan 19-1902: Enrollment cancelled by Department.					

210

Choctaw By Blood Enrollment Cards 1898-1914

RESIDENCE: Towson COUNTY.   **Choctaw Nation**   **Choctaw Roll** CARD No.

POST OFFICE: Alikchi, I.T.   (Not Including Freedmen)   FIELD NO. 511

Dawes' Roll No.		NAME	Relationship to Person First Named	AGE	SEX	BLOOD	TRIBAL ENROLLMENT		
							Year	County	No. P.R.
VOID.	1	Willis, Emerson	Named	22	M	Full	1893	Towson	418
1042	2	" Eden	Brother	13	"	"	1893	"	419
1043	3	" Louis ¹⁴	"	11	"	"	1893	"	420
	4								
	5								
	6	ENROLLMENT							
	7	OF NOS. 2 and 3 HEREON APPROVED BY THE SECRETARY							
	8	OF INTERIOR DEC 12 1902							
	9								
	10								
	11	No2 Died June 10, 1900: proof of death filed Nov. 24, 1902							
	12								
	13								
	14								
	15								
	16								
	17								

DIED PRIOR TO SEPTEMBER 25, 1902

TRIBAL ENROLLMENT OF PARENTS

	Name of Father	Year	County	Name of Mother	Year	County
1	Dixon Willis	Dead	Towson	Elizabeth Willis	Dead	Towson
2	" "	"	"	" "	"	"
3	" "	"	"	" "	"	"
4						
5						
6						
7						
8						
9						
10						
11	No1 on 1893 roll as Emmerson					
12	No2 also on 1896 roll, Page 347, No 13200,					
13	Towson County, as Eden Wellis					
14	No3 also on 1896 roll, Page 347, No 13201				Date of Application for Enrollment.	
15	Towson County as Louis Wellis					
16	No2 died June 10-1900: Enrollment cancelled by Department				April 18/99	
17	No1 on card No 1351.					

Emerson Willis No 1 is a duplication of Emerson D. Willis on Choctaw card
#1351, and is cancelled hereon. Jan. 25, 1900

211

Choctaw By Blood Enrollment Cards 1898-1914

RESIDENCE: Red River   COUNTY.   **Choctaw Nation**   **Choctaw Roll**   CARD No.
POST OFFICE: Janis, I.T.   (Not Including Freedmen)   FIELD No. 512

Dawes' Roll No.	NAME	Relationship to Person First Named	AGE	SEX	BLOOD	TRIBAL ENROLLMENT		
						Year	County	No.
1044	1 Morris, Charles 27	First Named	24	M	Full	1896	Red River	8657
1045	2 " Rhoda 36	Wife	33	F	"	1893	" "	2671
1046	3 Camp, Eliza 9	S. Dau	6	"	"	1896	" "	2671
	4							
	5							
	6							
	7							
	8							
	9	ENROLLMENT OF NOS. 1 2 and 3 HEREON APPROVED BY THE SECRETARY OF INTERIOR Dec 12 1902						
	10							
	11							
	12							
	13	No2 on 1896 roll as Rurie Camp						
	14							
	15							
	16							
	17							

TRIBAL ENROLLMENT OF PARENTS

	Name of Father	Year	County	Name of Mother	Year	County
1	George Morris	1896	Red River	Lisa Morris	Dead	Red River
2	Cooper	Dead	Kiamitia		"	Kiamitia
3	Dixon Camp	"	Red River	No 2		
4						
5						
6						
7						
8						
9						
10						
11						
12						
13						
14					Date of Application for Enrollment.	
15						
16					April 18/99	
17	Nowood[sic], I.T. 11/25/02					

212

Choctaw By Blood Enrollment Cards 1898-1914

RESIDENCE: Red River COUNTY. **Choctaw Nation** Choctaw Roll CARD NO.
POST OFFICE: Janie, I.T. (Not Including Freedmen) FIELD NO. 513

Dawes' Roll No.	NAME		Relationship to Person First Named	AGE	SEX	BLOOD	TRIBAL ENROLLMENT		
							Year	County	No.
1047	1 Thomas, Daniel	37	First Named	36	M	Full	1896	Red River	12328
1048	2 " Cillen	26	Wife	23	F	"	1896	" "	12329
1049	3 " Mary DIED PRIOR TO SEPTEMBER 25, 1902		Dau	5	"	"	1896	" "	12330
DEAD.	4 " Lucy		"	2	"	"			
1050	5 " Missie		"	6mo	"	"			
14563	6 " Cornelius		Son	5mo	M	Full			
	7								
	8 ENROLLMENT								
	9 OF NOS. 1 2 3 and 5 HEREON APPROVED BY THE SECRETARY								
	10 OF INTERIOR DEC 12 1902								
	11 ENROLLMENT								
	12 OF NOS. 6 HEREON APPROVED BY THE SECRETARY								
	13 OF INTERIOR MAY 20 1903								
	14 No. 4 HEREON DISMISSED UNDER								
	15 ORDER OF THE COMMISSION TO THE FIVE								
	16 CIVILIZED TRIBES OF MARCH 31, 1905.								
	17								

TRIBAL ENROLLMENT OF PARENTS

Name of Father	Year	County	Name of Mother	Year	County
1 Ta-mu-ley	Dead	Atoka	Sallie	Dead	Bok Tuklo
2 Falen Tuska	"	Red River	Silnay Tuska	1896	Red River
3 No 1			No 2		
4 No 1			No 2 No		
5 No.1			No.2		
6 No 1			No 2		
7					
8					
9 For child of Nos 1&2 see N.B. (Apr 26-06) Card #577					
10 No4 – Affidavit of birth to be supplied.					
11 No 3 also on 1896 roll Page 319, No 12276					
12 as Mary Tushka, also on " 320 " 12327					
13 " " " Red River Co					
14 No.5 Enrolled June 23d, 1900					
15 No6 born July 11 1902; enrolled Dec 2, 1902			No3 died Feb 2, 1900; proof of death filed Dec. 4, 1902	Date of Application for Enrollment: #1 to 4 inc	
16 No4 " May 19, 1900; " " " " " 4, 1902			April 19/99		
17 No3 died Feb 2, 1900; Enrollment cancelled by Department Sept 16 1904					

Choctaw By Blood Enrollment Cards 1898-1914

RESIDENCE: Bok Tuklo   COUNTY.   **Choctaw Nation**   **Choctaw Roll**   CARD NO.
POST OFFICE: Lukfata, I.T.   *(Not Including Freedmen)*   FIELD NO.   514

Dawes' Roll No.	NAME		Relationship to Person First Named	AGE	SEX	BLOOD	TRIBAL ENROLLMENT		
							Year	County	No.
1051	1 James, Silley	48	First Named	45	F	Full	1896	Bok Tuklo	6925
1052	2 " Sarah	11	Dau	8	"	"	1896	" "	6926
	3								
	4								
	5								
	6								
	7								
	8	ENROLLMENT							
	9	OF NOS. 1 and 2 HEREON APPROVED BY THE SECRETARY							
	10	OF INTERIOR DEC 12 1902							
	11								
	12								
	13	No2 has been adopted by Susan Parsons Choc card #1144 11/28/02							
	14								
	15								
	16								
	17								

TRIBAL ENROLLMENT OF PARENTS

	Name of Father	Year	County	Name of Mother	Year	County
1	Willis Nicketomby	Dead	Bok Tuklo	Ish-ta-o-na	Dead	Bok Tuklo
2	Lap James	"	" "	No 1		
3						
4						
5						
6						
7						
8						
9						
10						
11						
12						
13						
14						
15				Date of Application for Enrollment.		April 18/99
16						
17						

214

Choctaw By Blood Enrollment Cards 1898-1914

RESIDENCE: Red River	COUNTY.	**Choctaw Nation**	**Choctaw Roll**	CARD NO.
POST OFFICE: Janis, I.T.			*(Not Including Freedmen)*	FIELD NO. 515

Dawes' Roll No.	NAME		Relationship to Person First Named	AGE	SEX	BLOOD	TRIBAL ENROLLMENT		
							Year	County	No.
1053	1 Morris, George	58	First Named	55	M	Full	1896	Red River	8678
1054	2 " David	18	Son	14	"	"	1896	" "	P.R. 511
1055	3 " Betsy	13	Dau	10	F	"	1896	" "	8683
1056	4 " Forbis	11	Son	8	M	"	1896	" "	8682
	5								
	6								
	7								
	8	ENROLLMENT							
	9	OF NOS. 1 2 3 and 4 HEREON APPROVED BY THE SECRETARY							
	10	OF INTERIOR DEC 12 1902							
	11								
	12	No2 on 1896 Choctaw census roll, page 217.							
	13	#8681, as Daniel Morris							
	14								
	15	For child of No3 see NB (April 26 1906) No 267							
	16	[Entry illegible]							
	17								

TRIBAL ENROLLMENT OF PARENTS						
Name of Father	Year	County	Name of Mother	Year	County	
1 Jim Moore[sic]	Dead	Nashoba	Un-te-nu-he	Dead	Eagle	
2 No 1			Eliza Morris	"	Red River	
3 No 1			" "	"	" "	
4 No 1			" "	"	" "	
5						
6						
7						
8						
9						
10						
11						
12						
13						
14						
15				Date of Application for Enrollment.		
16				April 19/99		
17						

Choctaw By Blood Enrollment Cards 1898-1914

RESIDENCE: Red River   COUNTY.   **Choctaw Nation**   **Choctaw Roll**   CARD NO.
POST OFFICE: Kullituklo, I.T.   *(Not Including Freedmen)*   FIELD NO. **516**

Dawes' Roll No.	NAME	Relationship to Person First Named	AGE	SEX	BLOOD	TRIBAL ENROLLMENT Year	County	No.
1057	1 Kanimaya, Hodges 38	First Named	35	M	Full	1896	Red River	7576
1058	2 " Jennie 39	Wife	36	F	"	1896	" "	7577
1059	3 " James 14	Son	11	M	"	1896	" "	7578
1060	4 Kaniatubbee, Rosa 25	S. Dau	22	F	"	1896	" "	13627
1061	5 Williston, Tobia 5	G.S.Son	3mo	M	"			
1062	6 Kaniatubbee, Nelson 2	Son of No4	6mo	M	"			
	7							
	8	ENROLLMENT						
	9	OF NOS. 1 2 3 4 5 and 6 HEREON APPROVED BY THE SECRETARY						
	10	OF INTERIOR Dec 12 1902						
	11							
	12							
	13							
	14							
	15							
	16							
	17							

TRIBAL ENROLLMENT OF PARENTS

Name of Father	Year	County	Name of Mother	Year	County
1 Hodges Kanimaya	Dead	Red River	Un-ta-ke-huna	Dead	Red River
2 Louis Josan	"	" "	Amy Josan	1896	" "
3 No 1			No 2		
4 Chas. Williston	Dead	Red River	No 2		
5 Johnson Cogswell	1896	" "	No 4		
6 Wilburn D Kaniatubbee	1896	" "	No 4		
7					
8					

9   No4 is now the wife of Wilburn Kaniatobe[sic] on Choctaw Card #1059 May 17, 1901
10   No4 Evidence of marriage filed May 17, 1901
11   No6 Enrolled May 17, 1901
12   For child of No4 see NB (Apr 26-06) Card #466
13   " " " " " " (Mar 3-05) " #929
   No6 died June 28, 1902: Proof of death filed Dec 4, 1902.
14   No6 died June 28, 1902: Enrollment cancelled by Department Sept. 16, 1904.
15   #1 to 4 inc

	Date of Application for Enrollment.	April 19/99

16

17   P.O. Idabel I.T. 4/11/05   No5 April 28/99

216

Choctaw By Blood Enrollment Cards 1898-1914

RESIDENCE: Nashoba COUNTY. **Choctaw Nation** **Choctaw Roll** CARD NO.
POST OFFICE: Alikchi, I.T. (Not Including Freedmen) FIELD NO. **517**

Dawes' Roll No.	NAME		Relationship to Person First Named	AGE	SEX	BLOOD	TRIBAL ENROLLMENT		
							Year	County	No.
1063	1 John, Cephus	30	First Named	27	M	Full	1896	Nashobe[sic]	6880
1064	2 " Bessie	24	Wife	21	F	"	1896	Cedar	9255
1065	3 " Felesten	4	Son	4mo	M	"			
	4								
	5								
	6	ENROLLMENT							
	7	OF NOS. 1 2 and 3 HEREON APPROVED BY THE SECRETARY							
	8	OF INTERIOR Dec 12 1902							
	9								
	10								
	11	No2 on 1896 roll as Bessie McFarland.							
	12								
	13	No3 – Affidavit of birth to be supplied: - Recd. April 19/99							
	14	For child of Nos 1&2 see NB (Apr 26-06) Card #588							
	15								
	16								
	17								

TRIBAL ENROLLMENT OF PARENTS

	Name of Father	Year	County	Name of Mother	Year	County
1	Lake John	Dead	Nashoba	Wynie John	1896	Nashoba
2	Sam McFarland	"	"	Listie McFarland	Dead	Cedar
3	No 1			No 2		
4						
5						
6						
7						
8						
9						
10						
11						
12						
13					Date of Application for Enrollment.	
14						
15					April 19/99	
16						
17						

Choctaw By Blood Enrollment Cards 1898-1914

RESIDENCE: Nashoba COUNTY.
POST OFFICE: Alikchi, I.T.

Choctaw Nation

Choctaw Roll
(Not Including Freedmen)

CARD No.
FIELD No. 518

Dawes' Roll No.	NAME	Relationship to Person First Named	AGE	SEX	BLOOD	TRIBAL ENROLLMENT Year	TRIBAL ENROLLMENT County	TRIBAL ENROLLMENT No.
1066	1 John, Wynie ⁵²	First Named	49	F	Full	1896	Nashoba	6879
1067	2 " Narie ¹⁸	Dau	15	"	"	1896	"	6882
1068	3 " Lorte ¹⁵	"	12	"	"	1896	"	6883
	4							
	5	ENROLLMENT						
	6	OF NOS. 1 2 and 3 HEREON APPROVED BY THE SECRETARY						
	7	OF INTERIOR DEC 12 1902						
	8							
	9							
	10	For child of No2 see NB (Apr 26-06) Card #421						
	11	" " " " 3 " " " " " "610						
	12							
	13							
	14							
	15							
	16							
	17							

TRIBAL ENROLLMENT OF PARENTS

Name of Father	Year	County	Name of Mother	Year	County
1 Ale-much-tubbee	Dead	Nashoba	Ho-ke	Dead	Nashoba
2 Morman Johnson	"	"	No 1		
3 Morris William	1896	"	No 1		
4					
5					
6					
7					
8					
9					
10					
11					
12					
13					
14					
15			Date of Application for Enrollment.	April 19/99	
16					
17					

218

Choctaw By Blood Enrollment Cards 1898-1914

RESIDENCE: Nashoba COUNTY. **Choctaw Nation** Choctaw Roll CARD No.
POST OFFICE: Alikchi, I.T. *(Not Including Freedmen)* FIELD No. **519**

Dawes' Roll No.	NAME		Relationship to Person	AGE	SEX	BLOOD	TRIBAL ENROLLMENT		
							Year	County	No.
1069	1 Noah, Nellis	31	First Named	28	M	Full	1896	Nashoba	9674
1070	2 " Elensie	28	Wife	25	F	"	1896	"	9675
	3								
	4	ENROLLMENT							
	5	OF NOS. 1 and 2 HEREON APPROVED BY THE SECRETARY							
	6	OF INTERIOR Dec 12 1902							
	7								
	8								
	9								
	10	For child of No2 see N.B. (Apr 26-06) Card #754							
	11	" " " " " " " (Mar 3-05) " #907							
	12								
	13								
	14								
	15								
	16								
	17								

TRIBAL ENROLLMENT OF PARENTS

	Name of Father	Year	County	Name of Mother	Year	County
1	Allison Noah	Dead	Nashoba	Celey Noah	Dead	Nashoba
2	David Jefferson	"	"	Sarah Jefferson	1896	"
3						
4						
5						
6						
7						
8						
9						
10						
11						
12						
13						
14						
15				Date of Application for Enrollment.		
16				April 19/99		
17						

Choctaw By Blood Enrollment Cards 1898-1914

RESIDENCE: Nashoba COUNTY.
POST OFFICE: Alikchi, I.T.

Choctaw Nation

Choctaw Roll
(Not Including Freedmen)

CARD No.
FIELD No. 520

Dawes' Roll No.	NAME	Relationship to Person	AGE	SEX	BLOOD	TRIBAL ENROLLMENT		
						Year	County	No.
1071	1 Stephen, Granson ²⁵	First Named	22	M	Full	1896	Nashoba	11410
1072	2 " Sarah ²⁸	Wife	25	F	"	1896	"	P.R. 6
	3							
	4							
	5	ENROLLMENT						
	6	OF NOS. 1 and 2 HEREON APPROVED BY THE SECRETARY						
	7	OF INTERIOR DEC 12 1902						
	8							
	9							
	10	No2 on 1893 Pay roll as Sarah Apeha						
	11	No2 also on 1896 roll, Page 30, No 1223 as						
	12	Sarah Ben						
	13							
	14							
	15							
	16							
	17							

TRIBAL ENROLLMENT OF PARENTS

	Name of Father	Year	County	Name of Mother	Year	County
1	James Stephen	Dead	Nashoba	Wynie John	1896	Nashoba
2	Ape-ha	"	Cedar	Sukey Ape-ha	Dead	Cedar
3						
4						
5						
6						
7						
8						
9						
10						
11						
12						
13						
14				Date of Application for Enrollment.		
15						
16				April 19/99		
17						

Choctaw By Blood Enrollment Cards 1898-1914

RESIDENCE: Red River COUNTY.
POST OFFICE: Kullituklo, I.T.

Choctaw Nation

Choctaw Roll *(Not Including Freedmen)*

CARD No.
FIELD No. **521**

Dawes' Roll No.	NAME	Relationship to Person First Named	AGE	SEX	BLOOD	TRIBAL ENROLLMENT		
						Year	County	No.
1073	1 Williston, John 41	First Named	38	M	Full	1896	Red River	13607
1074	2 " Annie 28	Wife	25	F	"	1896	Towson	183
1075	3 Haiakonubbee, Mary 18	Dau	15	"	"	1896	Red River	13608
1076	4 Williston, Jane 16	"	13	"	"	1896	" "	13609
1077	5 " Denison 8	Son	5	M	"	1896	" "	13610
1078	6 Haiakonubbee, Albert 1	Gr Son	7wks	M	"			
	7							
	8	ENROLLMENT OF NOS. 1 2 3 4 5 and 6 HEREON						
	9	APPROVED BY THE SECRETARY						
	10	OF INTERIOR Dec 12 1902						
	11							
	12							
	13							
	14							
	15							
	16							
	17							

TRIBAL ENROLLMENT OF PARENTS

	Name of Father	Year	County	Name of Mother	Year	County
1	Hully Williston	Dead	Red River	Lydie Williston	Dead	Red River
2	Mullis Isaac	"	" "	Phoebe Austin	"	Bok Tuklo
3	No 1			Liza A Williston	"	Red River
4	No 1			" " "	"	" " "
5	No 1			" " "	"	" " "
6	Willington Haiakonubbi	1896	Red River	No 3		
7						
8						
9	No2 on 1896 roll as Annie Austin					
10	No4 " 1896 " " Janer Williston					
11	For child of No.3 see NB (March 3, 1905) #955					
12	No2 also on 1896 roll Anna Isaac, Page 154.					
13	No6 299 Red River Co.					
14	N°3 is now the wife of Wellington Haiakonubbi on Choctaw card #1224. Evidence of marriage filed Aug. 28, 1902.					
15	N°6 Born July 16, 1902; enrolled Aug. 29, 1902.					
16	No1 and 2 have seperated[sic].					
17	No3 P.O. Idabel I.T. 4/10/05					

Date of Application for Enrollment. #1 to 5

April 19/99

Choctaw By Blood Enrollment Cards 1898-1914

Choctaw Nation

Choctaw Roll *(Not Including Freedmen)*

CARD NO.
FIELD NO. **522**

Dawes' Roll No.	NAME	Relationship to Person First Named	AGE	SEX	BLOOD	TRIBAL ENROLLMENT		
						Year	County	No.
1079	1 Baker, Elizabeth 19		16	F	Full	1896	Red River	13611
1080	2 Williston, Joseph 14	Brother	11	M	"	1893	" "	P.R. 727
1081	3 Baker, Rena 1	Dau	1mo	F	"			
	4							
	5	ENROLLMENT						
	6	OF NOS. 1 2 and 3 HEREON APPROVED BY THE SECRETARY						
	7	OF INTERIOR Dec 12 1902						
	8							
	9							
	10	No1 is now the wife of Noel Baker on Choctaw card #751: Evidence						
	11	of marriage requested May 28, 1902						
	12	No 3 Born April 18, 1902: enrolled May 28, 1902.						
	13							
	14							
	15							
	16							
	17							

TRIBAL ENROLLMENT OF PARENTS

	Name of Father	Year	County	Name of Mother	Year	County
1	Payson Williston	Dead	Red River	Sarah Williston	Dead	Red River
2	" "	"	" "	Sosphia "	"	Towson
3	Noel Baker	1893	Nashoba	No 1		
4						
5						
6						
7						
8						
9						
10						
11						
12						
13						
14					#1 to 2 inc	
15					Date of Application for Enrollment.	April 19/99
16						
17						

Choctaw By Blood Enrollment Cards 1898-1914

RESIDENCE: Bok Tuklo   COUNTY.   **Choctaw Nation**   **Choctaw Roll**   CARD NO.
POST OFFICE: Lukfata, I.T.   *(Not Including Freedmen)*   FIELD NO.   523

	NAME		Relationship to Person First Named	AGE	SEX	BLOOD	TRIBAL ENROLLMENT		
							Year	County	No.
1	Anderson, Colbert	32	First Named	29	M	Full	1896	Bok Tuklo	252
2	" Maggie	27	Wife	24	F	"	1896	" "	253
3	" Noel	10	Son	7	M	"	1896	" "	254
4	" Mary	6	Dau	3	F	"	1896	" "	255
5	" Lucy	2	Dau	8mo	F	"			
6	" Nellie	1	Dau	5mo	F	"			
7									
8	ENROLLMENT								
9	OF NOS. 1 2 3 4 5 and 6 HEREON								
10	APPROVED BY THE SECRETARY OF INTERIOR DEC 12 1902								
11									
12									
13									
14									
15									
16									
17									

TRIBAL ENROLLMENT OF PARENTS

	Name of Father	Year	County	Name of Mother	Year	County
1	Apo-an-teby	Dead	Bok Tulo	No-ley	Dead	Bok Tuklo
2	Davis Noknediah	"	Eagle	Co-nun-tema	"	Eagle
3	No 1			No 2		
4	No 1			No 2		
5	No.1			No.2		
6	Nº1			Nº2		
7						
8						
9	No5 Enrolled March 19th, 1901					
10	Given name of No.2 appears in application for en-					
11	rollment of No. 5 as Nukey					
12	Nº6 Born April 23, 1902. enrolled Sept. 15, 1902.					
13	For child of Nos 1&2 see NB (March 3, 1905) #874					
14						#1 to 4 inc
15						Date of Application for Enrollment.
16						April 19/99
17						

Choctaw By Blood Enrollment Cards 1898-1914

RESIDENCE: Nashoba COUNTY.
POST OFFICE: Smithsville[sic], I.T.

Choctaw Nation

Choctaw Roll
(Not Including Freedmen)

CARD No.
FIELD No. **524**

Dawes' Roll No.	NAME	Relationship to Person First Named	AGE	SEX	BLOOD	TRIBAL ENROLLMENT		
						Year	County	No.
1088	1 Going, Peter 23	First Named	20	M	Full	1896	Nashoba	4753
DEAD	2 " Sainey 20	wife	17	F	"	1896	"	10793
	3							
	4							
	5	ENROLLMENT OF NOS. 1 HEREON APPROVED BY THE SECRETARY OF INTERIOR Dec. 12, 1902						
	6							
	7							
	8							
	9	No. 2 hereon dismissed under order of the Commission to the Five Civilized Tribes of March 31, 1905.						
	10							
	11							
	12							
	13							
	14							
	15							
	16							
	17							

TRIBAL ENROLLMENT OF PARENTS

	Name of Father	Year	County	Name of Mother	Year	County
1	Gibson Going	1896	Nashoba	Elzena Going	Dead	Nashoba
2	Morgan Robert	Dead	"	Nancy Robert	"	"
3						
4	No.2 on 1896 roll as Sainey Robert.					
5	No.1 is now the husband of Lizzie Robinson on Choctaw card #2073: March 13, 1902.					
6	No2 died July 26, 1900: proof of death filed Oct. 6, 1902					
7	For child of No1 see NB (March 3, 1905) #1379					
8						
9						
10						
11						
12						
13						
14						
15				Date of Application for Enrollment.	April 19/99	
16						
17						

Choctaw By Blood Enrollment Cards 1898-1914

RESIDENCE: Nashoba COUNTY. **Choctaw Nation** **Choctaw Roll** CARD NO.
POST OFFICE: Smithsville[sic], I.T. *(Not Including Freedmen)* FIELD NO. **525**

Dawes' Roll No.	NAME	Relationship to Person First Named	AGE	SEX	BLOOD	TRIBAL ENROLLMENT		
						Year	County	No.
1089	1 Robert, Semiton 20	First Named	17	M	Full	1896	Nashoba	10794
1090	2 " Watkin 17	brother	14	"	"	1896	"	10795
	3							
	4 ENROLLMENT							
	5 OF NOS. 1 and 2 HEREON APPROVED BY THE SECRETARY							
	6 OF INTERIOR Dec 12 1902							
	7							
	8							
	9							
	10							
	11							
	12							
	13							
	14							
	15							
	16							
	17							

TRIBAL ENROLLMENT OF PARENTS

	Name of Father	Year	County	Name of Mother	Year	County
1	Morgan Robert	Dead	Nashoba	Nancy Robert	Dead	Nashoba
2	" "	"	"	" "	"	"
3						
4						
5						
6						
7						
8						
9						
10						
11						
12						
13						
14					Date of Application for Enrollment.
15				Date of application for enrollment April 19/99
16						
17						

Choctaw By Blood Enrollment Cards 1898-1914

RESIDENCE:	Nashoba	COUNTY.	Choctaw Nation	Choctaw Roll	CARD NO.	
POST OFFICE:	Smithsville[sic], I.T.			(Not Including Freedmen)	FIELD NO.	526

Dawes' Roll No.	NAME		Relationship to Person First Named	AGE	SEX	BLOOD	TRIBAL ENROLLMENT		
							Year	County	No.
1091	1 Going, Gibson	39		36	M	Full	1896	Nashoba	4751
1092	2 " Sophia	29	Wife	26	F	"	1896	"	4752
1093	3 " Osborne	21	Son	18	M	"	1896	"	4754
1094	4 " Vinson	17	"	14	"	"	1896	"	4755
1095	5 " Salina	9	Dau	6	F	"	1896	"	4756
1096	6 " Rayson	6	Son	2	M	"			
1097	7 John	DIED PRIOR TO SEPTEMBER 25 1902	"	5mo	"	"			
1098	8 Isam	DIED PRIOR TO SEPTEMBER 25, 1902	Son	11mo	M	"			
	9								
	10								
	11	ENROLLMENT OF NOS. 1234567and8 HEREON							
	12	APPROVED BY THE SECRETARY							
	13	OF INTERIOR Dec 12, 1902							
	14								
	15								
	16								
	17								

TRIBAL ENROLLMENT OF PARENTS

	Name of Father	Year	County	Name of Mother	Year	County
1	John Going	Dead	Eagle	Montema	Dead	Eagle
2	Adam Epalumbe	1896	Nashoba	Lucy Epalumbe	"	Nashoba
3	No 1			Sallie Going	"	"
4	No 1			" "	"	"
5	No 1			No 2		
6	No 1			No 2		
7	No 1			No 2		
8	No 1			No 2		
9						
10	No.2 on 1896 roll as Sophina Going					
11	No.5 " 1896 " " Selaway "					
12	No.8 Enrolled September 3, 1901.					
	No.7 died Sept 14, 1900: proof of death filed Dec. 11, 1902					
13	No.7 died Sept 14-1900: No.8 died Feb 23-1902: Enrollment cancelled by Department July8,1904					
14	For child of Nos 1&2 see NB (Apr 26-06) card #604					
15	" " " " 3 " " " " " #609					
16	" " " " 1&2 " (Mar 3-05) " #894			Date of Application for Enrollment.		
	" " " " 4 " " " " " " #926				April 19/99	
17	" " " " 3 " " " " " " #974					

226

Choctaw By Blood Enrollment Cards 1898-1914

RESIDENCE: Red River COUNTY.	Choctaw Nation	Choctaw Roll (Not Including Freedmen)	CARD NO.
POST OFFICE: Shawneetown, I.T.			FIELD NO. 527

Dawes' Roll No.	NAME	Relationship to Person First Named	AGE	SEX	BLOOD	TRIBAL ENROLLMENT		
						Year	County	No.
1099	1 Wright, Bicy 48	First Named	45	F	Full	1896	Red River	7565
	2							
	3 ENROLLMENT							
	OF NOS. 1 HEREON							
	4 APPROVED BY THE SECRETARY							
	5 OF INTERIOR Dec 12 1902							
	6							
	7							
	8							
	9	On 1896 roll as Bicy King						
	10							
	11							
	12							
	13							
	14							
	15							
	16							
	17							

TRIBAL ENROLLMENT OF PARENTS

	Name of Father	Year	County	Name of Mother	Year	County
1	Davis King	Dead	Skullyville	Jincy King	Dead	Skullyville
2						
3						
4						
5						
6						
7						
8						
9						
10						
11						
12						
13					Date of Application for Enrollment.	
14						
15					April 19/99	
16						
17						

Choctaw By Blood Enrollment Cards 1898-1914

RESIDENCE: Eagle   COUNTY.   **Choctaw Nation**   **Choctaw Roll**   CARD NO.
POST OFFICE: Eagletown, Ind. Ter.   *(Not Including Freedmen)*   FIELD NO.   528

Dawes' Roll No.	NAME		Relationship to Person	AGE	SEX	BLOOD	TRIBAL ENROLLMENT		
							Year	County	No.
1100	1 Wilson, David	34	First Named	36	M	Full	1893	Eagle	P.R. 706
1101	2 " Wicy		Wife	38	F	"	1893	"	707
1102	3 " Helen	18	Dau	15	"	"	1893	"	708
1103	4 " Lucy	16	"	13	"	"	1893	"	709
1104	5 " Mikey	9	Son	6	M	"	1893	"	712
14564	6 " Cabiu	7	"	3	M	"			
1104	7 " Lena	3	Dau	8mo	F	"			
	8								
	9	No4 Died prior to September 25, 1902, not entitled to land or money. See decision in Office Letter April 5, 1908 (I.T. 9099-1908)							
	10	N°6 Proof of birth received and filed Dec 24, 1902.							
	11	ENROLLMENT							
	12	OF NOS. 1 2 3 4 5 and 7 HEREON APPROVED BY THE SECRETARY							
	13	OF INTERIOR DEC 12 1902							
	14								
	15	ENROLLMENT							
	16	OF NOS. 6 HEREON APPROVED BY THE SECRETARY OF INTERIOR MAY 20 1903							
	17								

TRIBAL ENROLLMENT OF PARENTS

	Name of Father	Year	County	Name of Mother	Year	County
1	Enu-lija	Dead	Eagle	Artill Wilson	Dead	Eagle
2	Sho-ma-ka	"	"	Pisa-li-hoke	"	"
3	No 1			No 2		
4	No 1			No 2		
5	No 1			No 2		
6	No 1			No 2		
7	No 1			No 2		
8						
9						
10						
11	No6 – Affidavit as to birth to be supplied: Recd May 9/99					
12	No3 also on 1896 roll; Page 354, No 13509					
13	No5 " " 1896 " " 354 No 13504					
14	No2 " " 1896 " " 354 No 13515 as Wicey Wilson					
	No1 " " 1896 " " 355 No 13529					
15	No4 " " 1896 " " 355 No 13554			# 1 to 6		
16	No.7 Enrolled April 15, 1901			Date of Application for Enrollment.	April 19/99	
17						

Choctaw By Blood Enrollment Cards 1898-1914

RESIDENCE: Eagle COUNTY.
POST OFFICE: Eagletown, Ind. Ter.
Choctaw Nation
Choctaw Roll (Not Including Freedmen)
CARD NO.
FIELD NO. **529**

Dawes' Roll No.	NAME	Relationship to Person	AGE	SEX	BLOOD	TRIBAL ENROLLMENT		
						Year	County	No.
1106	1 Haiakonobi, Wilson 63	First Named	60	M	Full	1893	Eagle	P.R. 320
DEAD	2 " Louisa	Wife	40	F	"	1893	"	321
1107	3 " Sillis 18	Dau	15	F	"	1893	"	323
1108	4 Haiakonobi Maike 15	Dau	12	F	"	1893	"	324
1109	5 " Adeline 11	"	8	"	"	1893	"	325
1110	6 " Mary 9	"	6	"	"	1893	"	326

ENROLLMENT OF NOS. 1,3,4,5 and 6 HEREON APPROVED BY THE SECRETARY OF INTERIOR Dec 12 1902

No3 is a girl sex changed under Departmental instructions of July 15, 1904 (D.C. #25570-1904)

For child of No3 see NB (Apr 26-06) Card #874

No1 on 1896 roll Eagle Co Page 137
No 5646 as Nickson Hayakonubbi
No2 on 1896 roll Eagle Co Page 137
No 5637 as Sillis Hayakonubbi
No3 on 1896 roll Eagle Co Page 137
No 5634 as Maikkie Hayakonubbi
No5 on 1896 roll Eagle Co Page 136
No6 " 1896 " " " 137

No1 on 1893 Pay roll as Wickson Hiakonabe
No2 " 1893 " " " Susiang "
No3 " 1893 " " " Sillis "
No4 " 1893 " " " Maike "
No5 " 1893 " " " Ateline "
No6 " 1893 " " " Mary "

	TRIBAL ENROLLMENT OF PARENTS					
	Name of Father	Year	County	Name of Mother	Year	County
1	Haiakonobi	Dead	Eagle	Putchee	Dead	Eagle
2	Ya-ho-te-by	"	Nashoba	Ho-ta-che	"	"
3	No 1			No 2		
4	No 1			No 2		
5	No 1			No 2		
6	No 1			No 2		
7				No. 2 hereon dismissed under order of		
8				the Commission to the Five Civilized		
9				Tribes of March 31, 1905.		
10	Amos Hayakonubbi, No 5595 on 1896 Roll as age 1 with Louisa Hayakonubbi					
11	But left off on this card No 529 Oct. 13, 1902					
12	No2 Died Sept. 1, 1899, proof of death filed					
13	No3 is now wife of Wright Anderson on					
14	Choctaw Card #1124					
15	No 5594 as Antaline Hayakonubbi			Date of Application for Enrollment.		
16	" 5635 " Mary "			April 19/99		
17						

Choctaw By Blood Enrollment Cards 1898-1914

RESIDENCE: Eagle   COUNTY.
POST OFFICE: Eagletown, Ind. Ter.

Choctaw Nation

Choctaw Roll
(Not Including Freedmen)

CARD NO.
FIELD NO. 530

Dawes' Roll No.	NAME	Relationship to Person First Named	AGE	SEX	BLOOD	TRIBAL ENROLLMENT		
						Year	County	No.
1111	1 Jones, George 54	First Named	51	M	Full	1893	Eagle	P.R. 437
1112	2 " Lienda 47	Wife	46	F	"	1893	"	438
1113	3 " Elson 19	Son	16	M	"	1893	"	439
1114	4 " Miston 14	"	11	"	"	1893	"	440
1115	5 " Houston 12	"	9	"	"	1893	"	441
1116	6 " Liney 10	Dau	7	F	"	1893	"	442
1117	7 " Louiston 4	Son	1	M	"			
1118	8 " Wilson 20	Nephew	17	"	"	1896	Atoka	7332
15779	9 " Alfus 9	Son	9	M	"	1896	Eagle	6945
	10 No1 on 1896 roll Page 170, No 6929							
	11 No2 " 1896 " " 171 " 6939 as Lente Jones							
	12 No3 " 1896 " " 170 " 6938							
	No4 " 1896 " " 171 " 6947							
	13 No5 " 1896 " " 171 " 6945							
	14 No6 " 1896 " " 171 " 6940 as Learnie Jones					ENROLLMENT		
	15 No8 is also on 1896 roll Page 170, No 6932					OF NOS. 1,2,3,4,5,6,7 and 8 HEREON APPROVED BY THE SECRETARY		
	No9 on 1896 roll page 171 No 6945 as Houston Jones					OF INTERIOR Dec 12 1902		
	16							
	17							

TRIBAL ENROLLMENT OF PARENTS

	Name of Father	Year	County	Name of Mother	Year	County
1	Louis Jones	Dead	Eagle	Emale Jones	Dead	Eagle
2	John Going	"	"	Montema Going	"	"
3	No 1			No 2		
4	No 1			No 2		
5	No 1			No 2		
6	No 1			No 2		
7	No 1			No 2		
8	Simon Jones	Dead	Eagle	Melissie Jones	Dead	Eagle
9	No 1			No 2		
10				ENROLLMENT		
11				OF NOS. 9 HEREON APPROVED BY THE SECRETARY		
12	No2 on 1893 Payroll as Leaton Jones			OF INTERIOR Mar 15 1905		
13	No6 " 1893 " " " Liney "					
14	No5 died - - 1901: Enrollment cancelled by Department July 8 – 1904					
15				Date of Application for Enrollment.		
16				April 19/99		
17						

Choctaw By Blood Enrollment Cards 1898-1914

RESIDENCE: Nashoba COUNTY.
POST OFFICE: Smithsville[sic], I.T.

Choctaw Nation

Choctaw Roll CARD No.
(Not Including Freedmen) FIELD No. 531

Dawes' Roll No.	NAME	Relationship to Person First Named	AGE	SEX	BLOOD	TRIBAL ENROLLMENT Year	TRIBAL ENROLLMENT County	TRIBAL ENROLLMENT No.
1119	1 McCoy, Iston 28	First Named	25	M	Full	1896	Nashoba	9280
1120	2 " Annie 33	Wife	30	F	"	1896	"	5527
	3							
	4	ENROLLMENT						
	5	OF NOS. 1 and 2 HEREON APPROVED BY THE SECRETARY						
	6	OF INTERIOR Dec 12 1902						
	7							
	8							
	9							
	10	No2 is well known as a full blood Choctaw. She has lived						
	11	in the Nation all her life under different names none of						
	12	which can be found on the Rolls.						
	13	No2 on 1896 Choctaw roll as Annie Hayes. Dec. 31st, 1900						
	14							
	15							
	16							
	17							

TRIBAL ENROLLMENT OF PARENTS

	Name of Father	Year	County	Name of Mother	Year	County
1	Ela-po-shema	Dead	Nashoba	Is-te-chee	Dead	Eagle
2	John Wallace	"		Ya-ko-tema	"	
3						
4						
5						
6						
7						
8						
9						
10						
11						
12						
13						
14						
15						
16						
17						

Date of Application for Enrollment. April 19/99

Choctaw By Blood Enrollment Cards 1898-1914

RESIDENCE: Red River   COUNTY.   **Choctaw Nation**   **Choctaw Roll**   CARD NO.
POST OFFICE: Garvin, I.T.   *(Not Including Freedmen)*   FIELD NO.   532

Dawes' Roll No.	NAME	Relationship to Person First Named	AGE	SEX	BLOOD	TRIBAL ENROLLMENT Year	County	No.
1121	1 Wesley, Tecumseh 51	First Named	48	M	Full	1896	Red River	13631
1122	2 " Louisa 36	Wife	33	F	"	1896	" "	13632
1123	3 " Emerson 16	Son	13	M	"	1896	" "	13633
1124	4 " Martha 12	Dau	11	F	"	1896	" "	13634
1125	5 " James 12	Son	9	M	"	1896	" "	13635
1126	6 " Rayson 10	"	7	"	"	1896	" "	13636
1127	7 " Sophy 8	Dau	5	F	"	1896	" "	13637
1128	8 " Minnie 3	"	7mo	"	"			
	9							
	10							
	11	ENROLLMENT						
	12	OF NOS. 12345678 HEREON APPROVED BY THE SECRETARY						
	13	OF INTERIOR Dec 12 1902						
	14							
	15							
	16							
	17							

TRIBAL ENROLLMENT OF PARENTS

	Name of Father	Year	County	Name of Mother	Year	County
1	Wesley	Dead	Red River	Betsy Wesley	Dead	Red River
2	Cabel Lewis	"	Cedar	Pearlie Lewis	"	Cedar
3	No 1			No 2		
4	No 1			No 2		
5	No 1			No 2		
6	No 1			No 2		
7	No 1			No 2		
8	No 1			No 2		
9						
10						
11						
12						
13						
14						
15					#1 to 7	
16				Date of Application for Enrollment.		April 19/99
17				No 8 enrolled Dec 16/99		

232

Choctaw By Blood Enrollment Cards 1898-1914

RESIDENCE: Eagle   COUNTY.   **Choctaw Nation**   **Choctaw Roll**   CARD NO.
POST OFFICE: Eagletown, I.T.   *(Not Including Freedmen)*   FIELD NO. 533

Dawes' Roll No.	NAME		Relationship to Person First Named	AGE	SEX	BLOOD	TRIBAL ENROLLMENT		
							Year	County	No.
1129	1	Battiest, Lawson ⁵⁴	First Named	49	M	Full	1896	Eagle	1293
1130	2	" Polly ⁵²	Wife	49	F	"	1896	"	1310
1131	3	" Wilsey ¹⁸	Dau	15	"	"	1896	"	1323
1132	4	" Marlis ¹³	Son	10	M	"	1896	"	1302
1133	5	" Kisson ¹⁸	Dau	16	F	"	1896	"	1322
15968	6	" Allittie ¹	Dau of No5	1	F	"			
	7								
	8	ENROLLMENT OF NOS. 1 2 3 4 and 5 HEREON							
	9	APPROVED BY THE SECRETARY							
	10	OF INTERIOR DEC 12 1902							
	11								
	12	ENROLLMENT							
	13	OF NOS. ～～ 6 ～～ HEREON							
	14	APPROVED BY THE SECRETARY OF INTERIOR MAR 14 1906							
	15								
	16								
	17								

TRIBAL ENROLLMENT OF PARENTS

	Name of Father	Year	County	Name of Mother	Year	County
1	[Illegible] Battiest	Dead	Eagle		Dead	Eagle
2		"	"		"	"
3	No 1			No 2		
4	No 1			No 2		
5	No 1			No 2		
6				No 5		
7						
8	No5 on 1896 roll as Stisin Battiest. Also on 1893 Pay roll Eagle Co No 111					
9						
10	Names of parents of No2 could not be ascertained Name " mother " No1 " " "					
11	No6 born Feb 22, 1902: application received and No6 placed on					
12	this card April 17, 1905 under Act of Congress approved March 3, 1905					
13						
14						
15					#1 to 5 inc	
16					Date of Application for Enrollment	April 19/99
17	No5 P.O. Lukfata I.T. 1/10/03					

Choctaw By Blood Enrollment Cards 1898-1914

RESIDENCE: Red River   COUNTY.   **Choctaw Nation**   Choctaw Roll   CARD NO.
POST OFFICE: Shawneetown, I.T.   *(Not Including Freedmen)*   FIELD NO. **534**

Dawes' Roll No.	NAME		Relationship to Person First Named	AGE	SEX	BLOOD	TRIBAL ENROLLMENT		
							Year	County	No.
1134	1	Williams, Watt ⁴⁷	First Named	44	M	Full	1896	Red River	13638
1135	2	" Eliza ⁴³	Wife	40	F	"	1896	" "	13639
1136	3	" Byington ²³	Son	20	M	"	1896	" "	13640
1137	4	" Abner ²⁰	"	17	"	"	1896	" "	13641
1138	5	" Wacy ¹⁸	Dau	15	F	"	1896	" "	13642
1139	6	" Levicey ¹⁷	"	14	"	"	1896	" "	13643
1140	7	" Phillis ¹⁴	Son	11	M	"	1896	" "	13644
	8								
	9								
	10								
	11	ENROLLMENT							
	12	OF NOS. 1,2,3,4,5,6 and 7 HEREON APPROVED BY THE SECRETARY							
	13	OF INTERIOR Dec 12 1902							
	14								
	15								
	16								
	17								

TRIBAL ENROLLMENT OF PARENTS

	Name of Father	Year	County	Name of Mother	Year	County
1	Parsey Williams	Dead	Towson	Betsy Williams	Dead	Red River
2	Alex Bond	"	Red River	Juliann Bond	"	" "
3	No 1			No 2		
4	No 1			No 2		
5	No 1			No 2		
6	No 1			No 2		
7	No 1			No 2		
8						
9						
10	No7 on 1896 roll as Phillip Williams					
11	No6 " 1896 " " Levicy "					
12	No4 is now the husband of Rocey Pigg. Evidence of marriage filed July 8, 1901					
	No6 on 1896 roll as Levicy Williams See Choctaw card D843					
13	No3 is now the husband of Isabel Johnson Choc. No 1263~~11/26/02					
14	For child of No4 see NB (March 3, 1905) #904					
15					Date of Application for Enrollment.	
16					April 19/99	
17						

Choctaw By Blood Enrollment Cards 1898-1914

RESIDENCE: Towson   COUNTY.   **Choctaw Nation**   **Choctaw Roll** *(Not Including Freedmen)*   CARD NO.
POST OFFICE: Fowlerville, I.T.   FIELD NO. **535**

Dawes' Roll No.	NAME		Relationship to Person First Named	AGE	SEX	BLOOD	TRIBAL ENROLLMENT		
							Year	County	No.
1141	1 Lucas, Luvicey	42	Named	40	F	Full	1896	Towson	193
1142	2 Austin, Minerva	19	Dau	16	"	"	1896	"	194
1143	3 Lucas, Phoebe	18	"	15	"	"	1896	"	195
1144	4 Austin, Narcissa	15	"	12	"	"	1896	"	196
1145	5 " Ida	13	"	10	"	"	1896	"	197
1146	6 " Samuel	11	Son	8	M	"	1896	"	198
1147	7 " Nellie	3	G Dau	4mo	F	1/2			
IW700	8 Lucas, Spencer	37	hus of No.3	37	M	I.W.			
	9								
	10								
	11								
	12								
	13								
	14								
	15								
	16								
	17								

ENROLLMENT
OF NOS. 123456and7 HEREON
APPROVED BY THE SECRETARY
OF INTERIOR Dec 12 1902

ENROLLMENT
OF NOS. ~ 8 ~ HEREON
APPROVED BY THE SECRETARY
OF INTERIOR May 7 1904

TRIBAL ENROLLMENT OF PARENTS

	Name of Father	Year	County	Name of Mother	Year	County
1	Morris Garland	Dead	Sans Bois	Laris LeFlore	Dead	Towson
2	Henry Austin	"	Towson	No 1		
3	" "	"	"	No 1		
4	" "	"	"	No 1		
5	" "	"	"	No 1		
6	" "	"	"	No 1		
7	John Williams		Non Citz	No2		
8	Nath Lucas	dead	non-citizen	Ann Lucas	dead	non-citizen
9						
10	No1 on 1896 roll as Luvicey Austin					
11	No5 "	1896	" " Edda			
12	No3 is now the wife of Spencer Lucas January 15, 1901 Husband of No.3 on Choctaw card D #612					
13	No1 is wife of Thomas L. Lucas on Choctaw card #5647					
14	No8 transferred from Choctaw Card #D612, See decision of Feby 29, 1904					
15						#1 to 6
16					Date of Application for Enrollment.	April 19/99
17					No7 enrolled Jany 17, 1900	

Choctaw By Blood Enrollment Cards 1898-1914

RESIDENCE: Towson COUNTY.
POST OFFICE: Fowlerville, I.T.

Choctaw Nation

Choctaw Roll
(Not Including Freedmen)

CARD No.
FIELD No. **536**

Dawes' Roll No.	NAME	Relationship to Person First Named	AGE	SEX	BLOOD	TRIBAL ENROLLMENT		
						Year	County	No.
1148	1 Harkens, Isaac 25	First Named	22	M	1/2	1896	Towson	5472
I.W. 559	2 " Alice 24	Wife	18	F	I.W.			
1149	3 " George 3	Son	3mo	M	1/4			
1150	4 " Arasona 2	Dau	2mo	F	1/4			
14565	5 " Leonie 1	Dau	5mo	F	1/4			
	6							
	7	ENROLLMENT OF NOS. 1 3 and 4 HEREON APPROVED BY THE SECRETARY OF INTERIOR Dec 12 1902						
	8							
	9							
	10							
	11	ENROLLMENT OF NOS. 5 HEREON APPROVED BY THE SECRETARY OF INTERIOR May 20 1903						
	12							
	13							
	14	ENROLLMENT OF NOS. ~~ 2 ~~ HEREON APPROVED BY THE SECRETARY OF INTERIOR Feb 8 1904						
	15							
	16							
	17							

TRIBAL ENROLLMENT OF PARENTS

	Name of Father	Year	County	Name of Mother	Year	County
1	Dick Harkins	Dead	Towson	Luvicey Lucas	1896	Towson
2	Leonard Romines		Non Citz	Betty Romines	Dead	Non Citz
3	No 1			No 2		
4	No 1			No 2		
5	No 1			No 2		
6						
7						
8	No 1 on 1896 roll as Isaac Harkin					
9	No.4 Enrolled June 4th, 1901					
10	No 5 born June 30, 1902: enrolled Dec 2 1902					
	For child of Nos 1&2 see NB (March 3, 1905) #1329					
11						
12						
13						
14						
15					#1&2	
16				Date of Application for Enrollment.	April 19/99	
17	P.O. Valliant I.T. 11/28/02			No 3 enrolled Nov 1/99		

236

Choctaw By Blood Enrollment Cards 1898-1914

| RESIDENCE: Eagle COUNTY. | POST OFFICE: Eagletown, I.T. | **Choctaw Nation** | Choctaw Roll (Not Including Freedmen) | CARD NO. FIELD NO. **537** |

Dawes' Roll No.	NAME		Relationship to Person	AGE	SEX	BLOOD	TRIBAL ENROLLMENT		
							Year	County	No.
1151	1 Dyer, James	64	First Named	61	M	Full	1896	Eagle	3416
1152	2 " Adeline	18	Dau	15	F	1/2	1896	"	3408
1153	3 " James Jr	14	Son	11	M	1/2	1896	"	3417
1154	4 " Aaron	12	"	9	"	1/2	1896	"	3409
1155	5 " Willy	9	"	6	"	1/2	1896	"	3425
1156	6 " Pearly	6	Dau	3	F	1/2	1896	"	3430
IW 1091	7 " Malinda	44	Wife	40	F	I.W.			14469
1157	8 " Nellie May	1	GrandDau	5mo	F	1/2			
	9								
	10	ENROLLMENT							
	11	OF NOS. 123456and8 HEREON APPROVED BY THE SECRETARY							
	12	OF INTERIOR Dec 12 1902							
	13								
	14	ENROLLMENT							
	15	OF NOS. ～ 7 ～ HEREON APPROVED BY THE SECRETARY							
	16	OF INTERIOR Nov 16 1904							
	17								

TRIBAL ENROLLMENT OF PARENTS

	Name of Father	Year	County	Name of Mother	Year	County	
1	Moses Dyer	Dead	Eagle		Dead	Eagle	
2	No 1			Malinda Dyer		Non Citz	
3	No 1			" "		" "	
4	No 1			" "		" "	
5	No 1			" "		" "	
6	No 1			" "		" "	
7	William Labor	dead	non-citizen	Preeca Labor	dead	" "	
8	Unknown			No 2			
9							
10	Evidence of marriage to be supplied. Recd and approved by Commiss-						
11	ioner McKennon, May 6/99						
12	No.7 Enrolled on this card Feby 18, 1902						
13	No.8 Born Sept. 29, 1901: enrolled March 4, 1902.						
14	For child of No1 see NB (Apr 26-06) Card #823					#1 to 6 inc	
15						Date of Application for Enrollment.	
16						April 19/99	
17	No2 P.O. Cope I.T. 5/23/05						

Choctaw By Blood Enrollment Cards 1898-1914

RESIDENCE: Eagle   COUNTY.   **Choctaw Nation**   Choctaw Roll   CARD No.
POST OFFICE: Eagletown, I.T.   *(Not Including Freedmen)*   FIELD No. **538**

Dawes' Roll No.	NAME	Relationship to Person First Named	AGE	SEX	BLOOD	TRIBAL ENROLLMENT		
						Year	County	No.
1158	₁ McClure, Preeman J. ³⁵	First Named	32	M	1/8	1896	Tobucksy	9179
1159	₂ " Laura ²¹	Wife	18	F	1/2	1896	"	3419
1160	₃ " Ida ⁴	Dau	5mo	"	5/16			
1161	₄ " Sarah Artemisso ¹	Dau	9mo	F	5/16			
	₅							
	₆							
	₇							
	₈							
	₉							
	₁₀							
	₁₁							
	₁₂							
	₁₃							
	₁₄							
	₁₅							
	₁₆							
	₁₇							

ENROLLMENT
OF NOS. 1, 2, 3 and 4 HEREON
APPROVED BY THE SECRETARY
OF INTERIOR Dec 12 1902
Dec 12 1902

TRIBAL ENROLLMENT OF PARENTS

	Name of Father	Year	County	Name of Mother	Year	County
₁	Isaac McClure	Dead	Blue	Laura McClure	Dead	Non Citz
₂	James Dyer	1896	Eagle	Malinda Dyer	"	" "
₃	No 1			No 2		
₄	No 1			No 2		
₅						
₆						
₇						
₈		No.1 is now guardian of Virginia Winship on Choctaw card #542.				
₉		Petition for adoption filed December 16, 1902.				
₁₀		No3 Affidavit of birth to be supplied: Recd Dec 19/99; but irregular and returned for correction; Filed Jany 17, 1900.				
₁₁		Evidence of marriage to be supplied: See card No 537				
₁₂		as to marriage of parents of No.2.				
₁₃		No.1 on 1896 roll as Preman J. McClure				
	No.4 Born January 31, 1901 and enrolled November 12, 1901.					
₁₄		No.1 as to proof of marriage of parents, see				
₁₅		testimony of S.E. Lewis attached to card			#1 to 3
₁₆		No. 3845.			Date of Application for Enrollment.	
₁₇	Lukfata I.T. 12/9/02				April 19/99	

238

Choctaw By Blood Enrollment Cards 1898-1914

RESIDENCE: Nashoba   COUNTY.   **Choctaw Nation**   **Choctaw Roll**   CARD NO.
POST OFFICE: Alikchi, I.T.   *(Not Including Freedmen)*   FIELD NO. **539**

Dawes' Roll No.	NAME	Relationship to Person First Named	AGE	SEX	BLOOD	TRIBAL ENROLLMENT Year	County	No.
Dead	Warnehtha ~DEAD		70	M	Full	1896	Nashoba	13355
1162	2 " Billy DIED PRIOR TO SEPTEMBER 25, '02	Wife	65	F	"	1893	"	P.R. 969
1163	3 Baker, Coleman ²⁰	S.Son	17	M	"	1896	"	1156
1164	4 Battiest, Enettie ¹⁹	S.Dau	16	F	"	1896	"	1155
1165	5 Baker, Malin ⁵	G.S.Dau	1	"	"			
1166	6 Battiest, Ella ¹	Dau of No.4	7mo	F	"			
	7 No. 1 hereon dismissed under order of							
	8 the Commission to the Five Civilized							
	Tribes of March 31, 1905.							
	9							
	10 ENROLLMENT							
	OF NOS. 2 3 4 5 and 6 HEREON							
	11 APPROVED BY THE SECRETARY							
	OF INTERIOR Dec 12, 1902							
	12							
	13 For child of No.4 See NB (Apr. 26-06) Card #606.							
	14 No.1 is also known as Tonih cha.							
	15							
	16							
	17							

TRIBAL ENROLLMENT OF PARENTS

	Name of Father	Year	County	Name of Mother	Year	County
1	Ok-la-kin-ta	Dead	Nashoba	I-en-sey		Died in Mississippi
2	Phila-ka-teby	"	"	E-me-ho-ne	Dead	Nashoba
3	Simon Baker	"	"	No.2		
4	" "	"	"	No.2		
5	Alenden Battice	1896	"	No.4		
6	Colbert Battiest	1896	"	No.4		
7						
8						
9			No.5: Affidavit of birth to be supplied: Recd April 24/99.			
10		No.2 died Oct. – 1900: Enrollment cancelled by Department July 8 – 1904.				
11			No.1 on 1896 roll as "Warnehcha"			
12			No.2 " 1893 Pay roll as "Baise"			
13		No.1 Died Oct. 16, 1900. Evidence of death filed Oct. 9, 1901.				
		No.4 is now the wife of Colbert Battiest on Choctaw card #924: Nov. 25, 1901.				
14		No.6 born April 7, 1901: Enrolled Nov. 25, 1901				
15		No.2 died Oct. 1900: proof of death filed Dec. 4, 1902.				
16				Date of Application for Enrollment April 19/99		
17				#1 to 5		

Choctaw By Blood Enrollment Cards 1898-1914

RESIDENCE: Eagle   COUNTY.   **Choctaw Nation**   **Choctaw Roll** (Not Including Freedmen)   CARD NO.
POST OFFICE: Eagletown, I.T/   FIELD NO. **540**

Dawes' Roll No.	NAME	Relationship to Person First Named	AGE	SEX	BLOOD	TRIBAL ENROLLMENT		
						Year	County	No.
1167	1 Colbert, Billis		42	M	Full	1896	Eagle	2594
1168	2 Colbert, Winey ³³	Wife	30	F	"	1896	"	2641
	3							
	4							
	5							
	6							
	7							
	8							
	9							
	10							
	11							
	12							
	13							
	14							
	15							
	16							
	17							

ENROLLMENT
OF NOS. 1 and 2 HEREON
APPROVED BY THE SECRETARY
OF INTERIOR Dec 12 1902

TRIBAL ENROLLMENT OF PARENTS

Name of Father	Year	County	Name of Mother	Year	County
1 David Colbert	Dead	Eagle	Ka-nun-te-ma	Dead	Eagle
2 General Cooper	"	"	Netsey Cooper	"	"
3					
4					
5					
6	No.2 on 1896 roll as Winney Cooper.				
7	No.2 is now wife of Thomas Sampson Choc #1057 (Card)				
8	No.1 Died January – 1902 Enrollment cancelled by Department May 3, 1906				
9					
10					
11					
12					
13					
14					
15			Date of Application for Enrollment.		April 19/99
16					
17					

240

Choctaw By Blood Enrollment Cards 1898-1914

RESIDENCE: Nashoba COUNTY.   **Choctaw Nation**   **Choctaw Roll** CARD No.
POST OFFICE: Alikchi, Ind. Ter.   *(Not Including Freedmen)*   FIELD No. **541**

Dawes' Roll No.	NAME		Relationship to Person First Named	AGE	SEX	BLOOD	TRIBAL ENROLLMENT		
							Year	County	No.
1169	1 Watkins, Nicholas	38	First Named	35	M	Full	1896	Nashoba	13378
1170	2 " Ennissie	48	Wife	45	F	"	1896	"	13379
1171	3 " Hickman	17	Son	14	M	"	1896	"	13380
1172	4 " Zona	19	Dau	16	F	"	1896	"	13381
1173	5 " Davis	15	Son	12	M	"	1896	"	13382
1174	6 " Louviney	13	Dau	10	F	"	1896	"	13383
1175	7 " Millawit	8	Son	5	M	"	1896	"	13384
1176	8 " Sealy	6	Dau	3	F	"	1896	"	13385
	9								
	10								
	11	ENROLLMENT							
	12	OF NOS. 12345678 HEREON APPROVED BY THE SECRETARY							
	13	OF INTERIOR Dec 12 1902							
	14								
	15								
	16								
	17								

TRIBAL ENROLLMENT OF PARENTS

	Name of Father	Year	County	Name of Mother	Year	County
1	Eastman Watkins	1896	Nashoba	Winey Watkins	1896	Nashoba
2	Jonas Watson	Dead	"	Autuna Watson	Dead	"
3	No 1			No 2		
4	No 1			No 2		
5	No 1			No 2		
6	No 1			No 2		
7	No 1			No 2		
8	No 1			No 2		
9						
10						
11			No2 on 1896 roll as Emisie Watkins			
12			No4 " 1896 " " Sonney "			
13			No5 " 1896 " " Dennis "			
			No7 " 1896 " " Matward "			
14			No8 " 1896 " " Sillie "			
15			For child of No6 see NB (Apr 26-06) Card #665			Date of Application for Enrollment.
16			" " " No4 " " (Mar 3-05) " #1085			April 19/99
17						

241

Choctaw By Blood Enrollment Cards 1898-1914

RESIDENCE: Eagle   COUNTY.
POST OFFICE: Eagletown, Ind. Ter.   **Choctaw Nation**   **Choctaw Roll** *(Not Including Freedmen)*   CARD NO.
FIELD NO. 542

Dawes' Roll No.	NAME	Relationship to Person First Named	AGE	SEX	BLOOD	TRIBAL ENROLLMENT Year	County	No.
1177	1 Winship, Simeon 30	First Named	27	M	1/2	1896	Eagle	13481
1178	2 " Nela 41	Wife	38	F	Full	1896	"	13483
1179	3 " Virginia 13	Dau	10	"	3/4	1896	"	13482
1180	4 " Andy 11	Son	8	M	3/4	1896	"	13484
1181	5 " Buddy 8	"	5	"	3/4	1896	"	13485
1182	6 " Tobias 6	"	3	"	3/4	1896	"	13486
1183	7 " Mitchell 10	"	7	"	3/4	1896	"	13487
1184	8 Christy, Charley 20	S.Son	17	"	Full	1896	"	2597
1185	9 " Amanda 18	S.Dau	15	F	"	1896	"	2626
1186	10 " Harmon 15	S.Son	12	M	"	1896	"	2609
14566	11 Winship, Rafy [or Rofy]1	Son	1	M	3/4			
	12							
	13 ENROLLMENT OF NOS. 1,2,3,4,5,6,7,8,9 and 10 HEREON							
	14 APPROVED BY THE SECRETARY OF INTERIOR Dec. 12, 1902							
	15							
	16							
	17							

No11 born August 9, 1901: enrolled December 5, 1902
No2 is on 1896 roll as four years of age
No1 " " 1896 " " Simon Winship
No9 " " 1896 " " Mandy Christy

TRIBAL ENROLLMENT OF PARENTS

	Name of Father	Year	County	Name of Mother	Year	County	
1	Tobias Winship	Dead	Nashoba	Mary Winship		Non Citz	For children of No.9 see NB (Mar 3 '05) #447
2	John Goings	"	Eagle	Tick-a-bon-tana	Dead	Eagle	
3	No. 1			Sarah Winship	"	"	
4	No. 1			" "	"	"	
5	No. 1			No.2			
6	No. 1			No.2			
7	No. 1			No.2			
8	Calvin Christy	Dead	Eagle	No.2			
9	" "	"	"	No.2			
10	" "	"	"	No.2			
11	No. 1			No2			
12					ENROLLMENT OF NOS. 11 HEREON		
13					APPROVED BY THE SECRETARY OF INTERIOR May 20, 1903		
14	No2 identified from 1893 payroll Eagle Co page 16 No 176 as Mela Christy						
15	No3 has been legally adopted by Preeman J McClure Choctaw Card #538						
16	Petition for adoption filed December 9 – 1902				Date of Application for Enrollment. #1to10		
17	No.3 P.O. Bennington, I.T. 3/18/07				April 19/99		

242

Choctaw By Blood Enrollment Cards 1898-1914

RESIDENCE: Eagle COUNTY.
POST OFFICE: Eagletown, I.T.

Choctaw Nation

Choctaw Roll
(Not Including Freedmen)

CARD NO.
FIELD NO. **543**

Dawes' Roll No.	NAME		Relationship to Person	AGE	SEX	BLOOD	TRIBAL ENROLLMENT		
							Year	County	No.
1187	1 Colbert, Amos	33	First Named	30	M	Full	1896	Eagle	2593
1188	2 " Selin		Wife	10	F	"	1896	"	2637
1189	3 " Sampson	4	Son	1	M	"			
1190	4 " John	9	brother	16	"	"	1896	Eagle	2617
	5 " Georgie **DEAD**		"	13	"	"	1896	"	2606
	6 No 2 hereon dismissed under order of								
	7 the Commission to the Five Civilized								
	8 Tribes of March 31, 1905.								
	9								
	10								
	11								
	12 ENROLLMENT								
	13 OF NOS. 1 2 3 and 4 HEREON APPROVED BY THE SECRETARY								
	14 OF INTERIOR Dec 12 1902								
	15								
	16								
	17								

DIED PRIOR TO SEPTEMBER 25, 190_

TRIBAL ENROLLMENT OF PARENTS

	Name of Father	Year	County	Name of Mother	Year	County
1	Alinton Colbert	Dead	Eagle	Manda Colbert	Dead	Eagle
2	Sam Houston	"	Red River	Okishtima	"	Red River
3	No 1			No 2		
4	Alinton Colbert	Dead	Eagle	Manda Colbert	Dead	Eagle
5	" "	"	"	" "	"	"
6						
7						
8	No5 died March 13th 1901: proof of death filed June 7th 1901.					
9	No2 died Jan. 9 – 1902: proof of death filed Dec. 24, 1902					
10	No.2 died Jan. 9 – 1902: Enrollment cancelled by Department July 8 – 1904.					
11						
12						
13						
14						
15				Date of Application for Enrollment.		
16				April 19/99		
17						

Choctaw By Blood Enrollment Cards 1898-1914

Dawes' Roll No.	NAME	Relationship to Person First Named	AGE	SEX	BLOOD	TRIBAL ENROLLMENT Year	County	No.
1191	1 Wall, Wilkin 40		37	M	Full	1893	Nashoba	P.R. 872
1192	2 " Elsie	Wife	35	F	"	1896	"	5522
1193	3 " Nelson 12	Son	9	M	"	1893	"	P.R. 874
1194	4 Christie, Caroline 16	Ward	13	F	3/4	1896	"	2485
1195	5 " Mary 13	"	10	"	3/4	1896	"	2486
	6							
	7							
	8							
	9							
	10							
	11	ENROLLMENT OF NOS. 1 2 3 4 and 5 HEREON						
	12	APPROVED BY THE SECRETARY						
	13	OF INTERIOR DEC 12 1902						
	14							
	15							
	16							
	17							

TRIBAL ENROLLMENT OF PARENTS

	Name of Father	Year	County	Name of Mother	Year	County
1	James Wall	1896	Eagle	Pisa-ho-tema	Dead	Eagle
2	Joel Hudson	Dead	"	Liza Hudson	"	"
3	No 1			Sissie Wall	"	Nashoba
4	Nelson Christie	Dead	Eagle	Dora Christie	"	Eagle
5	" "	"	"	" "	"	"
6						
7						
8						
9						
10			No3 on 1893 Pay roll as Nelson M Wall			
11			No2 " 1896 roll " Elsie Hudson			
12			No1 also on 1896 roll, Page 348, No 13241 as Wilkin Waul			
13			No3 also on 1896 roll, Page 348, No 13242			
14			as Nelson Waul			
15			No2 died Aug, 10-1902. No5 died [remainder illegible]			
16				Date of Application for Enrollment.	April 19/99	
17						

244

Choctaw By Blood Enrollment Cards 1898-1914

RESIDENCE: Eagle COUNTY. **Choctaw Nation** **Choctaw Roll** (Not Including Freedmen) CARD NO. FIELD NO. **545**
POST OFFICE: Eagletown, I.T.

Dawes' Roll No.	NAME	Relationship to Person First Named	AGE	SEX	BLOOD	TRIBAL ENROLLMENT Year	County	No.
1196	Ward, Alfred ⁴³	First Named	40	M	Full	1896	Eagle	13475
1197	" Sallie ⁵³	Wife	50	F	"	1896	"	13476
1198	Charley ³	Son	18	M	"	1896	"	13478
4								
5	ENROLLMENT							
6	OF NOS. 1 2 and 3 HEREON APPROVED BY THE SECRETARY							
7	OF INTERIOR Dec 12 1902							
8								
9								
10								
11								
12								
13								
14								
15								
16								
17								

(notations overstruck: DIED PRIOR TO SEPTEMBER 25, 1902)

TRIBAL ENROLLMENT OF PARENTS

	Name of Father	Year	County	Name of Mother	Year	County
1	William Ward	Dead	Wade	Mary Ward	Dead	Eagle
2	Big John	"	Eagle	Sukey Wade	"	"
3	No.1			No. 2		
4						
5						
6						
7						
8	N⁰3 Died Feby 15, 1900, proof of death filed Dec. 24, 1902.					
9	N⁰2 Died Dec. 26, 1901, proof of death filed Dec. 24, 1902					
10	No.2 died Dec. 20 – 1902: No.3 died Feb. 15 – 1900: Enrollment cancelled by Department July 8 - 1904					
11						
12						
13						
14						
15						
16				Date of Application for Enrollment.		April 19/99
17						

Choctaw By Blood Enrollment Cards 1898-1914

RESIDENCE: Eagle COUNTY.
POST OFFICE: Eagletown, I.T.

Choctaw Nation

Choctaw Roll
(Not Including Freedmen)

CARD NO.
FIELD NO. 546

Dawes' Roll No.	NAME	Relationship to Person First Named	AGE	SEX	BLOOD	TRIBAL ENROLLMENT Year	County	No.
1199	1 Colbert, Nancy 33	Named	30	F	Full	1896	Eagle	2627
1200	2 " Josie 18	Dau	16	"	"	1896	"	2612
1201	3 " Joel 16	Son	13	M	"	1896	"	2613
1202	4 " Tobias 13	Son	10	"	"	1896	"	2638
	5							
	6							
	7							
	8							
	9							
	10							
	11	ENROLLMENT OF NOS. 1 2 3 and 4 HEREON APPROVED BY THE SECRETARY OF INTERIOR DEC 12 1902						
	12							
	13							
	14							
	15							
	16							
	17							

TRIBAL ENROLLMENT OF PARENTS

Name of Father	Year	County	Name of Mother	Year	County
1 Ka-nan-tuby	Dead	Eagle	Mary	Dead	Eagle
2 Jonas Colbert	"	Nashoba	No 1		
3 " "	"	"	No 1		
4 " "	"	"	No 1		
5					
6					
7					
8					
9					
10					
11					
12					
13					
14					
15					
16			Date of Application for Enrollment.		April 19/99
17					

246

Choctaw By Blood Enrollment Cards 1898-1914

RESIDENCE: Eagle COUNTY.
POST OFFICE: Ulti Mathule, Ark.

Choctaw Nation

Choctaw Roll
(Not Including Freedmen)

CARD No.
FIELD NO. 547

Dawes' Roll No.	NAME		Relationship to Person First Named	AGE	SEX	BLOOD	TRIBAL ENROLLMENT		
							Year	County	No.
1203	1 Wall, Samuel	53	First Named	50	M	Full	1896	Eagle	13456
1204	2 " William	18	Son	15	"	"	1896	"	13458
1205	3 " Noel	16	"	13	"	"	1896	"	13455
1206	4 " Chubby	15	Nephew	12	"	"	1896	"	13459
	5								
	6								
	7								
	8								
	9								
	10								
	11	ENROLLMENT OF NOS. 1 2 3 and 4 HEREON							
	12	APPROVED BY THE SECRETARY							
	13	OF INTERIOR DEC 12 1902							
	14								
	15								
	16								
	17								

TRIBAL ENROLLMENT OF PARENTS

	Name of Father	Year	County	Name of Mother	Year	County
1	John Yohambe	Dead	Eagle	Nancy Wall	1896	Eagle
2	No 1			Belinda Wall	Dead	"
3	No 1			" "	"	"
4	Jim Billy	Dead	Eagle	Cissie Stephen	"	"
5						
6						
7						
8						
9						
10						
11						
12						
13						
14						
15				DATE OF APPLICATION FOR ENROLLMENT.	April 19/99	
16						
17	P.O. Johnson, I.T. 1/26/03					

Choctaw By Blood Enrollment Cards 1898-1914

RESIDENCE: Eagle   COUNTY.   **Choctaw Nation**   **Choctaw Roll**   CARD NO.
POST OFFICE: Ulti Mathule, Ark   *(Not Including Freedmen)*   FIELD NO. 548

Dawes' Roll No.	NAME	Relationship to Person	AGE	SEX	BLOOD	TRIBAL ENROLLMENT		
						Year	County	No.
1207	1 Wall, Nancy 73	First Named	70	F	Full	1896	Eagle	13461
	2							
	3							
	4	ENROLLMENT						
	5	OF NOS. 1 HEREON APPROVED BY THE SECRETARY						
	6	OF INTERIOR DEC 12 1902						
	7							
	8							
	9							
	10							
	11							
	12							
	13							
	14							
	15							
	16							
	17							

TRIBAL ENROLLMENT OF PARENTS

	Name of Father	Year	County	Name of Mother	Year	County
1			Died in Mississippi			Died in Mississippi
2						
3						
4						
5						
6						
7						
8						
9						
10						
11						
12						
13						
14						
15				Date of Application for Enrollment.		April 19/99
16						
17						

248

Choctaw By Blood Enrollment Cards 1898-1914

RESIDENCE: Eagle	COUNTY.	**Choctaw Nation**	**Choctaw Roll** *(Not Including Freedmen)*	CARD NO.
POST OFFICE: Ulti Mathule, Ark.				FIELD NO. 549

Dawes' Roll No.	Ultima Thule, Ark. NAME	Relationship to Person	AGE	SEX	BLOOD	TRIBAL ENROLLMENT		
						Year	County	No.
1208	1 Wall, Frances 63	First Named	60	F	Full	1896	Eagle	13453
	2							
	3							
	4	ENROLLMENT OF NOS. 1 HEREON						
	5	APPROVED BY THE SECRETARY						
	6	OF INTERIOR DEC 12 1902						
	7							
	8							
	9							
	10							
	11							
	12							
	13							
	14							
	15							
	16							
	17							

TRIBAL ENROLLMENT OF PARENTS

	Name of Father	Year	County	Name of Mother	Year	County
1		Died in Mississippi			Died in Mississippi	
2						
3						
4						
5						
6						
7						
8						
9						
10						
11						
12						
13						
14						
15				Date of Application for Enrollment.	April 19/99	
16						
17						

Choctaw By Blood Enrollment Cards 1898-1914

RESIDENCE: Eagle   COUNTY.   **Choctaw Nation**   **Choctaw Roll**   CARD NO.
POST OFFICE: Eagletown, I.T.   (Not Including Freedmen)   FIELD NO.   550

Dawes' Roll No.	NAME	Relationship to Person First Named	AGE	SEX	BLOOD	TRIBAL ENROLLMENT		
						Year	County	No.
1209	1 Fobb, Simon ²⁹	First Named	26	M	Full	1896	Eagle	4182
1210	2 " Adeline ²⁶	Wife	23	F	"	1896	"	12251
1211	3 " Edmond ⁴	Son	4mo	M	"			
1212	4 Thompson, Quatambe¹⁰	S. Son	6	"	"	1896	Eagle	9931
15566	5 Ishtimonehoke ⁸	S. Dau	4	F	"			
14567	6 Fobb, Lawson ¹	Son	1	M	"			
⁴	7							
	8	ENROLLMENT OF NOS. 1 2 3 and 4 HEREON APPROVED BY THE SECRETARY OF INTERIOR DEC 12 1902						
	9							
	10							
	11							
	12	ENROLLMENT OF NOS. 6 HEREON APPROVED BY THE SECRETARY OF INTERIOR MAY 20 1903						
	13							
	14							
	15				ENROLLMENT OF NOS. ~ 5 ~ HEREON APPROVED BY THE SECRETARY OF INTERIOR SEP 22 1904			
	16							
	17							

TRIBAL ENROLLMENT OF PARENTS

	Name of Father	Year	County	Name of Mother	Year	County
1	Frank Fobb	Dead	Wade	Wicey Fobb	Dead	Eagle
2	Geo. Thompson	18966	Eagle	Sonney Thompson	1896	Bok Tuklo
3	No 1			No 2		
4				No 2		
5	Jones James	1896	Eagle	No 2		
6	Nº1			Nº2		
7						
8	No2 on 1896 roll as Adaline Thompson					
9	No4 " 1896 Payroll as Quatambi					
10	For child of Nos 1&2 see N.B. (Apr 26, 1906) Card No. 107					
	No3: Affidavit as to birth to be supplied. Recd May 6/99					
11						
12	No5 " " " " " " " " 6/99					
13	Nº6 Born Nov. 18, 1901. Enrolled Nov. 20, 1902					
	For child of Nos 1&2 see NB (March 3, 1905) #1 29					
14						
15						#1 to 5 inc
16						Date of Application for Enrollment.
17						April 19/99

Choctaw By Blood Enrollment Cards 1898-1914

RESIDENCE: Eagle COUNTY.
POST OFFICE: Eagletown, I.T.

Choctaw Nation

Choctaw Roll
(Not Including Freedmen)

CARD NO.
FIELD NO. 551

Dawes' Roll No.	NAME	Relationship to Person	AGE	SEX	BLOOD	TRIBAL ENROLLMENT		
						Year	County	No.
14568	DIED PRIOR TO SEPTEMBER 25, 1902 1 Stephen, Sinie	First Named	40	F	Full	1896	Eagle	4181
	2							
	3							
	4							
	5							
	6	ENROLLMENT						
	7	OF NOS. 1 HEREON						
	8	APPROVED BY THE SECRETARY OF INTERIOR MAY 20 1903						
	9							
	10							
	11							
	12	On 1896 roll as Sinie Fobb.						
	13							
	14	No 1 died May – 1902. Enrollment cancelled by Department [remainder illegible]						
	15							
	16							
	17							

TRIBAL ENROLLMENT OF PARENTS

	Name of Father	Year	County	Name of Mother	Year	County
1	Noah-tambe	Dead	Eagle	Lo-le-hu-ma	Dead	Eagle
2						
3						
4						
5						
6						
7						
8						
9						
10						
11						
12						
13						
14						
15						
16				Date of Application for Enrollment.		April 19/99
17						

251

Choctaw By Blood Enrollment Cards 1898-1914

RESIDENCE: Cedar COUNTY.
POST OFFICE: Doaksville, I.T.

Choctaw Nation

Choctaw Roll
(Not Including Freedmen)

CARD No.
FIELD No. 552

Dawes' Roll No.	NAME		Relationship to Person First Named	AGE	SEX	BLOOD	TRIBAL ENROLLMENT		
							Year	County	No.
1213	1 Lewis, James	46	First Named	43	M	Full	1896	Cedar	7908
1214	2 " Beckie	52	Wife	49	F	"	1896	"	7909
	3								
	4								
	5	ENROLLMENT OF NOS. 1 and 2 HEREON							
	6	APPROVED BY THE SECRETARY							
	7	OF INTERIOR DEC 12 1902							
	8								
	9								
	10								
	11								
	12								
	13								
	14								
	15								
	16								
	17								

TRIBAL ENROLLMENT OF PARENTS

	Name of Father	Year	County	Name of Mother	Year	County
1	Lum-ba	Dead	Red River		Dead	Sugar Loaf
2	Ma-na-hubbee	"	" "	Ish-e-huna	Dead	Towson
3						
4						
5						
6						
7						
8						
9						
10						
11						
12						
13						
14						
15			Date of Application for Enrollment.	April 19/99		
16						
17						

252

Choctaw By Blood Enrollment Cards 1898-1914

RESIDENCE:	Nashoba	COUNTY.								

Choctaw Nation (Not Including Freedmen)

Choctaw Roll

CARD NO.
FIELD NO. **553**

POST OFFICE: Alikchi, I.T.

Dawes' Roll No.	NAME	Relationship to Person First Named	AGE	SEX	BLOOD	TRIBAL ENROLLMENT		
						Year	County	No.
1215	1 Watkins, Elam ³⁰	First Named	27	M	Full	1896	Nashoba	13388
1216	2 " Susan ³²	Wife	29	F	"	1896	"	13389
1217	3 Joel, Hampton ¹⁷	S. Son	14	M	"	1896	"	6834
	4							
	5							
	6	ENROLLMENT OF NOS. 1 2 and 3 HEREON APPROVED BY THE SECRETARY						
	7	OF INTERIOR Dec 12 1902						
	8							
	9							
	10	For child of No.3 see NB (March 3, 1905) #1309						
	11							
	12							
	13							
	14							
	15							
	16							
	17							

TRIBAL ENROLLMENT OF PARENTS

	Name of Father	Year	County	Name of Mother	Year	County
1	Ismon Watkins	1896	Nashoba	Winey Watkins	1896	Nashoba
2	Cole Nelson	Dead	Jacks Fork	Rhoda Nelson	1896	Jacks Fork
3	John Joel	"	" "	No.2		
4						
5						
6						
7						
8						
9						
10						
11						
12						
13						
14						
15					Date of Application for Enrollment.	
16					April 19/99	
17						

Choctaw By Blood Enrollment Cards 1898-1914

RESIDENCE: Eagle COUNTY.	Choctaw Nation	Choctaw Roll	CARD NO.
POST OFFICE: Ulti Mathule, Ark		(Not Including Freedmen)	FIELD NO. 554

Dawes' Roll No.	NAME	Relationship to Person First Named	AGE	SEX	BLOOD	TRIBAL ENROLLMENT		
						Year	County	No.
1218	1 Joseph, George	First Named	72	M	Full	1896	Eagle	6948
1219	2 " Lottie	Wife	40	F	"	1896	"	6950
	3							
	4							
	5	ENROLLMENT						
	6	OF NOS. 1 and 2 HEREON APPROVED BY THE SECRETARY						
	7	OF INTERIOR DEC 12 1902						
	8							
	9							
	10							
	11							
	12							
	13							
	14							
	15							
	16							
	17							

TRIBAL ENROLLMENT OF PARENTS

	Name of Father	Year	County	Name of Mother	Year	County
1	Ok-cha-lintubbee	Died	in Mississippi	Ma-a-sho-na	Dead	Eagle
2	A-sha-lin-tubbee	Dead	Eagle	Yan-tay	"	"
3						
4						
5						
6						
7						
8						
9						
10						
11						
12						
13						
14						
15						
16			Date of Application for Enrollment.		April 19/99	
17						

254

Choctaw By Blood Enrollment Cards 1898-1914

RESIDENCE:	Towson COUNTY.				Choctaw Nation		Choctaw Roll *(Not Including Freedmen)*		CARD NO.
POST OFFICE:	Alikchi, I.T.							FIELD NO.	**555**

Dawes' Roll No.	NAME		Relationship to Person First Named	AGE	SEX	BLOOD	TRIBAL ENROLLMENT		
							Year	County	No.
1220	1 Jacob, Simeon	29	First Named	26	M	Full	1896	Towson	6788
1221	2 " Sophie	28	Wife	25	F	"	1896	"	6789
1222	3 " Grayson	5	Son	1	M	"			
1223	4 " Daniel	17	brother	14	"	"	1896	Towson	6791
~~1224~~	~~5 " Mary~~ DIED PRIOR TO SEPTEMBER 25, 189?		~~sister~~	~~16~~	~~F~~	~~"~~	~~1896~~	~~"~~	~~6790~~
1225	6 " James	3	Son	6mo	M	"			
	7								
	8								
	9								
	10								
	11	ENROLLMENT OF NOS. 1 2 3 4 5 and 6 HEREON							
	12	APPROVED BY THE SECRETARY							
	13	OF INTERIOR Dec 12 1902							
	14								
	15								
	16								
	17								

TRIBAL ENROLLMENT OF PARENTS

	Name of Father	Year	County	Name of Mother	Year	County
1	Grayson Jacob	Dead	Towson	Sophiney Jacob	Dead	Towson
2	Joseph Morris	"	Nashoba	Liney Morris	"	Nashoba
3	No 1			No 2		
4	Grayson Jacob	Dead	Towson	Sophiney Jacob	Dead	Towson
5	" "	"	"	" "	"	"
6	No 1			No 2		
7						
8						
9						
10						
11	No.3: Affidavit of birth to be supplied. Recd April 20/99					
12	No.4 also on 1896 Choctaw roll as Daniel Jacob, page 175; #7124.					
13	No.5 died January 20, 1901: proof of death filed Dec. 9, 1902.					
13	No.5 died Jan. 20, 1901: Enrollment cancelled by Department Sept. 16, 1904. #1 to 5					
14	For child of Nos 1&2 see NB (March 3, 1905) #937					
15						Date of Application for Enrollment.
16						April 19/99
17	P.O. Valliant, I.T. 4/10/05					No 6 enrolled Nov. 1/99

Choctaw By Blood Enrollment Cards 1898-1914

RESIDENCE: Towson COUNTY.
POST OFFICE: Fowlerville, I.T.

Choctaw Nation

Choctaw Roll
(Not Including Freedmen)

CARD NO.
FIELD NO. **556**

Dawes' Roll No.	NAME		Relationship to Person	AGE	SEX	BLOOD	TRIBAL ENROLLMENT		
							Year	County	No.
1226	1 Austin, David	39	First Named	36	M	Full	1896	Towson	190
1227	2 " Emily	34	Wife	31	F	"	1896	"	191
1228	3 " Simon	10	Son	7	M	"	1896	"	192
1229	4 " Rosa	6	Dau	2	F	"			
1230	5 Aaron, Sallie	17	Ward	14	"	"	1896	Towson	215
1231	6 Austin, William	2	Son	2mo	M	"			
15761	7 " John	1	Son	1mo	M	"			
	8								
	9								
	10	ENROLLMENT							
	11	OF NOS. 1,2,3,4,5 and 6HEREON APPROVED BY THE SECRETARY							
	12	OF INTERIOR Dec 12 1902							
	13								
	14	ENROLLMENT							
	15	OF NOS. ~ 7 ~ HEREON APPROVED BY THE SECRETARY							
	16	OF INTERIOR Dec 28 1904							
	17								

TRIBAL ENROLLMENT OF PARENTS

	Name of Father	Year	County	Name of Mother	Year	County
1	Samuel Austin	Dead	Red River	Viney Austin	Dead	Towson
2	James Aaron	"	Towson	Saliney Aaron	"	"
3	No 1			No 2		
4	No 1			No 2		
5	Joseph Aaron	Dead	Towson	Narcissie Aaron	Dead	Towson
6	No 1			No. 2		
7	No 1			No. 2		
8				No		
9						
10	No4: Affidavit of birth to be supplied: Recd May 24/99					
11						
12	No.6 Enrolled Dec 14, 1900					
13	No.7 was born Sept 21, 1902: application was made for his enrollment at Garvin, I.T. Nov. 27, 1902, by David Austin. Placed on this card Dec. 8, 1904					
14						
15	For child of No5 see NB. (Mar 3-05) #94					
16				Date of Application for Enrollment.		#1 to 5 April 19/99
17	P.O. Chula, I.T. 10/29/03					

P.O. Valliant I.T. 12/31/04

256

Choctaw By Blood Enrollment Cards 1898-1914

RESIDENCE: Towson   COUNTY.   **Choctaw Nation**   **Choctaw Roll** *(Not Including Freedmen)*   CARD NO. FIELD NO. **557**

POST OFFICE: Alikchi, I.T.

Dawes' Roll No.	NAME	Relationship to Person First Named	AGE	SEX	BLOOD	TRIBAL ENROLLMENT Year	County	No.
1232	1 Wallace, Amos ⁷⁰		67	M	Full	1896	Towson	13195
1233	2 " Bessie ³⁰	Wife	27	F	"	1896	"	13196
1234	3 " Salie ¹¹	Dau	8	"	"	1896	"	13197
1235	4 " Agnes ⁹	Dau	6	"	"	1896	"	13198
	5							
	6							
	7							
	8							
	9							
	10							
	11	ENROLLMENT						
	12	OF NOS. 1 2 3 and 4 HEREON APPROVED BY THE SECRETARY						
	13	OF INTERIOR DEC 12 1902						
	14							
	15							
	16							
	17							

TRIBAL ENROLLMENT OF PARENTS

	Name of Father	Year	County	Name of Mother	Year	County
1	Wallace Patabee	Dead	Towson	Susan Patabee	Dead	Towson
2	Lawson	"	Nashoba	Josie Battiest	"	Cedar
3	No 1			No 2		
4	No 1			No 2		
5						
6						
7	No3 on 1896 roll as Lillie Wallace					
8	N°1 has legally adopted Sampson Momintubbi on Choctaw card # 348, Jany 2 1903.					
9	For child of No.2 see NB (March 3 1905) 692					
10						
11						
12						
13						
14					Date of Application for Enrollment	
15						
16	P.O. Rufe I.T. 3/12/07				April 19/99	
17	P.O. Doaksville I.T. 1/27/02					

Choctaw By Blood Enrollment Cards 1898-1914

RESIDENCE: Towson COUNTY.	Choctaw Nation	Choctaw Roll *(Not Including Freedmen)*	CARD No. FIELD No. 558
POST OFFICE: Alikchi, I.T.			

Dawes' Roll No.	NAME	Relationship to Person First Named	AGE	SEX	BLOOD	TRIBAL ENROLLMENT		
						Year	County	No.
1236	1 Tobby, Willis ^48	First Named	45	M	Full	1896	Sans Bois	11832
1237	2 " Kitty ^58	Wife	55	F	"	1896	" "	11833
14882	3 " Sampson ^12	Ward	9	M	"	1896	Cedar	2414
	4							
	5 ENROLLMENT							
	6 OF NOS. 1 and 2 HEREON							
	7 APPROVED BY THE SECRETARY OF INTERIOR Dec 12 1902							
	8							
	9 ENROLLMENT							
	10 OF NOS. 3 HEREON							
	11 APPROVED BY THE SECRETARY OF INTERIOR May 21 1903							
	12							
	13							
	14 No3 on 1896 roll as Sampson Choate							
	15							
	16							
	17							

TRIBAL ENROLLMENT OF PARENTS

	Name of Father	Year	County	Name of Mother	Year	County
1	Sam Tobby	Dead	Skullyville	Annette Tobby	Dead	Skullyville
2	Kan-cha-by	"	Sans Bois	Ma-te-o-na	"	Sans Bois
3	Stephen Gibson	1896	Nashoba	Kitty Gibson	"	Cedar
4						
5						
6						
7						
8						
9						
10						
11						
12						
13						
14						
15						
16				Date of Application for Enrollment	April 19/99	
17						

258

Choctaw By Blood Enrollment Cards 1898-1914

RESIDENCE: Towson COUNTY.
POST OFFICE: Alikchi, I.T.

Choctaw Nation

Choctaw Roll
(Not Including Freedmen)

CARD NO.
FIELD NO. **559**

Dawes' Roll No.	NAME		Relationship to Person First Named	AGE	SEX	BLOOD	TRIBAL ENROLLMENT		
							Year	County	No.
1238	1 Jacob, Eastman	39	First Named	36	M	Full	1896	Towson	6779
1239	2 " Elizabeth	41	Wife	38	F	"	1896	"	6780
1240	3 " Emily	21	Dau	18	"	"	1896	"	6783
1241	4 " Robert	10	Son	7	M	"	1896	"	6782
1242	5 " Ednie	7	Dau	4	F	"	1896	"	6781
	6								
	7								
	8	ENROLLMENT OF NOS. 1 2 3 4 and 5 HEREON APPROVED BY THE SECRETARY OF INTERIOR Dec 12, 1902							
	9								
	10								
	11								
	12		No3 now wife of Timothy Cephus on Choc card #752						
	13		For child of No1 see N.B. (March 3, 1905) #1105						
	14								
	15								
	16								
	17								

TRIBAL ENROLLMENT OF PARENTS

	Name of Father	Year	County	Name of Mother	Year	County
1	Julius Patabee	Dead	Towson	Alahotema	Dead	Towson
2	Lewis Christie	"	"	Mary Christie	"	"
3	No 1			No 2		
4	No 1			No 2		
5	No 1			No 2		
6						
7						
8						
9						
10						
11						
12						
13						
14						
15					Date of Application for Enrollment.
16					April 19/99
17	2/1/08 Rufe, Ok					

Choctaw By Blood Enrollment Cards 1898-1914

RESIDENCE: Eagle COUNTY. **Choctaw Nation** Choctaw Roll CARD NO.
POST OFFICE: Eagletown, I.T. *(Not Including Freedmen)* FIELD NO. **560**

Dawes' Roll No.	NAME	Relationship to Person First Named	AGE	SEX	BLOOD	TRIBAL ENROLLMENT		
						Year	County	No.
1243	1 Gardner, Jefferson 58	First Named	55	M	1/2	1896	Eagle	4780
1244	2 " Judy 40	Wife	37	F	3/4	1896	"	4781
1245	3 " Willie 23	Son	20	M	5/8	1896	"	4783
1246	4 " Emma 21	Dau	18	F	5/8	1896	"	4787
1247	5 " Scott 19	Son	16	M	5/8	1896	"	4782
1248	6 " Agnes 11	Dau	8	F	5/8	1896	"	4785
1249	7 " Zachariah 9	Son	6	M	5/8	1896	"	4784
1250	8 " Jefferson Jr. 6	"	2	"	5/8			
	9							
	10							
	11	ENROLLMENT						
	12	OF NOS. 1,2,3,4,5,6,7 and 8 HEREON APPROVED BY THE SECRETARY						
	13	OF INTERIOR Dec. 12 1902						
	14							
	15							
	16							
	17							

TRIBAL ENROLLMENT OF PARENTS

	Name of Father	Year	County	Name of Mother	Year	County
1	Noel Gardner	Dead	Towson	Hannah Gardner	Dead	Towson
2	Joe Christie	"	Eagle	Emily Christie	1896	Eagle
3	No 1			Lucy Gardner	Dead	"
4	No 1			" "	"	"
5	No 1			" "	"	"
6	No 1			No 2		
7	No 1			No 2		
8	No 1			No 2		
9						
10						
11	No8 Affidavit of birth to be supplied. Recd July 27/99					
12	No3 died Aug. 14 – 1900: Enrollment cancelled by Department, July 8 – 1904					
13	No3 died Aug 14, 1900: proof of death filed Dec. 13, 1902					
14						
15					Date of Application for Enrollment.	
16					April 20/99	
17						

Choctaw By Blood Enrollment Cards 1898-1914

RESIDENCE: Eagle COUNTY. **Choctaw Nation** **Choctaw Roll** CARD NO.

POST OFFICE: Eagletown, Ind. Ter. *(Not Including Freedmen)* FIELD NO. 561

Dawes' Roll No.	NAME	Relationship to Person	AGE	SEX	BLOOD	TRIBAL ENROLLMENT		
						Year	County	No.
1251	1 John, Matsy 23	First Named	20	F	Full	1896	Eagle	6979
	2							
	3							
	4							
	5	ENROLLMENT						
	6	OF NOS. 1 HEREON APPROVED BY THE SECRETARY						
	7	OF INTERIOR DEC 12 1902						
	8							
	9							
	10							
	11	For child of No.1 see NB (March 3 1905) #971						
	12							
	13							
	14							
	15							
	16							
	17							

TRIBAL ENROLLMENT OF PARENTS

Name of Father	Year	County	Name of Mother	Year	County
1 Isaac John	Dead	Eagle	Hotena-huma	Dead	Eagle
2					
3					
4					
5					
6					
7					
8					
9					
10					
11					
12					
13					
14					
15					
16			Date of Application for Enrollment	April 20/98	
17					

Choctaw By Blood Enrollment Cards 1898-1914

RESIDENCE: Eagle   COUNTY.   **Choctaw Nation**   **Choctaw Roll** CARD NO.
POST OFFICE: Eagletown, Ind. Ter.   *(Not Including Freedmen)*   FIELD NO. 562

Dawes' Roll No.	NAME	Relationship to Person First Named	AGE	SEX	BLOOD	TRIBAL ENROLLMENT		
						Year	County	No.
1252	1 Wilson, Lisive		28	F	Full	1896	Eagle	1354
	2							
	3							
	4	ENROLLMENT						
	5	OF NOS. 1 HEREON						
	6	APPROVED BY THE SECRETARY OF INTERIOR DEC 12 1902						
	7							
	8							
	9							
	10	No1 died Aug 15, 1900: proof of death filed Dec 13, 1902.						
	11							
	12							
	13							
	14							
	15							
	16							
	17							

TRIBAL ENROLLMENT OF PARENTS

	Name of Father	Year	County	Name of Mother	Year	County
1	Isaac John	Dead	Eagle	Hotena-hema	Dead	Eagle
2						
3						
4						
5						
6						
7						
8						
9						
10						
11						
12						
13						
14						
15				Date of Application for Enrollment.	April 20/99	
16						
17						

Choctaw By Blood Enrollment Cards 1898-1914

RESIDENCE: Eagle COUNTY. **Choctaw Nation** **Choctaw Roll** CARD No.
POST OFFICE: Eagletown, I.T. (Not Including Freedmen) FIELD No. 563

Dawes' Roll No.	NAME	Relationship to Person First Named	AGE	SEX	BLOOD	TRIBAL ENROLLMENT		
						Year	County	No.
1253	1 McKinney, Frances 68	First Named	65	F	Full	1896	Eagle	9306
	2							
	3							
	4							
	5	ENROLLMENT						
	6	OF NOS. 1 HEREON APPROVED BY THE SECRETARY						
	7	OF INTERIOR DEC 12 1902						
	8							
	9							
	10							
	11	On 1896 roll as Francis McKinney						
	12							
	13							
	14							
	15							
	16							
	17							

TRIBAL ENROLLMENT OF PARENTS

	Name of Father	Year	County	Name of Mother	Year	County
1	Bow-ellie	Dead	Eagle	Ish-te-malahona	Dead	Eagle
2						
3						
4						
5						
6						
7						
8						
9						
10						
11						
12						
13						
14						
15				Date of Application for Enrollment.		
16				April 20/99		
17						

Choctaw By Blood Enrollment Cards 1898-1914

RESIDENCE: Eagle COUNTY.
POST OFFICE: Eagletown, I.T.

Choctaw Nation

Choctaw Roll
(Not Including Freedmen)

CARD NO.
FIELD NO. 564

Dawes' Roll No.	NAME	Relationship to Person First Named	AGE	SEX	BLOOD	TRIBAL ENROLLMENT		
						Year	County	No.
1254	1 Christy, Emily 58	First Named	55	F	Full	11896	Eagle	2603
	2							
	3							
	4							
	5							
	6							
	7							
	8							
	9							
	10							
	11							
	12							
	13							
	14							
	15							
	16							
	17							

ENROLLMENT
OF NOS. 1 HEREON
APPROVED BY THE SECRETARY
OF INTERIOR DEC 12 1902

TRIBAL ENROLLMENT OF PARENTS

Name of Father	Year	County	Name of Mother	Year	County
1 Silas Bohanan	Dead	Kiamitia	E-lap-a-ho-na	Dead	Eagle
2					
3					
4					
5					
6					
7					
8					
9					
10					
11					
12					
13					
14					
15					
16			Date of Application for Enrollment	April 20/99	
17					

264

Choctaw By Blood Enrollment Cards 1898-1914

RESIDENCE: Nashoba   COUNTY.   **Choctaw Nation**   **Choctaw Roll**   CARD NO.

POST OFFICE: Alikchi, I.T.   *(Not Including Freedmen)*   FIELD NO.   565

Dawes' Roll No.	NAME	Relationship to Person First Named	AGE	SEX	BLOOD	TRIBAL ENROLLMENT Year	County	No.
1255	1 Watkins, Stephen ⁵⁵		52	M	Full	1896	Nashoba	13369
DEAD.	2 " Alice	Wife	18	F	"	1896	"	6833
1256	3 " Emma ¹⁶	Dau	13	"	"	1896	"	13372
1257	4 " Mattie ¹²	G.Dau	9	"	"	1896	"	13373
	5							
	6							
	7	ENROLLMENT						
	8	OF NOS. 1 3 and 4 HEREON APPROVED BY THE SECRETARY						
	9	OF INTERIOR DEC 12 1902						
	10							
	11							
	12	No. 2 HEREON DISMISSED UNDER						
	13	ORDER OF THE COMMISSION TO THE FIVE CIVILIZED TRIBES OF MARCH 31, 1905.						
	14							
	15							
	16							
	17							

TRIBAL ENROLLMENT OF PARENTS

	Name of Father	Year	County	Name of Mother	Year	County
1	John Lewis	Dead	Nashoba	Pe-sa-che-hona	Dead	Nashoba
2	John Joel	"	Jacks Fork	Sukey Watkins	1896	"
3	No 1			Sarah Watkins	Dead	"
4	Silas Homa	Dead	Nashoba	Mary Watkins	1896	Eagle
5						
6						
7	No2 on 1896 roll as Alice Joel					
8	No2 died Feby 13, 1900. Proof of death filed Sept 17, 1901.					
9	Nº1 is now the husband of Sinsie J Taylor on Choctaw card #729 Sept 21,1902.					
10	For child of No.3 see NB (March 3, 1905) #906.					
11						
12						
13						
14						
15						
16				Date of Application for Enrollment	April 20/99	
17	[Address Illegible]					

Choctaw By Blood Enrollment Cards 1898-1914

RESIDENCE: Nashoba   COUNTY.   **Choctaw Nation**   **Choctaw Roll**   CARD NO.
POST OFFICE: Alikchi, I.T.   *(Not Including Freedmen)*   FIELD NO. **566**

Dawes' Roll No.	NAME	Relationship to Person First Named	AGE	SEX	BLOOD	TRIBAL ENROLLMENT Year	TRIBAL ENROLLMENT County	TRIBAL ENROLLMENT No.
4258	1 Jefferson, Sweny 61	First Named	58	M	Full	1896	Nashoba	6862
14569	2 " Ellen 21	Wife	18	F	"	1896	Kiamitia	5772
DEAD	3 Colbert, Sammy	S. Dau	3mo	"	"			
	4							
	5	ENROLLMENT OF NOS. 1 HEREON APPROVED BY THE SECRETARY OF INTERIOR Dec 12 1902						
	6							
	7							
	8							
	9							
	10	ENROLLMENT OF NOS. 2 HEREON APPROVED BY THE SECRETARY OF INTERIOR May 20 1903						
	11							
	12							
	13							
	14	No 3 Hereon dismissed under order of						
	15	the Commission to the five civilized						
	16	tribes of March 31, 1905.						
	17							

TRIBAL ENROLLMENT OF PARENTS

	Name of Father	Year	County	Name of Mother	Year	County
1	Ho-ka-tubbee	Dead	Bok Tuklo	Ka-ne-a-hema	Dead	Bok Tuklo
2	Joe Hicks	"	Nashoba	Losanna Hicks	"	Nashoba
3	William Colbert	1896	Bok Tuklo	No 2		
4						
5						
6						
7		No2 on 1896 roll as Ellen Hayes				
8		No1 " 1896 " " Sweeny Jefferson				
9		No3 is an illegitimate child				
10		No3 died Feb. 18, 1901; proof of death filed Dec. 5, 1901				
11						
12						
13						
14						
15				Date of Application for Enrollment.		April 20/99
16						
17						

266

Choctaw By Blood Enrollment Cards 1898-1914

RESIDENCE: Eagle COUNTY.
POST OFFICE: Eagletown, I.T.

Choctaw Nation

Choctaw Roll (Not Including Freedmen)

CARD NO.
FIELD NO. 567

Dawes' Roll No.	NAME		Relationship to Person	AGE	SEX	BLOOD	TRIBAL ENROLLMENT		
							Year	County	No.
1259	1 Dyer, Elliston E	26	First Named	23	M	1/2	1896	Eagle	3413
IW 503	2 " Nancy J	26	Wife	23	F	I.W.	1896	"	14470
1260	3 DIED PRIOR TO SEPTEMBER 25, 1902 Gertrude M		Dau	3	"	1/4	1896	"	3431
1261	4 DIED PRIOR TO SEPTEMBER 25, 1902 Burney F		Son	7mo	M	1/4			
1262	5 " Flordelle	1	Dau	5mo	F	1/4			
	6								
	7								
	8 No3 died Feb. 10-1900. Proof [sic] Death								
	filed Nov 25-1902								
	9 No4 died Dec 9-1899. Proof Death								
	10 filed Nov. 25, 1902								
	11								
	12 ENROLLMENT OF NOS. 1 3 4 and 5 HEREON								
	13 APPROVED BY THE SECRETARY OF INTERIOR DEC 12 1902								
	14								
	15 For child of Nos 1&2 see NB (March 3 05) # 264								
	16								
	17								

TRIBAL ENROLLMENT OF PARENTS

Name of Father	Year	County	Name of Mother	Year	County
1 Jame[sic] Dyer	1896	Eagle	Malinda Dyer		Non Citz
2 Dave Wilson		Non Citz	Martha Wilson		" "
3 No 1			No 2		
4 No 1			No 2		
5 No.1			No 2		
6					
7 No1 on 1896 roll as Ediston E. Dyer.					
8 No2 " 1896 " " Jennie Dyer					
9 No4: Affidavit of birth to be supplied. Recd May 4/99 Evidence of marriage " " " filed July 7' 1900					
10 No3 died Feb 10-1900. No4 died Dec 9-1899. Enrollment cancelled [remainder illegible]					
11 As to marriage of parents of No1 – see Card of father, James Dyer, No 537					
12					
13 No5 Enrolled Sept 21 1901					
14					
15			ENROLLMENT OF NOS. ~ 2 ~ HEREON		Date of Application for Enrollment.
16			APPROVED BY THE SECRETARY		April 20/99
17 Durant, I.T. 11/21/02			OF INTERIOR DEC 24 1903		

Choctaw By Blood Enrollment Cards 1898-1914

RESIDENCE: Eagle COUNTY.
POST OFFICE: Eagletown, I.T.

Choctaw Nation

Choctaw Roll
(Not Including Freedmen)

CARD NO.
FIELD NO. 568

Dawes' Roll No.	NAME	Relationship to Person First Named	AGE	SEX	BLOOD	TRIBAL ENROLLMENT		
						Year	County	No.
1263	1 Christy, Dallas 44	First Named	41	M	Full	1896	Eagle	2598
1264	2 " Elzire 29	Wife	26	F	"	1896	"	2599
1265	3 " Lula 12	Dau	9	"	"	1896	"	2620
1266	4 " Francis 6	"	2	"	"			
DEAD	5 " Jefferson 5	Son	3	M	"			
1267	6 " Janattie C. 3	Dau.	7mo	F	"			
	7							
	8							
	9							
	10							
	11	ENROLLMENT						
	12	OF NOS. 1 2 3 4 and 6 HEREON APPROVED BY THE SECRETARY						
	13	OF INTERIOR DEC 12 1902						
	14	No. 5 HEREON DISMISSED UNDER						
	15	ORDER OF THE COMMISSION TO THE FIVE CIVILIZED TRIBES OF MARCH 31, 1905.						
	16							
	17							

TRIBAL ENROLLMENT OF PARENTS

	Name of Father	Year	County	Name of Mother	Year	County
1	Joseph Christy	Dead	Eagle	Emery Christy	1896	Eagle
2	Jefferson Gardner	1896	"	Lucinda Gardner	Dead	Towson
3	No 1			No 2		
4	No 1			No 2		
5	No 1			No 2		
6	No. 1			No. 2		
7						
8						
9						
10	Affidavits of birth for Nos 4&5 to be supplied. Recd May 9/99					
11						
12	No.6 Enrolled April 7, 1906					
13	No5 appears to be No2611 on 1896 Choctaw roll					
	Nº5 Died Oct. 26, 1901, proof of death filed Nov. 11, 1902					
14						#1 to 5
15						
16						April 20/99
17						

268

Choctaw By Blood Enrollment Cards 1898-1914

RESIDENCE: Eagle COUNTY. **Choctaw Nation** **Choctaw Roll** (Not Including Freedmen) CARD NO. FIELD NO. **569**
POST OFFICE: Eagletown, I.T.

Dawes' Roll No.	NAME	Relationship to Person First Named	AGE	SEX	BLOOD	TRIBAL ENROLLMENT Year	County	No.
1268	1 Thompson, Wash 28	First Named	25	M	1/2	1896	Eagle	12250
1269	2 " Josephine 21	Wife	18	F	1/2	1893	"	195
1270	3 " Clayton 6	Son	2	M	1/2			
1271	4 " Nela 4	Dau	1	F	1/2			
1272	5 " William McKinley 2	Son	2mo	M	1/2			
14570	6 " Arrebella 1	Dau	1mo	F	1/2			
	7							
	8							
	9							
	10	ENROLLMENT OF NOS. 1 2 3 4 and 5 HEREON APPROVED BY THE SECRETARY OF INTERIOR Dec 12 1902						
	11							
	12							
	13							
	14	ENROLLMENT OF NOS. 6 HEREON APPROVED BY THE SECRETARY OF INTERIOR May 20 1903						
	15							
	16							
	17							

TRIBAL ENROLLMENT OF PARENTS

	Name of Father	Year	County	Name of Mother	Year	County
1	Jack Thompson	Dead	Skullyville	Mary Thompson	Dead	Skullyville
2	James Dyer	1896	Eagle	Manda Dyer		non Citz
3	No.1			No.2		
4	No.1			No.2		
5	No.1			No.2		
6	No.1			No.2		
7						
8	No.3 – Affidavit of birth to be supplied. Recd June 16/99.					
9	No.4 " " " " " " " " 16/99.					
10	See evidence of marriage of parents of No.2 attached to Card No. 537.					
11						
12	No.2 on 1893 Pay roll as Josie Dyer, Page 19, No. 195, Eagle Co.					
13	No.2 " 1896 roll as Josie Thompson " 318 " 12253 " "					
	No.5 Enrolled January 29, 1901.					
14	No.6 Born Sept. 16, 1902 enrolled Oct. 13, 1902.				#1 to 4 Date of Application for Enrollment.
15						
16						April 20/99
17	P.O. Durant, Okla.					

269

Choctaw By Blood Enrollment Cards 1898-1914

RESIDENCE: Nashoba COUNTY. **Choctaw Nation** **Choctaw Roll** CARD NO.
POST OFFICE: Alikchi, I.T. *(Not Including Freedmen)* FIELD NO. 570

Dawes' Roll No.	NAME	Relationship to Person First Named	AGE	SEX	BLOOD	TRIBAL ENROLLMENT Year	County	No.
1273	1 John, Rayson 33	First Named	30	M	Full	1896	Nashoba	6841
1274	2 " Mary 31	Wife	28	F	"	1896	"	6842
1275	3 " Mattie 12	Dau	9	"	"	1896	"	6843
1276	4 " Gabriel 6	Son	2	M	"			
	5	ENROLLMENT OF NOS. 1 2 3 and 4 HEREON APPROVED BY THE SECRETARY						
	6	OF INTERIOR DEC 12 1902						
	7							
	8							
	9							
	10							
	11							
	12							
	13							
	14	No 4: Affidavit of birth to be supplied – Recd April 24/99						
	15							
	16							
	17							

TRIBAL ENROLLMENT OF PARENTS

Name of Father	Year	County	Name of Mother	Year	County
1 William John	Dead	Red River	Meha John	Dead	Nashoba
2 John Cephus	"	Nashoba	Chibbie Cephus	"	"
3 No 1			No 2		
4 No 1			No 2		
5					
6					
7					
8					
9					
10					
11					
12					
13					
14					
15				Date of Application for Enrollment.	April 20/99
16					
17 Bethel IT 12/9/02					

Choctaw By Blood Enrollment Cards 1898-1914

RESIDENCE: Nashoba COUNTY. **Choctaw Nation** **Choctaw Roll** CARD No.
POST OFFICE: Alikchi, I.T. *(Not Including Freedmen)* FIELD NO. **571**

Dawes' Roll No.	NAME		Relationship to Person First Named	AGE	SEX	BLOOD	TRIBAL ENROLLMENT		
							Year	County	P.R. No.
1277	1	McAlester, Wallace 59	First Named	56	M	Full	1893	Nashoba	514
1278	2	" Nancy 39	Wife	36	F	"	1893	"	515
1279	3	" Aves 12	Son	9	M	"	1893	"	517
	4								
	5								
	6	ENROLLMENT OF NOS. 1 2 and 3 HEREON							
	7	APPROVED BY THE SECRETARY							
	8	OF INTERIOR Dec 12 1902							
	9								
	10								
	11	No1 on 1896 roll Page 61 No 2530 as Wallace Carlester							
	12	No2 " " " ' 61 " 2531 " Nancy "							
	13	No3 " " " ' 61 " 2532 " Eris "							
	14								
	15								
	16								
	17								

TRIBAL ENROLLMENT OF PARENTS

	Name of Father	Year	County	Name of Mother	Year	County
1	Car-lis-ter	Dead	Cedar	A mok-le-to-na	Dead	Cedar
2	O-na-hubbee	"	"	Ma-lee	"	Towson
3	No 1			No 2		
4						
5						
6						
7						
8						
9						
10						
11						
12						
13						
14						
15				Date of Application for Enrollment.		
16				April 20/99		
17						

Choctaw By Blood Enrollment Cards 1898-1914

RESIDENCE: Cedar   COUNTY.   **Choctaw Nation**   **Choctaw Roll** CARD NO.

POST OFFICE: Alikchi, I.T.   (Not Including Freedmen) FIELD NO. **572**

Dawes' Roll No.	NAME	Relationship to Person First Named	AGE	SEX	BLOOD	TRIBAL ENROLLMENT Year	County	No.
1280	1 McAlester, James ³²	Named	29	M	Full	1896	Cedar	9266
1281	2 ~~Narcissa~~ DIED PRIOR TO SEPT. APR. 25, 1942	Wife	40	F	"	1896	Nashoba	13312
1282	3 " Ellen ⁶	Dau	1	"	"			
1283	4 Wallace, Sam ¹⁷	S.Son	14	M	"	1896	Nashoba	13314
	5							
	6							
	7							
	8	ENROLLMENT OF NOS. 1 2 3 and 4 HEREON						
	9	APPROVED BY THE SECRETARY OF INTERIOR Dec 12 1902						
	10							
	11							
	12							
	13							
	14							
	15							
	16							
	17							

TRIBAL ENROLLMENT OF PARENTS

	Name of Father	Year	County	Name of Mother	Year	County
1	Wallace McAlester	1896	Nashoba	Eliza McAlester	Dead	Cedar
2	~~Stim-a-la-chubbe~~	~~Dead~~	~~Towson~~	~~Mollie~~	"	~~Towson~~
3	No 1			No 2		
4	Johnson Wallace	Dead	Nashoba	No 2		
5						
6						
7						
8		No2 on 1896 roll as Narcissa Wallis				
9		No.4 on Choctaw roll as Sam Wallis				
10		No3: Affidavit as to birth to be supplied. Recd April 24/99				
11		~~No2 identified from 1893 payroll Nashoba Co page 66 No 765 as Narcissa Wallace~~ No2 Died Jany. 28, 1902. Proof of death filed Dec. 24, 1902.				
12	No2 died Jan. 28,1901: Enrollment cancelled by Department, July 8 – 1904					
13		For child of No.1 See N.B. (Apr 26-06) Card #597				
14		" " " " " (March 3, 1905) " #1454				
15					Date of Application for Enrollment.	
16					April 20/99	
17						

272

Choctaw By Blood Enrollment Cards 1898-1914

RESIDENCE: Nashoba COUNTY. **Choctaw Nation** **Choctaw Roll** CARD NO.
POST OFFICE: Alikchi, I.T. (Not Including Freedmen) FIELD NO. **573**

Dawes' Roll No.	NAME		Relationship to Person First Named	AGE	SEX	BLOOD	TRIBAL ENROLLMENT		
							Year	County	No.
1284	1 Jones, James			53	M	Full	1896	Nashoba	6858
1285	2 " Agnes	48	Wife	45	F	"	1896	"	6859
1286	3 " Isaac	19	Son	16	M	"	1896	"	6860
1287	4 " Jeffrey	8	"	5	"	"	1896	"	6861
1288	5 " James Jr.	6	"	1	"	"			
	6								
	7								
	8								
	9								
	10								
	11	ENROLLMENT							
	12	OF NOS. 1 2 3 4 and 5 HEREON APPROVED BY THE SECRETARY							
	13	OF INTERIOR Dec 12 1902							
	14								
	15								
	16								
	17								

DIED PRIOR TO SEPTEMBER 25, 1902 (row 1)

TRIBAL ENROLLMENT OF PARENTS

	Name of Father	Year	County	Name of Mother	Year	County
1	Yo-chubee	Dead	Nashoba		Dead	Nashoba
2	Tusk-ki-fa	"	Towson	Mary	"	Towson
3	No 1			Rhoda Jones	"	Nashoba
4	No 1			Ensie Jones	"	"
5	No 1			No 2		
6						
7			No5 Affidavit as to birth to be supplied. Rec'd April 20/99			
8						
9			No4 on 1896 roll as Jeoffrey Jones.			
10			No1 died Nov. 16, 1900: Enrollment cancelled by Department Dec. 24, 1904. For child of No3 see N.B. (March 3, 1905) #939			
11						
12						
13						
14						
15				Date of Application for Enrollment.		
16				April 20/99		
17						

273

Choctaw By Blood Enrollment Cards 1898-1914

RESIDENCE: Towson   COUNTY.   **Choctaw Nation**   Choctaw Roll   CARD NO.
POST OFFICE: Alikchi, I.T.   *(Not Including Freedmen)*   FIELD NO.   574

Dawes' Roll No.	NAME	Relationship to Person First Named	AGE	SEX	BLOOD	TRIBAL ENROLLMENT		
						Year	County	No.
1289	1 Williams, Lonie	Named	24	F	Full	1896	Towson	13202
1290	2 " Francis	Dau ?	3	M	"	1896	"	13203
1291	3 Hoyoputubbe, Sarah	Sister	18	F	"	1896	"	6785
1292	4 James, Levi 18	Brother	15	M	"	1896	"	6786
1293	5 " Elizabeth 15	Sister	12	F	"	1896	"	P.R. 194
1294	6 Hoyoputubbi, Stanley	Son of No3	2mo	M	"			
	7							
	8							
	9							
	10							
	11							
	12							
	13							
	14							
	15							
	16							
	17							

DIED PRIOR TO SEPTEMBER 25, 1902

ENROLLMENT
OF NOS. 1 2 3 4 5 and 6 HEREON
APPROVED BY THE SECRETARY
OF INTERIOR DEC 12 1902

TRIBAL ENROLLMENT OF PARENTS

	Name of Father	Year	County	Name of Mother	Year	County
1	William James	Dead	Bok Tuklo	Melissie James	Dead	Towson
2	Cephus Williams	"	Towson	No 1		
3	William James	Dead	Bok Tuklo	Melissie James	Dead	Towson
4	" "	"	" "	" "	"	"
5	" "	"	" "	" "	"	"
6	Wash Hoyoputubbi	1896	Towson	No 3		
7						
8	No2 on 1896 roll as female Feby 25/03					
9	No2 on 1896 roll as Vensie Williams					
10	No.3 is now the wife of Wash Hoyopatubbi on Choctaw card #1115					
11	No.6 Enrolled April 25, 1901.					
12	Nº3 Died Aug 13, 1902, proof of death filed					
13	No.3 died Aug 13, 1902. Enrollment cancelled by Department [remainder illegible]					
14	For child of No.5 see NB (March 3, 1905) #1259					
15						#1 to 5
16						Date of Application for Enrollment.
17						April 29/99

274

Choctaw By Blood Enrollment Cards 1898-1914

RESIDENCE: Eagle COUNTY.		Choctaw Nation				Choctaw Roll *(Not Including Freedmen)*		CARD NO.	
POST OFFICE: Eagletown, I.T.								FIELD NO. 575	

Dawes' Roll No.	NAME		Relationship to Person First Named	AGE	SEX	BLOOD	TRIBAL ENROLLMENT		
							Year	County	No.
1295	1 Anna, Lucy	53	First Named	50	F	Full	1896	Red River	331
	2								
	3								
	4	ENROLLMENT OF NOS. 1 HEREON APPROVED BY THE SECRETARY OF INTERIOR DEC 12 1902							
	5								
	6								
	7								
	8								
	9								
	10								
	11								
	12	On 1896 roll as Lucy Ann							
	13	No2 also on 1896 Census roll as Lucy Ann Hotambi page 137 #5626							
	14								
	15								
	16								
	17								

TRIBAL ENROLLMENT OF PARENTS

Name of Father	Year	County	Name of Mother	Year	County
1 Wish-e-machteby	Dead		Pisa-to-na	1896	Eagle
2					
3					
4					
5					
6					
7					
8					
9					
10					
11					
12					
13					
14					
15			Date of Application for Enrollment	April 20/99	
16					
17					

Choctaw By Blood Enrollment Cards 1898-1914

RESIDENCE: Bok Tuklo   COUNTY.   **Choctaw Nation**   **Choctaw Roll**   CARD No.
POST OFFICE: Lukfata, I.T.   *(Not Including Freedmen)*   FIELD No.   **576**

Dawes' Roll No.	NAME	Relationship to Person First Named	AGE	SEX	BLOOD	TRIBAL ENROLLMENT		
						Year	County	No.
1	Tikbombe, Salina	Named	60	F	Full	1896	Bok Tuklo	12184
2								
3								
4								
5								
6								
7								
8	No. ~1~ HEREON DISMISSED UNDER							
9	ORDER OF THE COMMISSION TO THE FIVE CIVILIZED TRIBES OF MARCH 31, 1905.							
10								
11								
12								
13	No1 did in 1897 Proof of death filed May 14, 1906							
14								
15								
16								
17								

TRIBAL ENROLLMENT OF PARENTS

	Name of Father	Year	County	Name of Mother	Year	County
1	E-lam-bey	Dead		Hosh-tey	Dead	Bok Tuklo
2						
3						
4						
5						
6						
7						
8						
9						
10						
11						
12						
13						
14						
15						
16				Date of Application for Enrollment.		April 20/99
17						

276

Choctaw By Blood Enrollment Cards 1898-1914

RESIDENCE: Red River COUNTY. **Choctaw Nation** **Choctaw Roll** CARD NO.
POST OFFICE: Janis, I.T. *(Not Including Freedmen)* FIELD NO. 577

Dawes' Roll No.	NAME	Relationship to Person First Named	AGE	SEX	BLOOD	TRIBAL ENROLLMENT		
						Year	County	No.
1296	1 Hale, Elizabeth 58	First Named	55	F	Full	1896	Red River	5716
1297	2 Logan, Adeline 3	Ward	10	"	"	1896	" "	8066
	3							
	4							
	5	ENROLLMENT						
	6	OF NOS. 1 and 2 HEREON APPROVED BY THE SECRETARY						
	7	OF INTERIOR DEC 12 1902						
	8							
	9							
	10	No2 on 1896 roll as Edline Logan						
	11							
	12							
	13							
	14							
	15							
	16							
	17							

TRIBAL ENROLLMENT OF PARENTS

	Name of Father	Year	County	Name of Mother	Year	County
1	Ya-kan-teby	Dead	Red River		Dead	Red River
2	Joe Logan	1896	" "	Elizabeth Logan	"	" "
3						
4						
5						
6						
7						
8						
9						
10						
11						
12						
13						
14						
15						
16				Date of Application for Enrollment.	April 20/99	
17						

Choctaw By Blood Enrollment Cards 1898-1914

RESIDENCE: Red River   COUNTY.   **Choctaw Nation**   **Choctaw Roll**   CARD NO.
POST OFFICE: Janis, I.T.   (Not Including Freedmen)   FIELD NO.   578

Dawes' Roll No.	NAME	Relationship to Person First Named	AGE	SEX	BLOOD	TRIBAL ENROLLMENT		
						Year	County	No.
1298	1 Watkins, Bacy		52	F	Full	1896	Red River	13666
	2							
	3							
	4							
	5	ENROLLMENT						
	6	OF NOS. 1 HEREON APPROVED BY THE SECRETARY						
	7	OF INTERIOR DEC 12 1902						
	8							
	9							
	10							
	11	No1 died March 5, 1899: proof of death filed Dec 4, 1902.						
	12	No1 died March 5, 1899: Enrollment cancelled by Department [remainder illegible]						
	13							
	14							
	15							
	16							
	17							

TRIBAL ENROLLMENT OF PARENTS

	Name of Father	Year	County	Name of Mother	Year	County
1	Isht-noah	Dead	Red River		Dead	Red River
2						
3						
4						
5						
6						
7						
8						
9						
10						
11						
12						
13						
14						
15						
16				Date of Application for Enrollment.	April 20/00	
17						

278

Choctaw By Blood Enrollment Cards 1898-1914

RESIDENCE: Nashoba COUNTY. **Choctaw Nation**
POST OFFICE: Alikchi, I.T.

Choctaw Roll (Not Including Freedmen)

CARD NO.
FIELD NO. **579**

Dawes' Roll No.	NAME		Relationship to Person	AGE	SEX	BLOOD	TRIBAL ENROLLMENT		
							Year	County	No.
1299	1 Carney, Edward	27	First Named	24	M	Full	1896	Nashoba	2521
1300	2 " Lizzie	22	Wife	19	F	"	1896	"	2522
1301	3 " Henry	4	Son	9mo	M	"			
~~Dead~~ Dead	4 " ~~Seamie~~ DEAD		~~Sister~~	~~16~~	~~F~~	~~"~~	~~1896~~	~~Nashoba~~	~~2528~~
1302	5 " Larten	7	Brother	4	M	"	1896	"	2529
1303	6 " Effrim	1	Son	5mo	M	"			
	7								
	8	ENROLLMENT							
	9	OF NOS. 1 2 3 5 and 6 HEREON APPROVED BY THE SECRETARY							
	10	OF INTERIOR Dec 12, 1902							
	11								
	12	No. 4 Hereon dismissed under order							
	13	of the Commission to the Five Civilized							
		Tribes of March 31, 1905.							
	14								
	15								
	16								
	17								

TRIBAL ENROLLMENT OF PARENTS

	Name of Father	Year	County	Name of Mother	Year	County
1	Wallace Carney	Dead	Nashoba	Phoebe Carney	Dead	Nashoba
2	John Joel	"	Jacks Fork	Sukey Joel	1896	"
3	No 1			No 2		
4	Wallace Carney	Dead	Nashoba	Phoebe Carney	Dead	Nashoba
5	" "	"	"	" "	"	"
6	No 1			No 2		
7						
8						
9	For child of 1 and 2 see N.B. (Apr. 26-06) No. 567					
10	No2 on 1896 roll as Lizzie W. Carney.					
11	No6 Born March 24, 1902. enrolled Aug. 29, 1902.					
	No4 Died Sept. 4, 1899: Proof of Death filed Nov. 4, 1902					
12						
13						
14						#1 to 5
15						Date of Application for Enrollment.
16						April 20/99
17						

Choctaw By Blood Enrollment Cards 1898-1914

RESIDENCE: Towson COUNTY. POST OFFICE: Doaksville, I.T.

Choctaw Nation

Choctaw Roll (Not Including Freedmen)

CARD NO. FIELD NO. **580**

Dawes' Roll No.	NAME		Relationship to Person First Named	AGE	SEX	BLOOD	TRIBAL ENROLLMENT		
							Year	County	No.
1304	1 Austin, Willis	46	First Named	43	M	Full	1896	Towson	188
1305	2 " Sillis	26	Wife	23	F	"	1893	"	P.R. 348
1306	3 " Ellis	6	Son	3	M	"	1896	"	189
1307	4 Louis		"	8mo	"	"			
1308	5 " Felker	2	"	2m	M	"			
	6								
	7								
	8								
	9								
	10								
	11	ENROLLMENT							
	12	OF NOS. 1 2 3 4 and 5 HEREON APPROVED BY THE SECRETARY							
	13	OF INTERIOR Dec 12 1902							
	14								
	15								
	16								
	17								

TRIBAL ENROLLMENT OF PARENTS

	Name of Father	Year	County	Name of Mother	Year	County
1	Samuel Austin	Dead	Red River	Viney Austin	Dead	Red River
2	Bill Thomas	"	" "	Daisy A. Thomas	"	" "
3	No 1			Mary Austin	"	Towson
4	No 1			No 2		
5	No 1			No 2		
6						
7			No4 Affidavit of birth to be supplied. Recd. April 25/99			
8		No.2 on 1896 Choctaw census roll, page 315, No 12132 as Celers Timaye.				
9			No 2 on 1893 Pay-roll as Sillis Thomas			
10			No.5 Enrolled February 1, 1901.			
11			No4 died Nov. 29, 1899: Proof of death filed Dec 4, 1902.			
12		No.4 died Nov. 29, 1899: Enrollment cancelled by Department Sept. 16, 1904				
13						
14						
15					Date of Application for Enrollment	
16						April 20/99
17	Fowlerville I.T. 11/26/02					

Choctaw By Blood Enrollment Cards 1898-1914

RESIDENCE: Towson COUNTY.
POST OFFICE: Fowlerville, I.T.

Choctaw Nation

Choctaw Roll
(Not Including Freedmen)

CARD NO.
FIELD NO. 581

Dawes' Roll No.	NAME		Relationship to Person First Named	AGE	SEX	BLOOD	TRIBAL ENROLLMENT		
							Year	County	No.
1309	1 Louis, Jesse	39	First Named	36	M	Full	1896	Towson	7919
1310	2 " Empsie	43	Wife	40	F	"	1896	"	7920
1311	3 " Williamson	12	Son	9	M	"	1896	"	7921
1312	4 " Wilbert	11	"	8	"	"	1896	"	7922
1313	5 " Willie		"	2	"	"			
1314	6 Austin, Annie	21	S. Dau	18	F	"	1893	Towson	P.K. 327
	7								
	8								
	9								
	10								
	11								
	12								
	13								
	14								
	15								
	16								
	17								

DIED PRIOR TO SEPTEMBER 25, 1902 (row 5)
DIED PRIOR TO SEPTEMBER 25, 1902 (row 6)

ENROLLMENT
OF NOS. 1 2 3 4 5 and 6 HEREON
APPROVED BY THE SECRETARY
OF INTERIOR DEC 12 1902

No. 5 died Feb. 9, 1902; No. 6 died July — 1899;
Enrollment cancelled by Department
Sept. 16, 1904.

TRIBAL ENROLLMENT OF PARENTS

	Name of Father	Year	County	Name of Mother	Year	County
1	James Louis	Dead	Cedar	Noah-hema	Dead	Towson
2	John Tuskkia[sic]	"	Towson	Maley Tushkia	"	"
3	No 1			No 2		
4	No 1			No 2		
5	No 1			No 2		
6	Henry Austin	Dead	Towson	No 2		
7						
8						
9						
10			No 1 on 1896 roll as Jessie Louis			
11						
12			No 5: Affidavit of birth to be supplied. Recd May 2/99			
13			No 5 died Feb. 9, 1902; proof of death filed Dec 3, 1902			
14			No 6 " July - 1899: " " " " " " "			
15						
16				Date of Application for Enrollment.		April 29/99
17						

281

Choctaw By Blood Enrollment Cards 1898-1914

RESIDENCE: Towson COUNTY.
POST OFFICE: Doaksville, I.T.

Choctaw Nation

Choctaw Roll CARD NO.
(Not Including Freedmen) FIELD NO. **582**

Dawes' Roll No.	NAME	Relationship to Person	AGE	SEX	BLOOD	TRIBAL ENROLLMENT Year	County	No.
1315	1 Williams, Jonas 48	First Named	45	M	Full	1896	Towson	13209
1316	2 " Phoebe 43	Wife	40	F	"	1896	"	13210
1317	3 Hermon Cillen 18	Dau	15	"	"	1896	"	13212
1318	4 Williams, Elizabeth 13	"	10	"	"	1896	"	13213
1319	5 " Sibbie 6	"	3	"	"	1896	"	13214
1320	6 " Agnes 19	S.Dau	16	"	"	1896	"	13211
1321	7 " Tonsie 5	S.G.Son	1	M	"			
I.W. 13	8 Hermon, Joseph G.	Husband of No3	54	M	I.W.	1896	Kiamitia	14641
	9							
	10							
	11							
	12							
	13							
	14							
	15							
	16							
	17							

ENROLLMENT
OF NOS. 123456and7 HEREON
APPROVED BY THE SECRETARY
OF INTERIOR Dec 12 1902

ENROLLMENT
OF NOS. ~ 8 ~ HEREON
APPROVED BY THE SECRETARY
OF INTERIOR Jun 13 1903

TRIBAL ENROLLMENT OF PARENTS

	Name of Father	Year	County	Name of Mother	Year	County
1	William Smith	Dead	Towson	Ta-ha-te-ma	Dead	Towson
2	Louis Thomas	"	"	Leviney Towson	"	"
3	No 1			Sophie Williams	"	"
4	No 1			" "	"	"
5	No 1			No 2		
6	Simon Cobb	Dead	Towson	No 2		
7	Damnsel Louis	"	"	No 6		
8	John Hermon	Dead	Non Citizen	Amanda Hermon	Dead	Non citz
9						
10						
11						
12	No7 Affidavit of birth to be supplied: Recd April 25/99					
13	No3 is now the wife of Joseph G. Hermon on Choctaw Card #D163 March 29, 1901					
14	No8 transferred from Choctaw Card #D163 March 29 1903					
	See decision of March 13, 1903.					
15						#1 to 7 in
16						Date of Application for Enrollment
17						April 20/99

Choctaw By Blood Enrollment Cards 1898-1914

	RESIDENCE: Towson	COUNTY.	Choctaw Nation		Choctaw Roll	CARD No.	
	POST OFFICE: Doaksville, I.T.				(Not Including Freedmen)	FIELD No. **583**	

Dawes' Roll No.	NAME	Relationship to Person First Named	AGE	SEX	BLOOD	TRIBAL ENROLLMENT		
						Year	County	No.
1322	1 Holman, Sally ⁸³	First Named	80	F	Full	1896	Towson	5507
	2							
	3 ENROLLMENT							
	4 OF NOS. 1 HEREON APPROVED BY THE SECRETARY							
	5 OF INTERIOR DEC 12 1902							
	6							
	7							
	8							
	9							
	10							
	11							
	12							
	13							
	14							
	15							
	16							
	17							

TRIBAL ENROLLMENT OF PARENTS

	Name of Father	Year	County	Name of Mother	Year	County
1		Died in Mississippi			Died in Mississippi	
2						
3						
4						
5						
6						
7						
8						
9						
10						
11						
12						
13						
14						
15						
16					Date of Application for Enrollment	April 20/99
17						

283

Choctaw By Blood Enrollment Cards 1898-1914

RESIDENCE: Towson	COUNTY.	**Choctaw Nation**	**Choctaw Roll**	CARD No.
POST OFFICE: Fowlerville, I.T.			*(Not Including Freedmen)*	FIELD No. 584

Dawes' Roll No.	NAME	Relationship to Person First Named	AGE	SEX	BLOOD	TRIBAL ENROLLMENT Year	County	No.
1323	1 Cobb, Gibson 37	First Named	34	M	Full	1896	Towson	2466
1324	2 " Nancy 34	Wife	31	F	"	1896	"	2467
1325	3 " Bettie 13	Dau	10	"	"	1896	"	2468
1326	4 " Sophie 12	"	9	"	"	1896	"	2469
	5							
	6	ENROLLMENT						
	7	OF NOS. 1 2 3 and 4 HEREON APPROVED BY THE SECRETARY						
	8	OF INTERIOR DEC 12 1902						
	9							
	10							
	11							
	12							
	13							
	14							
	15							
	16							
	17							

TRIBAL ENROLLMENT OF PARENTS

	Name of Father	Year	County	Name of Mother	Year	County
1	Mike Cobb	Dead	Towson	Siney Cobb	Dead	Towson
2	Willis Willis	"	Red River	Sophie Willis	"	Red River
3	No 1			No 2		
4	No 1			No 2		
5						
6			No1 is now husband of Sallie Choate on Choctaw card #1081; evidence			
7			of marriage filed December 3, 1902			
8			No2 died June 19, 1900; proof of death filed Dec 4, 1902			
9			No.2 died June 19, 1900; Enrollment cancelled by Department [remainder illegible]			
10						
11						
12						
13						
14						
15				Date of Application for Enrollment.		
16				April 20/99		
17						

Choctaw By Blood Enrollment Cards 1898-1914

RESIDENCE:	Red River	COUNTY.		Choctaw Nation			Choctaw Roll	CARD NO.	
POST OFFICE:	Janis, I.T.						(Not Including Freedmen)	FIELD NO.	585

Dawes' Roll No.	NAME		Relationship to Person First Named	AGE	SEX	BLOOD	TRIBAL ENROLLMENT		
							Year	County	No.
1327	1 Hall, Sampson	57	First Named	54	M	Full	1896	Red River	5705
1328	2 " Sokey	DIED PRIOR TO SEPTEMBER 25, 1902	Wife	51	F	"	1896	" "	5706
1329	3 " Siney	25	Dau	22	"	"	1896	" "	5707
1330	4 " Joshua	23	Son	20	M	"	1896	" "	5708
1331	5 " Ellis	21	Dau	18	F	"	1896	" "	5709
1332	6 " Jonas	17	Son	14	M	"	1896	" "	5710
1333	7 Parker, Dennis	13	G.Son	10	"	"	1896	" "	10419
1334	8 " Lena	7	G.Dau	4	F	"	1896	" "	10420
15933	9 Billy, Levisee		Dau of No.3	6	F	"			
	10								
	11	ENROLLMENT OF NOS. 1234567and8 HEREON APPROVED BY THE SECRETARY							
	12	OF INTERIOR Dec 12 1902							

13 No.9 was born Jan.6,1897. appli- | No.2 died Nov.17,1901 proof of death filed Dec 3,1902
14 cation received and No 9 listed on | No 4 now married to Fannie Jefferson on Choctaw Card#810
15 this card. April 10, 1905, under Act | No.2 died Nov.17,1901:Enrollment cancelled by DepartmentSept.16,1904.
16 of Congress approved | No.2 died Nov.17,1901:Enrollment cancelled by DepartmentSept.16,1904. For child of No.4 see NB (March 3, 1905) #1100.
17 March3, 1905. | " " " " " (April 26, 1906) #578

TRIBAL ENROLLMENT OF PARENTS

	Name of Father	Year	County	Name of Mother	Year	County
1	Ka-no-te-ka-be	Dead	Red River	Ok-lo-ho-tena	Dead	Red River
2	We-ha-ta-ke	"	Eagle	To-lo-ach-ee	"	" "
3	No.1			No.2		
4	No.1			No.2		
5	No.1			No.2		
6	No.1			No.2		
7	Julius Jefferson	1896	Red River	Salissie Jefferson	Dead	Red River
8	Solomon Parker	Dead	" "	" "	"	" " "
9	David Billy			No.3		
10					ENROLLMENT OF NOS. ~ 9 ~ HEREON APPROVED BY THE SECRETARY OF INTERIOR Nov. 24 1905	
11						
12						
13			No.5 Sex changed under Departmental instructions of July 28, 1904. (D.C. #27369-1904)			
14			No.7 on 1896 roll as Denis Parker.			
15						#1 to 8 inc
16						Date of Application for Enrollment.
17						April 20/99

Choctaw By Blood Enrollment Cards 1898-1914

RESIDENCE: Red River COUNTY.
POST OFFICE: Janis, I.T.

Choctaw Nation

Choctaw Roll
(Not Including Freedmen)

CARD NO.
FIELD NO. 586

Dawes' Roll No.	NAME	Relationship to Person First Named	AGE	SEX	BLOOD	TRIBAL ENROLLMENT		
						Year	County	No.
1335	1 Logan, Thompson 48	First Named	45	M	Full	1896	Red River	8061
Dead	2 " Sallie DEAD	Wife	24	F	"	1896	" "	8062
1336	3 " Bias 16	Son	13	M	"	1896	" "	8063
1337	4 " Sam 12	Nephew	9	"	"	1896	" "	8064
	5							
	6	ENROLLMENT OF NOS. 1 – 3 and 4 HEREON APPROVED BY THE SECRETARY OF INTERIOR Dec 12 1902						
	7							
	8							
	9							
	10							
	11							
	12	No. 2 Hereon dismissed under order of						
	13	the Commission to the Five Civilized						
	14	Tribes of March 31, 1905.						
	15							
	16							
	17							

TRIBAL ENROLLMENT OF PARENTS

	Name of Father	Year	County	Name of Mother	Year	County
1	Bog Logan	Dead	Red River	I-yo-lee	Dead	Red River
2	Stephen Fisher	"	" "	Silaway Fisher	1896	" "
3	No 1			Sallie Logan	Dead	" "
4	Griggs Logan	Dead	Red River	Elizabeth Logan	"	" "
5						
6						
7						
8						
9	No3 on 1896 roll as Tobias Logan					
10	No.2 Died May 14, 1899. Evidence of death filed April6 1901					
11						
12						
13						
14						
15					Date of Application for Enrollment.	
16						April 20/99
17						

286

Choctaw By Blood Enrollment Cards 1898-1914

RESIDENCE: Towson COUNTY. **Choctaw Nation** **Choctaw Roll** CARD No.
POST OFFICE: Doaksville, I.T. *(Not Including Freedmen)* FIELD NO. 587

Dawes' Roll No.	NAME		Relationship to Person	AGE	SEX	BLOOD	TRIBAL ENROLLMENT		
							Year	County	No.
1338	1 Wilson, Nannie	37	First Named	34	F	1/2	1896	Towson	13205
1339	2 " Rufus L	16	Son	13	M	1/4	1896	"	13206
1340	3 " Cleopatra	11	Dau	8	F	1/4	1896	"	13207
1341	4 " Edward O	7	Son	4	M	1/4	1896	"	13208
	5								
	6								
	7	ENROLLMENT							
	8	OF NOS. 1 2 3 and 4 HEREON APPROVED BY THE SECRETARY							
	9	OF INTERIOR DEC 12 1902							
	10								
	11								
	12	Husband of No1 and father of her children is on Chickasaw Card No 1410.							
	13								
	14	For child of No2 see NB (Mar 3-1905) Card #95.							
	15								
	16								
	17								

TRIBAL ENROLLMENT OF PARENTS

	Name of Father	Year	County	Name of Mother	Year	County
1	Cornelius Carney	Dead	Towson	Rosanna Watson	1896	Towson
2	W. W. Wilson	1896	Chick residing in Choc. Natn	No 1		
3	" " "	1896	" "	No 1		
4	" " "	1896	" "	No 1		
5						
6						
7						
8						
9						
10						
11						
12						
13						
14						
15						
16				Date of Application for Enrollment.		April 20/99
17						

Choctaw By Blood Enrollment Cards 1898-1914

RESIDENCE: Red River   COUNTY.   **Choctaw Nation**   **Choctaw Roll**   CARD NO.

POST OFFICE: Janis, I.T.   *(Not Including Freedmen)*   FIELD NO.   588

Dawes' Roll No.	NAME	Relationship to Person First Named	AGE	SEX	BLOOD	TRIBAL ENROLLMENT Year	County	No.
Dead	1 Calvin, Melissa	Named	50	M	Full	1896	Red River	2675
1342	2 " Ellis [13]	Son	10	"	"	1896	" "	2676
	3							
	4 No. 1 HEREON DISMISSED UNDER							
	ORDER OF THE COMMISSION TO THE FIVE							
	5 CIVILIZED TRIBES OF MARCH 31, 1905.							
	6							
	7 ENROLLMENT							
	OF NOS. 2 HEREON							
	8 APPROVED BY THE SECRETARY							
	9 OF INTERIOR DEC 12 1902							
	10							
	11							
	12 No1 on 1896 roll as Malissa Calvin							
	13 No.1 Died June 14, 1899. Evidence of death filed April 18, 1901.							
	14							
	15							
	16							
	17							

TRIBAL ENROLLMENT OF PARENTS

Name of Father	Year	County	Name of Mother	Year	County
1 Isht-noah	Dead	Red River		Dead	Red River
2 Eden Calvin	"	" "	No 1		
3					
4					
5					
6					
7					
8					
9					
10					
11					
12					
13					
14					
15					
16			Date of Application for Enrollment.		April 20/99
17					

288

Choctaw By Blood Enrollment Cards 1898-1914

RESIDENCE: Red River COUNTY.
POST OFFICE: Kullituklo, I.T.

Choctaw Nation

Choctaw Roll
(Not Including Freedmen)

CARD No.
FIELD No. 589

Dawes' Roll No.	NAME		Relationship to Person First Named	AGE	SEX	BLOOD	TRIBAL ENROLLMENT		
							Year	County	No.
1343	1 Fisher, Thomas	23	First Named	20	M	Full	1896	Red River	4201
	2								
	3								
	4								
	5								
	6								
	7	ENROLLMENT							
	8	OF NOS. 1 HEREON APPROVED BY THE SECRETARY							
	9	OF INTERIOR DEC 12 1902							
	10								
	11								
	12								
	13								
	14	No.1 is now the husband of Kitsy Johnson							
	15	on Choctaw card #606 March 1st, 1900.							
	16								
	17								

TRIBAL ENROLLMENT OF PARENTS

	Name of Father	Year	County	Name of Mother	Year	County
1	Rogers Fisher	Dead	Red River	Elsie Fisher	1896	Red River
2						
3						
4						
5						
6						
7						
8						
9						
10						
11						
12						
13						
14						
15						
16				Date of Application for Enrollment.		April 20/99
17						

Choctaw By Blood Enrollment Cards 1898-1914

RESIDENCE: Towson   COUNTY.   **Choctaw Nation**   **Choctaw Roll**   CARD NO.
POST OFFICE: Fowlerville, I.T.   *(Not Including Freedmen)*   FIELD NO. **590**

Dawes' Roll No.		NAME		Relationship to Person First Named	AGE	SEX	BLOOD	TRIBAL ENROLLMENT		
								Year	County	No.
1344	1	Willis, John	35	First Named	32	M	Full	1896	Towson	13165
I.W. 560	2	" Sammie	32	Wife	28	F	I.W.	1896	"	15170
1345	3	" Betty	11	Dau	8	"	1/2	1896	"	13167
1346	4	" Nancy	9	"	6	"	1/2	1896	"	13166
1347	5	" Frances	6	"	3	"	1/2	1896	"	13168
1348	6	" Georgiana	4	"	9mo	"	1/2			
1349	7	~~" Lena~~ DIED PRIOR TO SEPTEMBER 25, 1902		Dau	7wks	F	1/2			
	8									
	9	ENROLLMENT								
	10	OF NOS. 13456and7 HEREON APPROVED BY THE SECRETARY								
	11	OF INTERIOR Dec 12, 1902								
	12									
	13	ENROLLMENT								
	14	OF NOS. ~~~ 2 ~~~ HEREON APPROVED BY THE SECRETARY								
	15	OF INTERIOR Feb 8, 1904								
	16									
	17									

TRIBAL ENROLLMENT OF PARENTS

	Name of Father	Year	County	Name of Mother	Year	County
1	Willis Willis	Dead	Red River	Sophie Willis	Dead	Red River
2	Al Romine	"	Non Citz	Bettie Romine	"	Non Citz
3	No 1			No 2		
4	No 1			No 2		
5	No 1			No 2		
6	No 1			No 2		
7	No 1			No 2		
8	No6 Affidavit of birth to be supplied Recd April 25/99					
9						
10	No7 Born Nov. 12, 1901: enrolled Jan. 3, 1902					
11	No7 died February 23, 1902: Proof of death filed Dec. 3, 1902					
12	No.7 died Feb 23, 1902: Enrollment cancelled by Department Sept. 16, 1904					
13	For child of No1 see N.B. (March 3, 1905) #933.					
14						
15						
16	P.O. Garvin I.T. 11/19/05 Valliant			Date of Application for Enrollment.	April 20/99	
17	P.O. seems to be ~~Garvin~~ I.T.					

290

Choctaw By Blood Enrollment Cards 1898-1914

Dawes' Roll No.		NAME		Relationship to Person	AGE	SEX	BLOOD	TRIBAL ENROLLMENT		
								Year	County	No.
IW 627	1	Stanley, William W	47	First Named	43	M	I W	1896	Towson	15045
1350	2	" Salena	32	Wife	29	F	1/8	1896	"	11361
1351	3	" James W	15	Son	12	M	1/16	1896	"	11362
1352	4	" Ada N.	13	Dau	10	F	1/16	1896	"	11363
DEAD.	5	" Lela C. DEAD.		"	8	"	1/16	1896	"	11364
1353	6	" Samuel M	9	Son	6	M	1/16	1896	"	11365
1354	7	" Helen A.	7	Dau	4	F	1/16	1896	"	11366
1355	8	" Bettie J	5	"	2	"	1/16			
DEAD.	9	" Allene DEAD.		Dau	3mo	F	1/16			
1356	10	" William R	1	Son	2m	M	1/16			
	11	ENROLLMENT OF NOS. 1 HEREON						No3 on 1896 roll as Jas. W. Stanley		
	12	APPROVED BY THE SECRETARY OF INTERIOR MAR 26 1904						No.9 Enrolled November 12th, 1900.		
	13	No10 Born May 24" 1902 Enrolled July 16"1902								
	14	No5 Died June 22nd 1902 Evidence of Death filed July 16"1902								
	15	ENROLLMENT OF NOS. 234678and9 HEREON								
	16	APPROVED BY THE SECRETARY OF INTERIOR DEC 12 1902						No9 Died Oct 9 1901: proof of death filed April 22		
	17									

TRIBAL ENROLLMENT OF PARENTS

	Name of Father	Year	County	Name of Mother	Year	County
1	James W. Stanley	Dead	Non Citz	Narcissa Stanley	1896	Non Citz
2	Cornelius Jones	"	Red River	Mahaley Jones	Dead	Red River
3	No 1			No 2		
4	No 1			No 2		
5	No 1			No 2		
6	No 1			No 2		
7	No 1			No 2		
8	No 1			No 2		
9	No.1			No.2		
10	No 1 No1 died 4/6/11 G.F.#22193			No 2		
11	For child of Nos1 and 2 see NB (Mar31905)#502			No. 5 and 9 HEREON DISMISSED UNDER		
12	Evidence of marriage to be supplied No8 Affidavit of birth " " " Recd April 26/99			ORDER OF THE COMMISSION TO THE FIVE CIVILIZED TRIBES OF MARCH 31, 1905.		
13	No4 on 1896 roll as Ada Stanley					
14	No5 " 1896 " " Lela "			Affidavit of Mahaley Jones as to marriage between		
15	No6 " 1896 " " Samuel " Nos 1and 2 filed July 21,1903					
16	No7 " 1896 " " Helen " No1 " 1896 " " Wm M "			Date of Application for Enrollment April 20/99		
17	Chula IT 11/26/02					

P.O. Parsons IT 4/4/03   P.O.#2 Valliant Okla see G.F.#22173 7/20/11   1 to 8

Choctaw By Blood Enrollment Cards 1898-1914

RESIDENCE: Towson COUNTY.
POST OFFICE: Fowlerville, I.T.

Choctaw Nation

Choctaw Roll
(Not Including Freedmen)

CARD NO.
FIELD NO. 592

Dawes' Roll No.	NAME	Relationship to Person	AGE	SEX	BLOOD	TRIBAL ENROLLMENT		
						Year	County	No.
1357	1 Jones, Mahaley 73	First Named	70	F	1/2	1896	Towson	6769
	2							
	3							
	4							
	5	ENROLLMENT						
	6	OF NOS. 1 HEREON APPROVED BY THE SECRETARY						
	7	OF INTERIOR DEC 12 1902						
	8							
	9							
	10							
	11							
	12							
	13							
	14							
	15							
	16							
	17							

TRIBAL ENROLLMENT OF PARENTS

Name of Father	Year	County	Name of Mother	Year	County
1 James Pickens	Dead	Bok Tuklo	Rachel Pickens	Dead	Bok Tuklo
2					
3					
4					
5					
6					
7					
8					
9					
10					
11					
12					
13					
14				Date of Application for Enrollment.	
15					
16				April 20/99	
17					

292

Choctaw By Blood Enrollment Cards 1898-1914

RESIDENCE: Towson COUNTY. POST OFFICE: Fowlerville, I.T.

Choctaw Nation

Choctaw Roll *(Not Including Freedmen)*

CARD NO. FIELD NO. 593

Dawes' Roll No.	NAME		Relationship to Person First Named	AGE	SEX	BLOOD	TRIBAL ENROLLMENT		
							Year	County	No.
1358	1 Baken, Lyman	33	First Named	30	M	Full	1896	Towson	1087
1359	2 " Winnie	15	Dau	12	F	"	1896	"	1089
1360	3 " Carsey	10	"	7	"	"	1896	"	1090
	4								
	5 ENROLLMENT								
	6 OF NOS. 1 2 and 3 HEREON APPROVED BY THE SECRETARY								
	7 OF INTERIOR DEC 12 1902								
	8 For child of No2 see NB (Apr 26-06) Card #638								
	9								
	10								
	11				No1 on 1896 roll as Laymon Baken.				
	12		No.3 also on 1896 Choctaw census roll, page 82: No. 3421						
	13		as Kissy Davis						
	14								
	15								
	16								
	17								

TRIBAL ENROLLMENT OF PARENTS

	Name of Father	Year	County	Name of Mother	Year	County
1	Ellis Baken	Dead	Towson	Pikey Baken	1896	Towson
2	No 1			Betsey Baken	Dead	"
3	No 1			Liddie Baken	1896	Bok Tuklo
4						
5						
6						
7	No1 now husband of Mollie Nokintaya on Choc #596					
8	For child of No.1 see N.B. (Apr. 26, 1906) Card No. 116.					
9	" " " " " " (March 3,1905) " " 786					
10						
11						
12						
13						
14				Date of Application for Enrollment.		
15						
16				April 20/99		
17						

Choctaw By Blood Enrollment Cards 1898-1914

RESIDENCE: Towson COUNTY.
POST OFFICE: Fowlerville, I.T.

Choctaw Nation

Choctaw Roll
(Not Including Freedmen)

CARD NO.
FIELD NO. **594**

Dawes' Roll No.	NAME	Relationship to Person First Named	AGE	SEX	BLOOD	TRIBAL ENROLLMENT Year	TRIBAL ENROLLMENT County	TRIBAL ENROLLMENT No.
1361	1 Baken, Parekie ~~DIED PRIOR TO SEPTEMBER 25, 1902~~ 63	First Named	60	F	Full	1896	Towson	1091
	2							
	3							
	4							
	5							
	6							
	7							
	8							
	9							
	10							
	11							
	12							
	13	No1 Died May 16, 1900: Proof of death filed Dec. 3, 1902						
	14	No1 died May 16, 1900: Enrollment cancelled by Department Sept. 16, 1904.						
	15							
	16							
	17							

ENROLLMENT
OF NOS. 1 HEREON
APPROVED BY THE SECRETARY
OF INTERIOR Dec. 12, 1902.

TRIBAL ENROLLMENT OF PARENTS

	Name of Father	Year	County	Name of Mother	Year	County
1	William Christie	Dead	Towson	Bicey Christie	Dead	Towson
2						
3						
4						
5						
6						
7						
8						
9						
10						
11						
12						
13						
14						
15						
16				Date of Application for Enrollment	April 20/99	
17						

294

Choctaw By Blood Enrollment Cards 1898-1914

RESIDENCE: Towson COUNTY.
POST OFFICE: Fowlerville, I.T.

Choctaw Nation

Choctaw Roll
(Not Including Freedmen)

CARD NO.
FIELD NO. 595

Dawes' Roll No.	NAME		Relationship to Person First Named	AGE	SEX	BLOOD	TRIBAL ENROLLMENT		
							Year	County	No.
1362	1 Davis, Alekton	31	First Named	28	M	Full	1896	Eagle	3412
1363	2 " Martha	27	Wife	24	F	"	1896	"	3424
1364	3 " Eliza	4	Dau	1	"	"			
	4								
	5								
	6 ENROLLMENT								
	7 OF NOS. 1 – 2 and 3 HEREON APPROVED BY THE SECRETARY								
	8 OF INTERIOR DEC 12 1902								
	9								
	10								
	11								
	12 For child of Nos. 1&2 see NB (March 4, 1905) 1467								
	13								
	14								
	15								
	16								
	17								

TRIBAL ENROLLMENT OF PARENTS

	Name of Father	Year	County	Name of Mother	Year	County
1	Davis Nakaneha	Dead	Bok Tuklo	Ko-no-te-ma	Dead	Bok Tuklo
2	Ellis Baken	"	Towson	Pikey Baken	1896	Towson
3	No 1			No 2		
4						
5						
6						
7						
8						
9						
10						
11						
12						
13						
14						
15				Date of Application for Enrollment.		April 20/99
16						
17	Valiant I.T. 11/27/02					

Choctaw By Blood Enrollment Cards 1898-1914

RESIDENCE: Eagle   COUNTY.   **Choctaw Nation**   **Choctaw Roll**   CARD NO.
POST OFFICE: Eagletown, I.T.   *(Not Including Freedmen)*   FIELD NO. 596

Dawes' Roll No.	NAME	Relationship to Person First Named	AGE	SEX	BLOOD	TRIBAL ENROLLMENT Year	County	No.
1365	1 Nakintaya, Mollie 21	First Named	18	F	Full	1896	Eagle	9725
	2							
	3							
	4							
	5	ENROLLMENT						
	6	OF NOS. 1 HEREON APPROVED BY THE SECRETARY						
	7	OF INTERIOR DEC 12 1902						
	8							
	9							
	10							
	11	On 1896 roll as Mali Nakintaya.						
	12	No1 is now wife of Lyman Baken Choc card #593.						
	13	For child of No.1 see N.B. (Apr 26,1906) Card No. 116.						
	14	" " " " " " " (March 3,1905) " " 786						
	15							
	16							
	17							

TRIBAL ENROLLMENT OF PARENTS

	Name of Father	Year	County	Name of Mother	Year	County
1	Davis Nakintaya	Dead	Bok Tuklo	Ko-no-te-ma	Dead	Bok Tuklo
2						
3						
4						
5						
6						
7						
8						
9						
10						
11						
12						
13						
14						
15					Date of Application for Enrollment.	April 20/99
16						
17	P.O. Valiant I.T. 11/27/02					

296

Choctaw By Blood Enrollment Cards 1898-1914

RESIDENCE: Towson COUNTY.　　**Choctaw Nation**　　**Choctaw Roll** CARD NO.
POST OFFICE: Doaksville, I.T.　　　　　　(Not Including Freedmen)　FIELD NO. 597

Dawes' Roll No.	NAME	Relationship to Person First Named	AGE	SEX	BLOOD	TRIBAL ENROLLMENT		
						Year	County	No.
1366	1 Christie, Gilbert 40	First Named	37	M	Full	1896	Towson	2471
1367	2 " Susanna 35	Wife	32	F	"	1896	"	229
1368	3 " Emiline 13	Dau	10	"	"	1896	"	2472
	4							
	5							
	6	ENROLLMENT						
	7	OF NOS. 1 – 2 and 3 HEREON APPROVED BY THE SECRETARY						
	8	OF INTERIOR DEC 12 1902						
	9							
	10							
	11							
	12	No2 on 1896 roll as Susanna Aaron.						
	13	No3 " " " " Emeline Christie						
	14							
	15							
	16							
	17							

TRIBAL ENROLLMENT OF PARENTS

Name of Father	Year	County	Name of Mother	Year	County
1 Lewis Christie	Dead	Towson	Maley Christie	Dead	Towson
2 Stephen Aaron	"	"	Mollie Aaron	"	"
3 No 1			Betsy Christie	"	"
4					
5					
6					
7			No2 died Feb 28, 1900; proof of death filed Dec 3, 1902		
8		No.2 died Feb 28, 1900. Enrollment cancelled by Department [remainder illegible]			
9					
10					
11					
12					
13					
14					
15					
16				Date of Application for Enrollment.	April 20/99
17 Fowlerville I.T. 11/27/02					

Choctaw By Blood Enrollment Cards 1898-1914

RESIDENCE: Red River COUNTY.
POST OFFICE: Kullituklo, I.T.

Choctaw Nation

Choctaw Roll
(Not Including Freedmen)

CARD NO.
FIELD NO. **598**

Dawes' Roll No.	NAME		Relationship to Person First Named	AGE	SEX	BLOOD	TRIBAL ENROLLMENT		
							Year	County	No.
1369	1 Battice, Thompson	35	First Named	32	M	Full	1896	Red River	1403
1370	2 " Sallie	24	Wife	32	F	"	1896	" "	1404
14571	3 " William	5	Son	2	M	"			
1371	4 " Lena	3	Dau	5mo	F	"			
	5								
	6								
	7		ENROLLMENT OF NOS. 1-2 and 4 HEREON APPROVED BY THE SECRETARY OF INTERIOR Dec 12, 1902						
	8								
	9								
	10								
	11		ENROLLMENT OF NOS. 3 HEREON APPROVED BY THE SECRETARY OF INTERIOR May 20, 1903						
	12								
	13								
	14								
	15								
	16								
	17								

TRIBAL ENROLLMENT OF PARENTS

	Name of Father	Year	County	Name of Mother	Year	County
1	Adam Battice	Dead	Red River	Bickie Battice	Dead	Red River
2	Fah-lin	"	" "	Bessie	1896	" "
3	No 1			No 2		
4	No 1			No 2		
5						
6	No3 Affidavit of birth to be supplied. Recd 5/3/99.					
7						
8	No4 enrolled Dec 19/99. Affidavit irregular and returned for correction. Returned corrected and filed March 27th 1900.					
9						
10	No3 Proof of birth received and filed Oct. 6, 1902					
11	For child of Nos 1&2 see N.B. (Apr 26-06) Card #515. " " " " " " " (Mar 3-05) " #962.					
12						
13						
14						
15						Date of Application for Enrollment.
16						April 20/99
17						

Choctaw By Blood Enrollment Cards 1898-1914

RESIDENCE: Red River COUNTY. **Choctaw Nation** **Choctaw Roll** CARD No.
POST OFFICE: Kullituklo, I.T. *(Not Including Freedmen)* FIELD No. **599**

Dawes' Roll No.	NAME		Relationship to Person First Named	AGE	SEX	BLOOD	TRIBAL ENROLLMENT		
							Year	County	No.
1372	1 Brown, Agnes	53	First Named	50	F	Full	1896	Red River	1371
1373	2 " Grayson	15	Son	12	M	"	1896	" "	1373
1374	3 " Mary	13	Dau	10	F	"	1896	" "	1374
1375	4 " Austin	10	Son	7	M	"	1896	" "	1375
	5								
	6	ENROLLMENT							
	7	OF NOS. 1 2 3 and 4 HEREON APPROVED BY THE SECRETARY							
	8	OF INTERIOR Dec 12 1902							
	9								
	10								
	11								
	12								
	13								
	14								
	15								
	16								
	17								

TRIBAL ENROLLMENT OF PARENTS

	Name of Father	Year	County	Name of Mother	Year	County
1	John	Dead	Blue		Dead	Bok Tuklo
2	Byington Brown	"	Red River	No 1		
3	" "	"	" "	No 1		
4	" "	"	" "	No 1		
5						
6						
7						
8						
9						
10						
11						
12						
13						
14						
15					Date of Application for Enrollment	
16					April 20/99	
17						

Choctaw By Blood Enrollment Cards 1898-1914

RESIDENCE: Nashoba   COUNTY.   **Choctaw Nation**   **Choctaw Roll** *(Not Including Freedmen)*

POST OFFICE: Alikchi, I.T.   CARD NO.   FIELD NO. **600**

Dawes' Roll No.	NAME	Relationship to Person First Named	AGE	SEX	BLOOD	TRIBAL ENROLLMENT Year	County	No.
DEAD	1 Johnson, Abel		61	M	Full	1896	Nashoba	6873
	2							
	3							
	4							
	5							
	6							
	7 No 1 HEREON DISMISSED UNDER							
	8 ORDER OF THE COMMISSION TO THE FIVE							
	CIVILIZED TRIBES OF MARCH 31, 1905.							
	9							
	10							
	11							
	12 No1 died about Feby 15, 1900, proof of death filed Sept 13, 1905							
	13							
	14							
	15							
	16							
	17							

TRIBAL ENROLLMENT OF PARENTS

	Name of Father	Year	County	Name of Mother	Year	County
1	Thleo hubbee	Dead	Nashoba	May a huma	Dead	Nashoba
2						
3						
4						
5						
6						
7						
8						
9						
10						
11						
12						
13						
14						
15						
16				Date of Application for Enrollment		April 20/99
17						

300

324

www.ingramcontent.com/pod-product-compliance
Lightning Source LLC
Chambersburg PA
CBHW030235030426
42336CB00009B/114